Target: China

How Washington and Wall Street Plan to Cage the Asian Dragon

© by F. William Engdahl

Progressive Press

2014

Target: China
How Washington and Wall Street Plan to Cage the Asian Dragon

First Print Edition, published November 11, 2014
by www. ProgressivePress.com, San Diego, Calif.

List Price: $24.95.
Length: 77,000 words on 251 pages
ISBN 1-61577-227-8, EAN 978-1-61577-227-8

BISAC Subject Area Codes
HIS008000 History / Asia / China
POL045000 Political Science / Colonialism & Post-Colonialism
POL062000 Political Science / Geopolitics

China today has become a world economic giant in just three decades. The country's central bank holds more than $3.5 trillion in foreign exchange reserves, mostly in dollars. Without the Chinese colossus, the USA might have long ago gone bankrupt, unable to finance its exploding national debt.

Now that China has emerged as the world's second largest economy, some powerful circles in Wall Street and Washington are alarmed that the Chinese might no longer follow the agenda, but decide for themselves what is best for China. They see China as a threat to their global power. The result is growing tension between Beijing and Washington – in the Middle East, Africa, and in Asia.

Especially alarming is covert US backing of Japan in a conflict with China over remote Pacific islands. China is beginning to feel escalating hostility, and not only from the Pentagon. Open conflict between the USA and China could deal a death-blow to the fragile world economy.

This book explains in clear terms what is at stake if Washington continues to try to turn the Chinese Dragon into an enemy state.

TABLE OF CONTENTS

"We have about 50% of the world's wealth, but only 6.3% of its population. ... In this situation, we cannot fail to be the object of envy and resentment. Our real task in the coming period is to devise a pattern of relationships which will permit us to maintain this position of disparity. ... To do so, we will have to dispense with all sentimentality and day-dreaming; and our attention will have to be concentrated everywhere on our immediate national objectives. ... We should cease to talk about vague and ... unreal objectives such as human rights, the raising of the living standards, and democratization. The day is not far off when we are going to have to deal in straight power concepts. The less we are then hampered by idealistic slogans, the better."

– George F. Kennan, US State Department Policy Planning Study 23 (PPS23), Foreign Relations of the United States (FRUS), 1948

Author's Introduction

Boiling Frogs Slowly...

Ancient folklore has it that if you want to boil a frog in a pot of water, you first gently place it in water that is cold, and ever so slowly turn up the heat until the stupefied frog allows itself to be boiled to death, never aware what is happening. It is a metaphor that describes the long-term strategy of powerful US and British leading circles towards the future sovereign existence of the Peoples' Republic of China. Some three decades ago China under Deng Xiaoping saw the introduction of a "socialist market economy." In many respects the policy succeeded beyond the wildest dreams of many Chinese and indeed, of much of the world. The industriousness and creativity of the Chinese people has been a major cause of the economic success that elevated China from an economically poor country in the 1970's to the economic colossus it is today.

The second factor that made the astonishing rise of China possible, however, was the growing interest of North American and certain European major powers in using the world's largest and cheapest labor pool to gain dramatic increases in manufacturing profit through what came to be called "outsourcing." The initiative for the China opening came from powerful circles inside the United States. The key figures preparing Nixon's historic 1972 Beijing meeting with Chairman Mao were then-National Security Advisor Henry Kissinger, and his assistant, Winston Lord, who would later become US Ambassador to China. Nixon's Beijing initiative was in reality decided by the Rockefeller faction in US foreign policy. Both Kissinger and Lord were close protégés of the Rockefeller group.

When Mao met with Nixon in 1972, the only other US official present in the room – in a meeting that excluded Secretary of State Rodgers – was Kissinger's assistant Winston Lord. For US policy circles, the US-China opening constituted a geopolitical strategy to win China as an ally against the Soviet Union during the Cold War.

In 1979 Deng, with strong encouragement from US circles, made the decisive shift to the "socialist market economy." It was a brilliant and daring move, but not one without danger. In 1989, at the same time as a US strategy had led to the downfall of the Soviet Union, the CIA, acting through US Ambassador to Beijing Winston Lord and his CIA-tied successor, James Lilley, set off a chain of events that came to be known as the "Tiananmen Square massacre." All indications are that it was intended to create political chaos inside China aimed at weakening the control of the Communist Party over China's economic transformation. In any case, the US plot failed, but not before exacting a high price in terms of isolating China in the world politically and economically.

After 1989, as the People's Republic moved to more open foreign investment and towards membership in the World Trade Organization, China became a preferred market for foreign direct investment by US and European multinationals. Over the past twenty or more years the results of that investment have been astonishing. China today is the world's largest exporting nation in dollar terms and the second largest oil importer after the United States.

However, Chinese policymakers must never lose sight of the fact that once all the friendly handshakes and smiles and many toasts to US-China friendship fade, at the end of the day, US foreign policy, like British foreign policy before it – notably during the Opium Wars – is driven by American national interests. It follows the dictum laid down by Britain's Lord Palmerston: "Nations have no permanent friends or allies, they only have permanent interests."

From the time of Washington's first China opening in 1972 until the fall of the Berlin Wall in 1989, the US "interest" in China was to subtly use the country as an antagonist against Soviet interests geopolitically. Once it became clear that various US policies had brought the Soviet regime of Gorbachev to its knees in 1989, the US intelligence circles around the Rockefeller-Bush faction attempted a similar destabilization of the CPC (Communist Party of China) regime in Beijing. They manipulated leading members of the CPC, including General Secretary Zhao Ziyang and others, to push for rapid economic reform – the kind of free-market "shock therapy" dictated by the International Money Fund (IMF) – that devastated Russia and most of eastern Europe after 1990.

Following the collapse of the USSR in the 1990's and the accession of China to the World Trade Organization (WTO), it was in the US security "interest" to flood China with investments aimed at making China a world export leader. However, the exports were US and European products, from cars to iPhones, that were now manufactured in China at extremely low wage levels. The profits largely went to US bank accounts, not Chinese.

Until around 2005, a policy of rapid economic growth in China was seen as no threat to US national "interest" – so long as the growth was based largely on the US-backed "free market" model. However, as China grew, her appetite for imports of oil, iron ore, copper and other commodities led China's leaders to engage in bold and effective foreign economic diplomacy. The initiatives spanned the world, from Africa to the Middle East. China was slowly shifting from a useful source of cheap labor for American multinationals like Walmart, to a potential threat to future US hegemony, especially in Africa, Asia and the oil-rich Middle East.

Step by step, just as with the boiling of frogs, Washington has been turning the heat up on China since about 2005. Today it is dangerously close to a boil. It is not too late for China, but its people and leaders must have absolutely no illusions about the ruthlessness and determination of their adversary, the elite policy circles of the Anglo-American axis. The book you are about to read details how US policy circles increasingly plan to mortally wound and eventually kill China's economic wonder.

– F. William Engdahl, Frankfurt am Main, April, 2014

Chapter One:
The Dollar-Renminbi War

Chinese dollar reserves from export earnings were rapidly approaching the staggering sum of $1 trillion by the end of 2005. That in effect meant that the US Government could run huge deficits to cover the costs of its wars in Iraq and Afghanistan, and be assured that China had almost no choice but to invest its growing dollar trade surpluses into US Government debt.

Alarm bells ring in Washington

By the middle of the first decade of this century, around 2005, China's unprecedented rate of economic growth began to set off alarm bells on Wall Street and in Washington.

In August of that year, China and Russia carried out their first joint military maneuvers, Peace Mission 2005, an 8-day training exercise on the Shandong peninsula.[1] It was a strong indication that the one geopolitical alliance Washington was most afraid of – namely, a political, military and economic alliance between former foes and former allies Russia and China – was imminent. The brazen US military occupation of Iraq two years earlier in March 2003 had sent shock waves around the world.

In Beijing it was duly noted that Washington's strategy was not about anything other than raw power.

Washington's response to the growing independence of Eurasian powers – China, Russia and the other nations of the Shanghai Cooperation Organization – was not long in coming. It began with a verbal attack on China's currency policy.

US is the real "currency manipulator"

The US Government began what was to become an ongoing verbal pressure campaign against what they claimed was a deliberate undervaluation of the Chinese currency, the renminbi (RMB), against the US dollar. Soon after the start of the second term of President George W. Bush, Washington began a relentless campaign to pressure China into revaluing the renminbi. The

Bush Administration was well aware that the RMB exchange rate is at the very heart of China's economy, which underpins the nation's political survival. For that very reason Washington has launched its relentless campaign threatening to label China a "currency manipulator."

On international currency markets China's currency was still not fully convertible into dollars or Euros or other currencies. But for accounting valuations of its trade, the Peoples National Bank of China had *de facto* pegged the renminbi's value to the US dollar, then China's major export market.

A sharp revaluation of the renminbi, as demanded by Washington, of between 20% and 40% beginning 2005, would have hit China's exports severely, creating economic difficulties.[2] However, a drastic fall in dollar export earnings by China would also have meant America's largest creditor would have fewer dollars with which to buy US Treasury bonds and the US home mortgage debt of Fannie Mae and Freddie Mac.

China dollar reserves from export earnings were headed rapidly towards the staggering sum of $1 trillion by the end of 2005. In effect, that meant that the US Government could run huge deficits to cover the costs of wars in Iraq and Afghanistan, with the assurance that China had almost no choice but to invest its growing dollar trade surpluses into US Government debt.

A perverse, unholy alliance was developing between the sole hegemonic superpower United States and the world's fastest growing economy, China. Washington never intended for China to massively revalue. It was a bluff, a pressure point to begin making Chinese officials nervous about their future economic security. It was the beginning of Washington's "Target China" strategy.

To ease the growing pressure from Washington, Beijing began in 2005 a policy of slow and cautious revaluation of the renminbi against the dollar. On July 21, 2005 China ended the fixed RMB-dollar peg, switching over to peg the renminbi to a basket of currencies, including mainly the US dollar, the Euro, the Japanese yen, and the Korean won.[3] By 2008 the RMB had risen some 20% against the US dollar, a major concession to the nominal US demands. Because the real US agenda is not about weakening Chinese exports, but rather about putting pressure on

China to weaken her overall economy, there was no end to Washington's currency wars.

With instant globalized financial and trade relations, a nation's currency security is even more critical than energy security. At the heart of this stability is the world reserve currency system. Since Washington largely wrote the rules of the international postwar monetary order at the Bretton Woods Conference in 1944, the US has resorted to manipulations, lies, cheating and even wars to maintain the US dollar as world "key currency," the leading Reserve Currency used in international trade. That "key currency" status has allowed Washington to manipulate the value of the dollar because the US remains the sole unchallenged world military leader, even as the health of the industrial economy backing the dollar has rotted much like Thatcher's England, into a post-industrial rust heap.

Several western economic commentators have pointed out the central irony in the US role as world reserve or key currency. Because other nations must hold large dollar reserves in order to defend their currency against speculative attack – such as hit East Asia in 1997-1998 – they are more or less forced to buy US Treasury debt. In other words, US Government deficits are being financed by the Peoples' National Bank of China. In effect the Bush Administration was financing its generous tax cuts to rich citizens and its "Global War on Terror" through the Peoples' Bank of China's huge purchases of US Treasury bills. This has been called by one noted Harvard professor, Niall Ferguson, "a kind of Chinese 'tribute' to the American Empire."[4]

By 2012 China's holdings of US Treasury debt were estimated at nearly $2 trillion, a staggering sum that leaves China vulnerable to a sudden dollar collapse.

In fact the only real currency manipulator in the world today is and has been for decades the US Government, not China. Since 1944, the dollar has lost 97% of its value against gold. The US has repeatedly made abrupt and rapid variations in the value of the dollar against other major currencies – often at 30% per year – in the service of its own economic interests. Now, the Federal Reserve continues to devalue the dollar by printing huge volumes of money since the financial crisis erupted in 2007, via successive "quantitative easing."

In 1985 the US manipulated its exchange rate to its advantage by forcing Japan into the so-called Plaza Accord. The effect of the Plaza Accord led Japan into the trap of the famous Japanese financial bubble, which collapsed in 1990, plunging Japan into a deflation and economic depression from which she has yet to recover. In 1989, Washington forced South Korea also to revalue the won to suit US interests. That, too, was "currency manipulation." The exchange rate realignments of the past, such as those with Japan in 1985 and South Korea in 1989, have been an attempt by the US to force other countries to adjust their policies in the name of "burden sharing." The only problem is that Washington never takes its share of the "burden."[5]

The most colossal US currency manipulation took place in 1973 when, as the dollar was in free-fall against leading world currencies, powerful Wall Street interests, in collusion with Secretary of State Henry Kissinger, manipulated a Yom Kippur Arab-Israeli war that led to a 400% rise in oil prices and a sharp rise in the US dollar that plunged the entire world into deep recession.[6]

By 2009, the manipulation of the value of the dollar through endless creation of new dollars by the Fed led the Chinese Premier, Wen Jiabao, to openly express China's alarm over the potential threat to the value of China's then $1 trillion investment in US Treasuries.[7] Because the US dollar remains the world's "key currency," Washington and Wall Street are able to use US monetary policy as a central pillar of US economic hegemony, and the floating dollar exchange rate as "a mechanism for plunder," as some Chinese analysts have rightly called it.[8]

Little surprise then that on 13 March, 2009, Premier Wen Jiabao openly aired his worries about China's $1 trillion investment in US Treasuries, hinting strongly that China was looking to diversify away from dollars to euros and other major currencies like the Japanese yen and Korean won. The Wall Street-Washington combine responded swiftly by launching the "euro crisis" in Greece in order to weaken the euro and strengthen the dollar, a covert "currency manipulation."[9]

He Zhicheng of the Agricultural Bank of China, argued that the free-floating renminbi exchange rate demanded by Washington would be a "trap" for China, because it would let foreign contractors determine the value of Chinese labor. In other words, a free-floating rate would surrender China's sovereignty over her currency to the international marketplace.[10]

In February 2011 the US Treasury, in its much-awaited report, while not quite labeling China a "currency manipulator," took a tougher line than in past years, saying the RMB is "substantially undervalued," warning "progress thus far is insufficient and that more rapid progress is needed." In its December 2011 report, the US Treasury kept up the pressure on China's currency.[11]

In May 2012 US Treasury Secretary Tim Geithner again pressured China to further revalue the renminbi against the dollar at a time when China's exports were slowing dramatically.[12]

And at the start of the US presidential campaign of 2012, candidate Mitt Romney said that

> "if he were elected president, he would label China a currency manipulator on his first day in office. One of his television ads predicts the expected actions of Mr. Romney's first day in office, with the narrator saying that, 'President Romney stands up to China on trade, and demands they play by the rules.'"[13]

The dollar-renminbi wars remain a major pressure on China's future economic security and sovereignty.

Not surprisingly, by early 2012 the signs were everywhere that the ASEAN+3 nations had grown tired of the US Dollar trade forcing them to "eat the inflation" that was being exported to their economies by Ben Bernanke and the Federal Reserve. There began a series of very rapid moves by these nations to link their collective fates to each other, banding together to create for themselves a currency and equity bloc to rival the West. A cross-border equity exchange that will link the exchanges of all members, with Singapore's and Malaysia's connecting first, opened in June 2012. Thailand was to join later in the year. China and its Asian trading partners moved to settle bilateral trade in mutual currency accounts, bypassing the dollar as medium of settlement.[14]

In reality, as with many geopolitical pressure tactics from Washington, the true goal of the pressure to revalue the renminbi was not merely a higher-value renminbi. It was a lever to pressure China to make the renminbi fully and freely a convertible currency in international foreign exchange trade like the dollar or euro, and also to pressure China to open its financial and capital markets fully to the Wall Street giant banks, to the "Gods of Money." Were Beijing to do this, as demanded by the US Treasury, the Federal Reserve and Wall Street banks, China would be vulnerable to speculator attacks, just as Thailand was in 1997.

The Dollar-Renminbi wars however, were but one flank in the growing campaign to target China. China's energy security and her access to foreign oil was the second major flank Washington and her NATO allies, especially Great Britain, would target to further weaken China's expansion into an economic great power.

Chapter Two:
Energy Wars: The War to Control China's Oil

"West Africa's oil has become of national strategic interest to us," stated US Assistant Secretary of State for Africa Walter Kansteiner in 2002. Darfur and Chad were but an extension of the US Iraq policy to control China's oil sources "with other means" – control of oil everywhere. China was challenging that control "everywhere," especially in Africa. Darfur was the beginning of the Pentagon's undeclared new Cold War, this one over oil.

China's energy Achilles heel

In 1994 China passed from being an exporter of oil to the world to becoming a net oil importer. The shift was to have profound implications for China's national security and her vulnerability to Anglo-American attempts to control her oil sources. By 2010 China had 90 times more cars than in 1990, and projections show that by 2030 or even sooner, China could surpass the US in the total number of cars. That, as well as demands for petroleum for the petrochemical industry, and for air and truck transport, have rapidly made securing adequate oil supplies a national security priority.

Beginning in 1999, China's major investments in oil extraction in Sudan began to sound alarm bells in Washington. Construction of a 900-mile long pipeline to carry oil from fields in southern Sudan to Port Sudan on the Red Sea, where it was loaded onto tankers bound for China, was not viewed favorably by certain powerful circles in the United States or the UK. When China then discovered a major new potential oilfield in Sudan's southwest Darfur Province, it was time to begin to draw the noose around the neck of Sudan.

In April 2005, Sudan Energy Minister Awad al-Jaz told reporters in Khartoum that an oil field had been found in southern Darfur, and it was expected to produce 500,000 barrels of oil per day within weeks. It was estimated by international geologists to be part of a huge complex of oil fields in a basin that went from

Darfur into neighboring Chad and on to Cameroon, perhaps one of the world's largest oil discoveries outside Saudi Arabia.[15]

Almost immediately, gangs of militia swept across the unmarked desert border from Chad, armed and aided by Western intelligence services and spreading murder, rape and chaos in the region. Washington had begun its Operation "Darfur Genocide." The ultimate aim was to provide an excuse to bring NATO troops into one of China's most promising new oil regions.

African oil diplomacy

Beijing launched a major new diplomatic initiative with most African states soon after the Darfur oil discovery, one designed to secure long-term raw materials sources from one of the planet's most endowed regions – the African continent. No raw material had higher priority in Beijing than oil. China's goal was the securing of long-term oil sources.

In 2006 China drew an estimated 30% of its crude oil from Africa. That explained a series of diplomatic initiatives which have left Washington furious. China used no-strings-attached dollar credits to gain access to Africa's vast raw material wealth, leaving Washington's typical control game via the World Bank and IMF out in the cold. Who needs the painful medicine of the IMF, when China gives easy terms and builds roads and schools to boot?

In November 2006, Beijing hosted an extraordinary summit of 40 African heads of state. China literally rolled out the red carpet for the leaders of Algeria, Nigeria, Mali, Angola, Central African Republic, Zambia, South Africa and Sudan, among others.

China signed an oil deal linking the Peoples' Republic of China with the continent's two largest nations – Nigeria and South Africa. China's CNOC would lift the oil in Nigeria via a consortium that included South African Petroleum Co., giving China access to what could be 175,000 barrels a day by 2008. The $2.27 billion deal gave state-controlled CNOC a 45% stake in a large off-shore Nigerian oil field. Previously, Nigeria had been considered in Washington to be an asset of the Anglo-American oil majors, ExxonMobil, Shell and Chevron.

China was generous in dispensing its soft loans, with zero interest or even outright grants to some of the poorest debtor states of Africa. The funds went to infrastructure, including highways, hospitals, and schools, a stark contrast to the brutal austerity demands of the IMF and World Bank. In 2006 China committed more than $8 billion to Nigeria, Angola and Mozambique, versus $2.3 billion to all sub-Saharan Africa from the US-controlled World Bank. Ghana was negotiating a $1.2 billion Chinese electrification loan. Unlike the World Bank, a *de facto* arm of US foreign economic policy, China shrewdly attached no strings to its loans.

The oil-related Chinese diplomacy led to the bizarre accusation from Washington that Beijing was trying to "secure oil at the sources," something Washington foreign policy had itself been doing intensively all across the globe for at least a century.[16]

Beijing's China National Petroleum Company, CNPC, became Sudan's largest foreign investor, with some $5 billion in oil field development. Since 1999 China has invested at least $15 billion in Sudan. It owns 50% of an oil refinery near Khartoum with the Sudanese government. The oil fields were concentrated in the south, site of a long-simmering civil war, partly financed covertly by the United States, to break the south from the Islamic Khartoum-centered north.

CNPC built an oil pipeline from its concession blocks 1, 2 and 4 in southern Sudan to a new terminal at Port Sudan on the Red Sea, where oil is loaded on tankers for China. In 2005, Sudan was China's fourth largest foreign oil source. By 2006 eight percent of China's oil came from southern Sudan.

In 2006 China surpassed Japan to become the world's second largest importer of oil after the United States, importing 6.5 million barrels a day of the black gold. China took from 65% to 80% of Sudan's 500,000 barrels/day of oil production. With its oil demand growing by an estimated 30% a year, China was expected to pass the US in oil import demand in a few years, according to USAID. That reality was the motor driving Chinese foreign policy in Africa.

China's CNPC held rights to block 6 – the only oil exploration area located entirely in North Sudan. Block 6 straddles Darfur, near the border to Chad and the Central African Republic. In April 2005 Sudan's government announced it had found oil in South Darfur, a major geopolitical event which major US and European media "forgot" to mention when discussing the sudden new "Darfur conflict."

Washington, using US Secretary of State Colin Powell, an African-American, to deliver the message, began accusing the Khartoum regime of "genocide" in Darfur, though no independent proof was given. Only Washington and the NGO's close to it used the term "genocide" to describe Darfur. If they could get a popular acceptance of the charge of genocide, it opened the possibility for drastic "regime change" interventions by NATO and by Washington in Sudan's sovereign affairs. The Washington Darfur smear campaign soon enlisted Hollywood stars like George Clooney in this effort. Washington and NATO launched a campaign to argue for a de facto NATO occupation of the region.

In an interview in November 2006, US Assistant Secretary of State Ellen Sauerbrey, head of the Bureau of Population, Refugees and Migration, said during a USINFO online interview: "The ongoing genocide in Darfur, Sudan – a 'gross violation' of human rights – is among the top international issues of concern to the United States." The Bush-Cheney administration insisted that genocide had been going on in Darfur since 2003. However, a UN mission, with a five-man panel led by Italian judge Antonio Cassese, reported in 2005 that genocide had not occurred in Darfur, but that some very grave human rights abuses were committed.[17]

The United States, acting through surrogate allies in Chad and neighboring states, trained and armed the Sudan Peoples' Liberation Army, headed until his death in July 2005 by John Garang, trained at the US Special Forces school in Fort Benning, Georgia. Washington poured arms first into south-eastern Sudan, and following the discovery of oil in Darfur in the southwest, into that region as well. Washington thus fuelled the conflict that led to tens of thousands dying and several million driven to flee their homes. Eritrea hosted and supported the SPLA (Sudanese Peoples' Liberation Army), the umbrella NDA (National Democratic Alliance) opposition group, and the Eastern Front and Darfur rebels.

There were two rebel groups fighting in Sudan's Darfur region against the Khartoum central government of President Omar al-Bashir: the Justice for Equality Movement (JEM), and the larger Sudan Liberation Army (SLA). In February 2003 the SLA launched attacks on Sudanese government positions in the Darfur region. SLA Secretary-General Minni Arkou Minnawi called for armed struggle, accusing the government of ignoring Darfur. "The objective of the SLA is to create a united democratic Sudan." In other words, regime change in Sudan.[18]

The US Senate adopted a resolution in February 2006 that requested North Atlantic Treaty Organization troops in Darfur, as well as a stronger UN "peacekeeping" force with a robust mandate. A month later, President Bush also called for additional NATO forces in Darfur. The aim was for NATO to gain control over China's huge new oil potential.

The Pentagon was busy providing training for African military officers in the US, much as it had for Latin American officers for decades. The International Military Education and Training (IMET) program had trained military officers from Chad, Ethiopia, Eritrea, Cameroon and the Central African Republic, in effect every country on Sudan's border. Much of the military equipment and arms that fuelled the killing in Darfur and the south were brought in via murky, protected private "merchants of death" such as Victor Bout, a notorious former KGB operative, now with offices in the US.

USAID development aid for all of Sub-Saharan Africa, including Chad, had been cut sharply in recent years, while its military aid rose as sharply.

Secretary of State Condoleezza Rice's Chevron Oil Co. was in neighboring Chad, together with the other US oil giant, ExxonMobil. They had built a $3.7 billion oil pipeline carrying 160,000 barrels/day of oil from Doba in central Chad, near Darfur, via Cameroon to Kribi on the Atlantic Ocean, destined for US refineries.

To accomplish this, they worked with Chad's "President for life," Idriss Deby, a corrupt despot who had been accused of feeding US-supplied arms to the Darfur rebels. Deby joined Washington's Pan Sahel Initiative run by the Pentagon's US-European Command, to train his troops to fight "Islamic terrorism." The majority of the tribes in Darfur region are Muslim.

Supplied with US military aid, training and weapons, in 2004 Deby launched the initial strike that set off the conflict in Darfur, using members of his elite Presidential Guard who originate from the province. He provided all-terrain vehicles, arms and anti-aircraft guns to Darfur rebels fighting the Khartoum government in southwest Sudan. The US military support to Deby was the trigger for the Darfur bloodbath. Khartoum reacted and the ensuing tragic debacle was unleashed in full force.[19]

Washington-backed NGO's and the US Government had begun the "Darfur genocide" campaign in 2003, at the same time the Chad-Cameroon pipeline oil began to flow. The US now had a base in Chad to go after Darfur oil and, potentially, co-opt China's new oil sources. Darfur was strategically located, straddling Chad, Central African Republic, Egypt and Libya.

According to Africa researcher Keith Harmon Snow: "US military objectives in Darfur – and the Horn of Africa more widely – are being served at present by the US and NATO backing of the African Union troops in Darfur. There, NATO provides ground and air support for AU troops who are categorized as 'neutral' and 'peacekeepers.' Sudan is at war on three fronts, each country – Uganda, Chad, and Ethiopia – with a significant US military presence and ongoing US military programs. The war in Sudan involves both US covert operations and US trained "rebel" factions coming in from South Sudan, Chad, Ethiopia and Uganda."[20]

Beijing responded with diplomatic counter-efforts in Chad and around Africa. In January 2007 Chinese President Hu Jintao made a state visit to Sudan and to Cameroon, among other African states. In 2006, China's leaders visited no less than 48 African states. In August 2006 Beijing had hosted Chad's Foreign Minister for talks and resumption of formal diplomatic ties that had been cut in 1997. China began to import oil from Chad as well as Sudan. Chad's Foreign Minister announced that talks with China over greater China participation in Chad's oil development were "progressing well." He referred to the terms the Chinese seek for oil development, calling them, "much more equal partnerships than those we are used to having."[21]

The Chinese economic presence in Chad, ironically, was more effective in calming the fighting and displacement of refugees in Darfur than any African Union or UN troop presence ever could. That was not welcome for some people in Washington and at Chevron headquarters.

New Cold War over oil

George W. Bush's interest in Africa included a new US base in Sao Tomé and Principe, 124 miles off the Gulf of Guinea, from which it can control the Gulf of Guinea oilfields from Angola in the south to Congo, Gabon, Equitorial Guinea, Cameroon and Nigeria. Those just happened to be the very same areas where recent Chinese diplomatic and investment activities have focused.

"West Africa's oil has become of national strategic interest to us," stated US Assistant Secretary of State for Africa Walter Kansteiner in 2002.[22] Darfur and Chad were but an extension of the US Iraq policy to control China's oil sources "with other means" – to control the oil everywhere. And China was challenging that control "everywhere," especially in Africa. Darfur was the beginning of the Pentagon's new undeclared Cold War, this one over oil.

In 2011 a new "republic" was declared in southern Sudan titled The Republic of South Sudan. It (conveniently for the Pentagon) controlled a major part of Sudan's oil flows to China. Washington covert aid and actions were behind the new state, although the US was careful not to be the first to diplomatically recognize it. The agenda began to become clear in January 2012, when the new state announced it was closing its entire oil facility, after failing to reach an agreement with the Sudan government on oil revenues. At the same time South Sudan's Information Minister Barnaba Marial Benjamin announced that South Sudan and Kenya had signed a memorandum of understanding to build an oil pipeline to the Kenyan port of Lamu. Construction of the pipeline will begin "as soon as sources of funding are made available," which should take about a month, he said, reckoning that the pipeline could be completed in 10 months.[23]

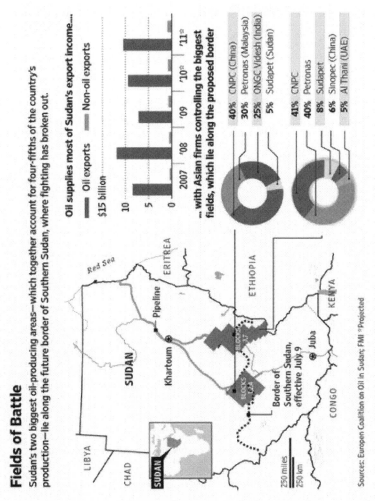

Fields of Battle

Sudan's two biggest oil-producing areas—which together account for four-fifths of the country's production—lie along the future border of Southern Sudan, where fighting has broken out.

Oil supplies most of Sudan's export income....

— Oil exports   — Non-oil exports

... with Asian firms controlling the biggest fields, which lie along the proposed border

| 40% CNPC (China) |
| 30% Petronas (Malaysia) |
| 25% ONGC Videsh (India) |
| 5% Sudapet (Sudan) |

| 41% CNPC |
| 40% Petronas |
| 8% Sudapet |
| 6% Sinopec (China) |
| 5% Al Thani (UAE) |

Sources: European Coalition on Oil in Sudan; FMI *Projected

Kenya was a major military bastion of the newly-created US Africa Command, AFRICOM. By routing the oil via pipeline through Kenya and not Sudan, Washington would gain a major control lever over a major source of China's oil. It was just one of many such moves that would occur after China's 2006 Africa diplomatic offensive. The border of South Sudan conveniently cut Sudan's oil fields down the middle in a disputed territory, and more than 350,000 barrels of oil destined for mainly Chinese ports was cut. This comprised some 90% of all Sudanese oil production. South Sudan also bordered the new oil areas of Darfur, potentially giving whoever controlled South Sudan the ability to sabotage Chinese oil infrastructure there, as well. Darfur itself was under a UN-African Union protectorate. The Sudan government accused the head of the UN Darfur mission, UNAMID, a Briton named Tony Prena, and his "peacekeepers" of using "humanitarian" convoys across Darfur as the main source of supplies and weapons for the rebel groups against the Khartoum central government.[24]

The US AFRICOM military and USAID forces were drawing a tight noose around the keystone to China's brilliant Africa oil strategy.

Creating AFRICOM to stop China

The covert target of US "surrogate warfare" in Africa today is China, which is the real threat to US control of Central Africa's vast mineral riches. The Democratic Republic of Congo was renamed from the Republic of Zaire in 1997, when the forces of Laurent-Désiré Kabila brought Mobutu's 32-year reign to an end. Locals call the country Congo-Kinshasa, in distinction to the smaller republic of Congo-Brazzaville.

The Kivu region has some of the world's greatest strategic reserves of minerals. The eastern border straddles Rwanda and Uganda, on the eastern edge of the Great African Rift Valley, believed by geologists to be one of the richest repositories of minerals on the face of the earth.

The Democratic Republic of Congo contains more than half the world's cobalt. It holds one-third of its diamonds, and, extremely significantly, fully three-quarters of the world resources of columbite-tantalite or "coltan" − a primary component of computer microchips and circuit boards, essential for mobile telephones, laptops and other modern electronic devices. And it is believed to hold huge oil riches.

America Minerals Fields, Inc., a company heavily involved in promoting the 1996 accession to power of Laurent Kabila, was, at the time of its involvement in the Congo's civil war, headquartered in Hope, Arkansas, an area where the Clinton family mafia is based. Major stockholders included long-time associates of former President Clinton going back to his days as Governor of Arkansas. From his base in Goma, Eastern Zaire, Kabila had renegotiated the mining contracts with several US and British mining companies, including American Mineral Fields, several months before the downfall of Zaire's French-backed dictator Mobutu. The US-directed International Monetary Fund (IMF) then helped bring Mobutu's corrupt rule to a bloody end.

Washington was not entirely comfortable with Laurent Kabila, who was finally assassinated in 2001. In a study released in April 1997, barely a month before President Mobutu Sese Seko fled the country, the IMF had recommended "halting currency issue completely and abruptly" as part of an "economic recovery" program. A few months later, the IMF ordered the new government of Laurent Kabila Desire to freeze civil service wages with a view to "restoring macro-economic stability." Eroded by hyperinflation, the average public sector wage had fallen to 30,000 New Zaires (NZ) a month, the equivalent of one US dollar.

According to Canadian researcher and economist Michel Chossudovsky, the IMF's demands were tantamount to maintaining the entire population in abysmal poverty. They precluded from the outset a meaningful post-war economic reconstruction, thereby continuing to fuel the Congolese civil war, in which close to 2 million people have died.

Laurent Kabila was succeeded by his son, Joseph Kabila, who went on to become the Congo's first democratically elected President, and appears to have held a closer eye to the welfare of his countrymen than did his father.

Since the Bush-Cheney Administration signed the directive creating it in February 2007, AFRICOM has been a direct response to China's successful African oil diplomacy. It defines its mission as follows: "Africa Command has administrative responsibility for US military support to US government policy in Africa, to include military-to-military relationships with 53 African nations." They openly admit to working intimately with US Embassies and the State Department across Africa, which would also include USAID: "US Africa Command provides personnel and logistical support to State Department-funded activities. Command personnel work closely with US embassies in Africa to coordinate training programs to improve African nations' security capacity."[25]

Speaking to the International Peace Operations Association in Washington, D.C. on Oct. 27, 2008, AFRICOM commander Gen. Kip Ward defined the command's mission thus: "In concert with other US government agencies and international partners, [to conduct] sustained security engagements through military-to-military programs, military-sponsored activities, and other military operations as directed to promote a stable and secure African environment in support of US foreign policy."[26]

Clearly, the "military operations as directed to promote a stable and secure African environment in support of US foreign policy," are aimed squarely at blocking China's growing economic presence in the region.

In fact, as various Washington sources state openly, AFRICOM was created to counter the growing efforts of China in Africa, including the Democratic Republic of Congo, to secure long-term economic agreements for African raw materials, in exchange for Chinese aid, production-sharing agreements and royalties. As noted, the Chinese approach has been far shrewder. Rather than offering only savage IMF-dictated austerity and economic chaos, China has been offering extensive credit, and soft loans to build roads and schools, in order to generate good will.

Dr. J. Peter Pham, a leading Washington insider who is an advisor of the US State and Defense Departments, stated openly that among the aims of the new AFRICOM, was the objective of "protecting access to hydrocarbons and other strategic resources which Africa has in abundance ... a task which includes ensuring against the vulnerability of those natural riches and ensuring that no other interested third parties, such as China, India, Japan, or Russia, obtain monopolies or preferential treatment."

In testimony before the US Congress supporting the creation of AFRICOM in 2007, Dr. Pham, who is closely associated with the neo-conservative Foundation for Defense of Democracies, stated:

> This natural wealth makes Africa an inviting target for the attentions of the People's Republic of China, whose dynamic economy, averaging 9 percent growth per annum over the last two decades, has an almost insatiable thirst for oil as well as a need for other natural resources to sustain it. China is currently importing approximately 2.6 million barrels of crude per day, about half of its consumption; more than 765,000 of those barrels – roughly a third of its imports – come from African sources, especially Sudan, Angola, and Congo (Brazzaville). Is it any wonder, then, that... perhaps no other foreign region rivals Africa as the object of Beijing's sustained strategic interest in recent years. Last year the Chinese regime

published the first ever official white paper elaborating the bases of its policy toward Africa...

Intentionally or not, many analysts expect that Africa – especially the states along its oil-rich western coastline – will increasingly become a theatre for strategic competition between the United States and its only real near-peer competitor on the global stage, China, as both countries seek to expand their influence and secure access to resources.[27]

In 2008, ahead of a twelve-day eight-nation tour of Africa – the third such journey since he took office in 2003 – Chinese President Hu Jintao announced a three-year, $3 billion program in preferential loans and expanded aid for Africa. These funds came on top of the $3 billion in loans and $2 billion in export credits that Hu announced in October 2006, at the opening of the historic Beijing summit of the Forum on China-Africa Cooperation (FOCAC). The Forum brought nearly fifty African heads of state and ministers to the Chinese capital. Making AFRICOM operational as soon as possible was an urgent geopolitical priority for Washington. AFRICOM began operations on October 1, 2008, from headquarters in Stuttgart, Germany.

In late October, 2008, only four weeks after creation of AFRICOM, the well-armed troops of Laurent Nkunda, a renegade Congolese general and warlord, surrounded Goma in North Kivu and demanded that Congo President Joseph Kabila negotiate with him. Among rebel leader Nkunda's demands was that Kabila cancel a $9 billion joint venture between the Congo and China, called Sicomines, signed in 2007. China was to acquire rights to the vast copper and cobalt resources of the region, in exchange for $6 billion worth of road construction, two hydroelectric dams, hospitals, schools and railway links to southern Africa, to Katanga and to the Congolese Atlantic port at Matadi. The other $3 billion was to be invested by China in development of new mining areas.[28] The aim was becoming clear to Beijing. The Sicomines project has been blocked blocked for years by the IMF and the World Bank,[29] although China's Ex-Im is still working on the deal.[30]

Libya and China oil

In October 2007, China's state oil giant CNPC signed a contract to build a refinery jointly with Chad's government. Two years later in 2009 they began construction of an oil pipeline to carry oil from a new Chinese field in the south some 300 kilometers to the refinery. Western-supported NGOs predictably began howling about environmental impacts of the Chinese oil pipeline. The same NGOs were curiously silent when Chevron struck oil in 2003 in Chad.

In July 2011 Chad and China celebrated opening of the joint venture oil refinery near Chad's capital of Ndjamena.[31] China's oil activities in Chad are in very close proximity to another major Chinese oil project in what then was Sudan's Darfur region bordering Chad.

According to geological estimates, the subsurface running from Darfur, in what was southern Sudan, through Chad into Cameroon, is one gigantic oil field. Its dimensions are perhaps equivalent to a new Saudi Arabia. Controlling southern Sudan as well as Chad and Cameroon is vital to the Pentagon strategy of "strategic denial" of China's future oil flows.

The next domino to fall in the war against Chinese oil security was Libya's Gaddafi, ironically aided by a Chinese government decision not to use its UN Security Council veto against the NATO "no-fly zone" bombing of Tripoli and all Libya.

So long as a stable and robust Gaddafi regime remained in power in Tripoli, control over the great African oil field remained a major problem for the US. The simultaneous splitting off of the Republic of South Sudan from Khartoum, and the toppling of Gaddafi in favor of weak rebel bands beholden to US support, were strategic priorities for the Pentagon's doctrine of Full Spectrum Dominance. AFRICOM has been the key force behind the recent wave of Western military attacks against Libya, and more covert regime changes such as those in Tunisia, Egypt and the fateful referendum in southern Sudan, which has now made that oil-rich region "independent."

If we take a careful look at a map of Africa and also look at the organization of the new Pentagon Africa Command – AFRICOM – the pattern that emerges constitutes a careful strategy of controlling one of China's most strategically important sources of oil and raw materials.

AFRICOM REGIONAL INTERESTS

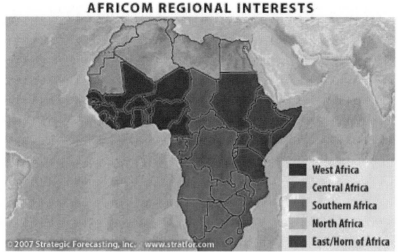

■	West Africa
■	Central Africa
■	Southern Africa
■	North Africa
■	East/Horn of Africa

Source: Strategic Forecasting Inc.

NATO's Libya campaign was and is all about oil. However, it is not about simply controlling Libyan high-grade crude because the USA is nervous about reliable foreign supplies. It is about controlling China's free access to long-term oil imports from Africa and from the Middle East. In other words, it is about controlling China itself.

Geographically Libya is bounded on its north by the Mediterranean directly across from Italy, where Italian ENI oil company has been the largest foreign operator in Libya for years. To its west it is bounded by Tunisia and Algeria. To its south it is bounded by Chad. To its east it is bounded by both Sudan (today Sudan and Southern Sudan) and by Egypt. That location reveals the strategic importance of Libya from the standpoint of the Pentagon-AFRICOM long-term strategy for controlling Africa, its resources, and which country is able to get those resources.

Gaddafi's Libya had maintained strict national state control over the rich reserves of high quality "light, sweet" Libyan crude oil. As of 2006, Libya had the largest proven oil reserves in Africa, some 35%, larger even than Nigeria.

Oil concessions had been extended to Chinese state oil companies as well as Russian and others in recent years.

Not surprisingly, a spokesman from the so-called opposition claiming victory over Gaddafi, Abdeljalil Mayouf, information manager at Libyan rebel oil firm AGOCO, told Reuters, "We don't have a problem with Western countries like the Italians, French and UK companies. But we may have some political issues with Russia, China and Brazil."[32] China, Russia and Brazil pressed for a negotiated settlement of the internal conflict and an end to NATO bombing.

It was no coincidence that the civil war in Sudan began in the oil-rich region of Darfur, while the insurrection in Libya started in the oil-rich eastern province of Cyrenaica. Few outside Beijing saw the connection. Yet Africa was only one theater of the global battlefield to control China's oil security. As then US Secretary of State Henry Kissinger is reported to have said during the 1970's, when he was arguably more powerful than the President of the United States, "If you control the oil, you control entire nations or groups of nations."

The Pentagon began quietly militarizing the key oil "choke points," those few very narrow water passages through which oil supertankers must pass as they bring oil from the Persian Gulf or Africa to China.

The world has seen a steady escalation of US military involvement in Yemen, a dismally poor land adjacent to Saudi Arabia on its north, the Red Sea on its west, the Gulf of Aden on its south, opening to the Arabian Sea, and overlooking another desolate land that has been in the headlines of late, Somalia. The Pentagon and US intelligence began moving to militarize another strategic chokepoint for the world's oil flows, Bab el-Mandab. By using the Somalia piracy incidents, together with claims of a new Al Qaeda threat arising from Yemen, the US aimed to militarize one of the world's most important oil transport routes. In addition, undeveloped petroleum reserves in the territory between Yemen and Saudi Arabia are reportedly among the world's largest.[33]

The intense destabilization of Yemen began with a sensational and quite fake arrest on December 25, 2009 by US authorities of a Nigerian named Abdulmutallab, who allegedly smuggled high explosives in his underwear aboard a Northwest Airlines flight from Amsterdam to Detroit. He was charged with having tried to blow up the plane with smuggled explosives. Following the arrest, reports were broadcast from CNN, the *New York Times* and other sources that he was "suspected" of having been trained in Yemen for his terror mission. He reportedly claimed he was sent on his mission by a new organization known as "Al Qaeda in the Arabian Peninsula" (AQAP), based in Yemen. That conveniently turned the world's attention on Yemen as a new center of the alleged Al Qaeda terror organization. In this way, the forgotten, dirt-poor state of Yemen became the latest target for the US "War on Terror."

Basic Yemeni geopolitics[34]

In early 2009 the chess pieces on the Yemeni board began to move. Tariq al-Fadhli, a former jihadist leader originally from South Yemen, broke a 15-year alliance with the Yemeni government of President Ali Abdullah Saleh, and announced he was joining the broad-based opposition coalition known as the Southern Movement (SM). Al-Fadhli had been a member of the Mujahideen movement in Afghanistan in the late 1980's where he was trained by the CIA, along with a then-unknown wealthy Saudi of Yemeni extraction, named Osama bin Laden. In fact several commentators have claimed that the real headquarters of "Al Qaeda" is at CIA headquarters in Langley, Virginia in the USA. Al-Fadhli's break with the Yemeni dictatorship gave new power to the Southern Movement (SM).

Yemen itself is a synthetic amalgam created after the collapse of the Soviet Union in 1990, when the southern Peoples' Democratic Republic of Yemen (PDRY) lost its main foreign sponsor. Unification of the northern Yemen Arab Republic and the southern PDRY state led to a short-lived optimism that ended in a brief civil war in 1994, as southern army factions organized a revolt against what they saw as the corrupt crony state rule of northern President Ali Abdullah Saleh. President Saleh began his autocratic rule of Yemen in 1978, first as President of North Yemen (the Yemen Arab Republic) and after 1990 as President of the unified Yemen.

During the 2011 "Arab Spring" he was badly injured in an assassination attempt, when the mosque he attended was bombed. He agreed to step down under pressure from Saudi Arabia and the Gulf Coordination Council in February 2012.

Before 1990, Washington and the Saudi Kingdom backed and supported Saleh and his policy of Islamization, as a bid to contain the communist south. Later, Saleh relied on a strong Salafist-jihadi movement to retain a one-man dictatorial rule. When al-Fadhli broke with Saleh and joined his former socialist foes in the southern opposition group, it marked a major setback for Saleh.

Soon after al-Fadhli joined the Southern Movement coalition, on April 28, 2009, protests in the southern Yemeni provinces of Lahj, Dalea and Hadramout intensified. There were demonstrations by tens of thousands of dismissed military personnel and civil servants demanding better pay and benefits, demonstrations that had been taking place in growing numbers since 2006.

Complicating the picture in Yemen – which some call a "failed state" – Saleh faced a rebellion in the north by the Shi'ite al-Houthi Zaydi clan. On September 11, 2009, in an Al-Jazeera TV interview, Saleh accused Iraq's Shi'ite opposition leader, Muqtada al-Sadr, and also Iran, of backing the north Yemen Shi'ite Houthist. He declared, "We cannot accuse the Iranian official side, but the Iranians are contacting us, saying that they are prepared for a mediation. This means that the Iranians have contacts with them [the Houthists], given that they want to mediate between the Yemeni government and them. Also,

Muqtada al-Sadr in al-Najaf in Iraq is asking that he be accepted as a mediator. This means they have a link."[35]

Yemen authorities claim they have seized caches of weapons made in Iran, while the Houthists claim to have captured Yemeni equipment with Saudi Arabian markings, accusing Sana'a (the capital of Yemen and site of the US Embassy) of acting as a Saudi proxy. Iran has rejected claims that Iranian weapons were found in north Yemen, calling claims of support to the rebels "baseless."[36]

Some 70% of Yemen's revenues derive from its oil sales. The central government of Saleh sits in former North Yemen in Sana'a, while the oil is in former South Yemen. Yet Saleh controls the oil revenue flows. Lack of oil revenue has made Saleh's usual option of buying off opposition groups all but impossible.

Into this chaotic domestic picture comes the January 2009 announcement, prominently featured on select Internet websites, that Al Qaeda, the alleged global terrorist organization created by the late CIA-trained Saudi, Osama bin Laden, has opened a major new branch in Yemen for both Yemen and Saudi operations.

Al Qaeda in Yemen released a statement through online jihadist forums Jan. 20, 2009 from the group's leader Nasir al-Wahayshi, announcing formation of a single al Qaeda group for the Arabian Peninsula under his command. According to al-Wahayshi, the new group, al Qaeda in the Arabian Peninsula, would consist of his former Al Qaeda in Yemen, as well as members of the defunct Saudi Al Qaeda group. The press release claimed, interestingly enough, that a Saudi national, a former Guantanamo detainee (Number 372), Abu-Sayyaf al-Shihri, would serve as al-Wahayshi's deputy.

Days later an online video from al-Wahayshi appeared under the alarming title, "We Start from Here and We Will Meet at al-Aqsa." Al-Aqsa refers to the al-Aqsa Mosque in Jerusalem that Jews know as Temple Mount, the site of the destroyed Temple of Solomon, which Muslims call Al Haram Al Sharif. The video threatens Muslim leaders – including Yemeni's President Saleh, the Saudi royal family, and Egyptian President Mubarak – and promises to take the jihad from Yemen to Israel to "liberate" Muslim holy sites and Gaza, something that would likely detonate World War III if anyone were mad enough to do it.

Also in that video, in addition to former Guantanamo inmate al-Shihri, is a statement from Abu-al-Harith Muhammad al-Awfi, identified as a field commander in the video, and allegedly former Guantanamo detainee 333. As it is well-established that torture methods are worthless for obtaining truthful confessions, some have speculated that the real goal of CIA and Pentagon interrogators at Guantanamo prison since September 2001, has been to use brutal techniques to train or recruit sleeper terrorists who can be activated on command by US intelligence, a charge difficult to prove or disprove. The presence of two such high-ranking Guantanamo graduates in the new Yemen-based Al Qaeda, however, is certainly grounds for questioning.

The curious emergence of a tiny but well-publicized al Qaeda in southern Yemen amid what observers call the Southern Movement, a broad-based and popular front that eschews the radical global agenda of al Qaeda, gave the Pentagon a kind of *casus belli* to escalate US military operations in the strategic region.

After declaring that the Yemen internal strife was Yemen's own affair, President Obama ordered air strikes against Yemen. The Pentagon claimed its attacks on December 17 and 24, 2009 killed three key al Qaeda leaders, but no evidence has yet proven this. Nonetheless the Christmas Day Detroit bomber drama gave new life to Washington's "War on Terror" campaign in Yemen. Obama has now offered military assistance to the Saleh Yemen government.

As if on cue, at the same time CNN headlines broadcast new terror threats from Yemen, the long-running Somalia pirate attacks on commercial shipping – in the same Gulf of Aden and Arabian Sea across from southern Yemen – escalated dramatically after having been reduced by multinational ship patrols.

On December 29, 2009 Moscow's *RIA Novosti* (the Russian Information Agency) reported that Somali pirates had seized a Greek cargo vessel in the Gulf of Aden off Somalia's coast. Earlier the same day a British-flagged chemical tanker and its 26 crew were also seized in the Gulf of Aden. Exhibiting sophisticated skills in using western media, pirate commander Mohamed Shakir told the British newspaper *The Times* by phone, "We have hijacked a ship with [a] British flag in the Gulf of Aden late yesterday." The US intelligence brief, Stratfor, reported that *The Times,* owned by neo-conservative financial backer, Rupert Murdoch, was sometimes used by Israeli intelligence to plant useful stories.

The two latest events were among a record number of attacks and hijackings during 2009. As of December 22, attacks by Somali pirates in the Gulf of Aden and the east coast of Somalia numbered 174, with 35 vessels hijacked and 587 crew taken hostage so far in 2009. Almost all the pirate activity had been successful, according to the International Maritime Bureau's Piracy Reporting Center. The question remained: who was providing the Somali "pirates" with arms and logistics sufficient to elude international patrols from numerous nations?

The waters between Yemen and Somalia are of strategic geopolitical significance. This is the site of the strait of Bab el-Mandab, which is on the US Government list of seven strategic world oil shipping chokepoints. The US Government Energy Information Agency states that "closure of the Bab el-Mandab could keep tankers from the Persian Gulf from reaching the Suez Canal/Sumed pipeline complex, diverting them around the southern tip of Africa. The Strait of Bab el-Mandab is a chokepoint between the horn of Africa and the Middle East, and a strategic link between the Mediterranean Sea and Indian Ocean."[37]

Bab el-Mandab, between Yemen, Djibouti, and Eritrea, connects the Red Sea with the Gulf of Aden and the Arabian Sea. Oil and other shipping from the Persian Gulf and Indian Ocean must pass through Bab el-Mandab before entering the Suez Canal to access the Mediterranean. In 2006, the Energy Department in Washington reported that an estimated 3.3 million barrels a day of oil flowed through this narrow waterway to Europe, the United States, and Asia. Most oil, or some 2.1 million barrels a day, goes north through the Bab el-Mandab strait to the Sumed pipeline near Suez and thence to the Mediterranean near Alexandria, avoiding the Suez Canal.

Since 2010, any excuse for a US or NATO militarization of the waters around Bab el-Mandab has given Washington another major link in the chain of control of the world's seven critical oil chokepoints – key to any future US strategy of denying oil to China, the EU or any region or country that opposes US policy.

Given that significant flows of Saudi oil pass through Bab el-Mandab, US military control of the strait could serve to deter the Saudi Kingdom from transacting future oil sales with China, or others no longer transacting in dollars.

The US would also be in a position to threaten China's oil transport from Port Sudan on the Red Sea just north of Bab el-Mandab, a major lifeline for China's national energy needs.

In addition to its geopolitical position as a major global oil transit chokepoint, Yemen has been reported to hold some of the world's greatest untapped oil reserves. Yemen's Masila Basin and Shabwa Basin are reported by international oil companies to contain "world class discoveries." France's Total and several smaller international oil companies are engaged in developing Yemen's oil production. Some fifteen years ago I was told in a private meeting with a well-informed Washington insider that Yemen contained "enough undeveloped oil to fill the oil demand of the entire world for the next fifty years."

Moving to China's borders

At the same time key oil sources for China in the Middle East and Africa have been militarized, step by careful step, the Pentagon and US secret intelligence services, deploying their in-house "Human Rights" NGOs, began a series of operations directly on and even inside Chinese borders in Myanmar, Tibet, and China's critical oil province Xianjiang.

The first moves in shifting the geopolitical orientation of Myanmar, formerly the British colony of Burma, took place in 2007 with the so-called Saffron revolution. Like all "Color Revolutions," from Ukraine to Georgia to Serbia, this color revolution was a project of the US State Department, Pentagon and CIA.

> Burma's "Saffron Revolution" followed the pattern of the Ukraine's "Orange Revolution," and Georgia's "Rose Revolution," and the various Color Revolutions instigated in recent years against strategic states surrounding Russia. It was another well-orchestrated exercise in Washington-run regime change, including the use of "hit-and-run" protests with "swarming" mobs of Buddhists in saffron, as well as internet blogs, mobile SMS links between protest groups, and well-organized protest cells that dispersed and

formed again. CNN made the blunder during a September 2007 broadcast of mentioning the active presence of the National Endowment for Democracy behind the protests in Myanmar.[38]

The NED is a US Government-controlled and financed NGO whose history of involvement in various strategic countries suggests strongly a sinister agenda of destabilizing regimes not "cooperative" with Washington.

Burma had one of the world's lowest standards of living. A dramatic collapse in purchasing power resulted from the Myanmar Government's ill-conceived 100% to 500% price hikes in gasoline and other fuels in August, 2007.

> Inflation, the nominal trigger for the mass protests led by Saffron-robed Buddhist monks, was unofficially estimated to have risen by 35% annually. Ironically, the demand to establish "market" energy prices was implemented under the orders of the IMF and World Bank, both controlled by Washington.

> The UN estimated that Burma's population of some 50 million inhabitants spends up to 70% of their monthly income on food alone. The fuel price hike, which was a direct result of the IMF "reforms," made matters unbearable for tens of millions.[39]

A motive of major geopolitical consequence lay behind the CNN News pictures of streams of saffron-robed Buddhist monks, marching in the streets of the largest city and former capital, Rangoon (Yangon), calling for more democracy in Myanmar. The US government still preferred to call it by the British colonial name, Burma.

Myanmar, with a land area about the size of Texas, was the victim of a drama scripted in Washington by its subversive NGOs: the National Endowment for Democracy (NED), the George Soros Open Society Institute, Freedom House, and the Albert Einstein Institution, all US intelligence assets used to spark "non-violent" regime change around the world on behalf of the US strategic agenda.

The US State Department admitted supporting the activities of the NED in Myanmar. The NED is a US Government-funded "private" entity whose activities are designed to support US foreign policy objectives, "doing today what the CIA did" during the Cold War, as its founder once admitted to the *Washington Post*. The NED in turn finances the Open Society Institute of George Soros, US billionaire speculator and convicted inside trader, which was enlisted to foster regime change in Myanmar.

In an October 30, 2003 press release, the State Department admitted, "The United States also supports organizations such as the National Endowment for Democracy, the Open Society Institute and Internews, working inside and outside the region on a broad range of democracy promotion activities."[40]

> The US State Department recruited and trained key local opposition leaders from numerous anti-government organizations within Myanmar. It has poured the huge sum (for Myanmar) of more than $2.5 million annually into NED activities in promoting regime change in Myanmar since at least 2003. The US regime change project, its Saffron Revolution, was largely run from the US Consulate General in bordering Chiang Mai, Thailand, according to informed reports. Activists are recruited and trained there and, in some cases, directly in the USA, before being sent back to organize inside Myanmar. The USA's NED admits to funding key opposition media, including the *New Era Journal*, *Irrawaddy* and the *Democratic Voice of Burma* radio.[41]

> The concert-master of the tactics of Saffron monk-led non-violent regime change was Gene Sharp, founder of the deceptively-named Albert Einstein Institution in Cambridge Massachusetts, a group funded by an arm of the NED to foster US-friendly regime change in key spots around the world. Sharp's institute has been active in Burma since 1989, just after the regime massacred some 3,000 protestors to silence internal opposition. CIA special operative and former US Military Attaché in Rangoon, Col. Robert Helvey, an expert in clandestine operations, introduced Sharp to Burma in 1989 to train the opposition there in non-violent strategy. Interestingly, Sharp was also in China two weeks before the dramatic events at Tiananmen Square.[42]

Geopolitical control was the aim of Washington's Saffron Revolution and of subsequent pressures that led to the "opening" of Myanmar to the West in 2011. For Washington, Myanmar is the key to ultimate control of the strategic waterways from the Persian Gulf to the South China Sea. The coastline of Myanmar provides naval access in vacinity of one of the world's most strategic shipping lanes, the Strait of Malacca, the ancient spice trade route to China.

> The Pentagon has been trying to militarize the region since September 11, 2001, using the argument of defending against possible terrorist attack. The US has managed to gain an airbase on Banda Aceh, the Sultan Iskandar Muda Air Force Base, on the northernmost tip of Sumatra, in Indonesia. The governments of the region, including Myanmar, however, adamantly refused US efforts to militarize the region. A glance at a map will confirm the strategic importance of Myanmar.[43]

The Strait of Malacca, linking the Indian and Pacific Oceans, is the shortest sea route between the Persian Gulf and China. It is the key chokepoint in Asia. More than 80% of China's oil imports are shipped by tankers passing through the Malacca Strait. The narrowest point is the Phillips Channel in the Singapore Strait, only 1.5 miles wide at its narrowest. Daily more than 12 million barrels in oil supertankers pass through here, most en route to China, the world's fastest-growing energy market, or to Japan.[44]

> If the Strait were closed, nearly half of the world's tanker fleet would be required to make longer voyages. Closure would immediately raise freight rates worldwide. More than 50,000 vessels per year transit the Strait of Malacca. The region from Myanmar to Banda Aceh in Indonesia is fast becoming one of the world's most strategic chokepoints. Whoever controls those waters controls China's energy supplies.[45]

> In recent years, Beijing has poured billions of dollars in military assistance into Myanmar, including fighter, ground-attack and transport aircraft; tanks and armored personnel carriers; naval vessels and surface-to-air missiles. China has built up Myanmar's railroads and roads, and won permission to station its troops in the country. According to Indian defense sources, China has also built a large electronic surveillance facility on

Myanmar's Coco Islands, and is building naval bases for access to the Indian Ocean.

In fact, Myanmar is an integral part of what the Pentagon terms China's "string of pearls," its strategy of establishing military bases in Myanmar, Thailand and Cambodia, in order to counter US control over the Strait of Malacca chokepoint. There is also energy onshore and offshore of Myanmar, and lots of it.[46]

The gas fields of Myanmar[47]

Oil and gas have been produced in Myanmar since the British set up the Rangoon Oil Company in 1871, later renamed Burmah Oil Co. The country has produced natural gas since the 1970's, and in the 1990's it granted gas concessions in the Gulf of Martaban to Elf Total of France and Premier Oil of the UK. Later Texaco and Unocal (now Chevron) won concessions at Yadana and Yetagun, as well. Yadana's field alone has estimated gas reserves of more than 5 trillion cubic feet, with an expected life of at least 30 years. Yetagun is estimated to have about a third the gas of the Yadana field.

In 2004 a large new gas field, Shwe field, off the coast of Arakan was discovered.

By 2002, both Texaco and Premier Oil had withdrawn from the Yetagun project, following UK government and NGO pressure. Malaysia's Petronas bought Premier's 27% stake. By 2004, Myanmar was exporting Yadana gas via pipeline to Thailand, bringing $1 billion annually to the Myanmar regime.

In 2005 China, Thailand and South Korea invested in expanding the Myanmar oil and gas sector, with the export of gas to Thailand rising 50%. Gas exports are now Myanmar's most important source of income. Yadana was developed jointly by ElfTotal, Unocal, PTT-EP of Thailand and Myanmar's state MOGE, and is operated by the French ElfTotal. Yadana supplies some 20% of Thailand's natural gas needs.

Today the Yetagun field is operated by Malaysia's Petronas along with MOGE and Japan's Nippon Oil and PTT-EP. The gas is piped onshore where it links to the Yadana pipeline. The Shwe field came online in 2009.

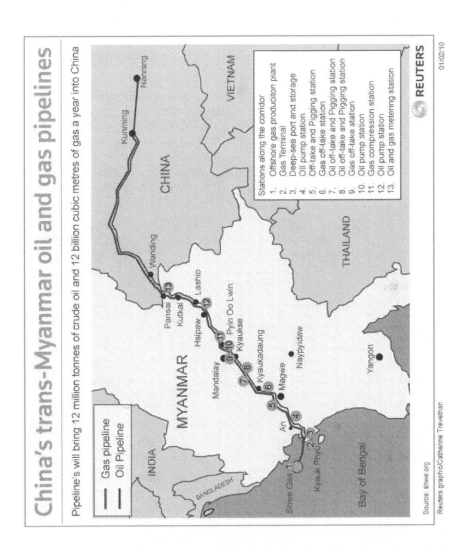

China, India, Myanmar and Bangladesh have had a boundary dispute over offshore energy rights, including the Shwe gas field reserves. In 2007 Myanmar signed a Memorandum of Understanding with PetroChina to supply large volumes of natural gas from reserves of the Shwe gas field in the Bay of Bengal. The contract runs for 30 years. India was the main loser. Myanmar had earlier given India a major stake in two offshore blocks to develop gas that would be transmitted via pipeline through Bangladesh to India's energy-hungry economy. Political bickering with Bangladesh brought the Indian plans to a standstill, although the two nations finally settled on a boundary agreement in 2014.

China took advantage of the stalemate, trumping India with an offer to invest billions in building a strategic oil and gas pipeline from Myanmar's deepwater port at Sittwe in the Bay of Bengal clear across the country to Kunming in China's Yunnan Province, a stretch of more than 2,300 kilometers. China plans an oil refinery in Kunming as well.

The Myanmar-China pipelines will allow oil and gas from Africa (Sudan among other sources) and the Middle East (Iran, Saudi Arabia) to bypass the vulnerable chokepoint of the Malacca Strait. Myanmar becomes China's "bridge," linking Bangladesh and countries westward to the China mainland, independent of any possible future moves by Washington to control the strait.

India's dangerous alliance shift[48]

It's no wonder that China is taking such precautions. Ever since the Bush Administration decided in 2005 to recruit India into the Pentagon's "New Framework for US-India Defense Relations," India has been pushed into a strategic alliance with Washington to counter China in Asia.

In an October 2002 Pentagon report, "The Indo-US Military Relationship," the Office of Net Assessments stated the reason for the India-USA defense alliance would be to have a "capable partner" who can take on "more responsibility for low-end operations" in Asia, provide new training opportunities and "ultimately provide basing and access for US power projection." Washington is also quietly negotiating for a base on Indian territory, a severe violation of India's traditional non-aligned status.

The Bush Administration also offered India to lift its nuclear sanctions of 30 years' standing, and to sell them advanced US nuclear technology, legitimizing India's open violation of the Nuclear Non-Proliferation Treaty – while at the same time putting sanctions on Iran for even thinking about violating same – an exercise in political hypocrisy, to say the least.

Notably, just as the Saffron-robed monks of Myanmar were taking to the streets, the Pentagon opened joint US-Indian naval exercises, Malabar 07, along with armed forces from Australia, Japan and Singapore. The US showed the awesome muscle of its

7th Fleet, deploying the aircraft carriers USS Nimitz and USS Kitty Hawk; guided missile cruisers USS Cowpens and USS Princeton and no less than five guided missile destroyers.[49]

Washington plays "Tibet Roulette" with China[50]

Washington had obviously decided on an ultra-high-risk geopolitical game by fanning the flames of violence inside China itself, in Tibet in early 2008, at a most sensitive time in their relations and on the run-up to the Beijing Olympics.

The 2008 Tibet operation got a green light in October 2007, when George Bush agreed to meet the 14th Dalai Lama for the first time publicly in Washington. The President of the United States was aware of the high stakes of such an insult to Beijing. Bush deepened the affront to America's largest trading partner by agreeing to attend the ceremony as the US Congress awarded the Dalai Lama the Congressional Gold Medal.

The wave of violent protests and documented attacks by Tibetan monks against Han Chinese residents began on March 10, 2008, when several hundred monks marched on Lhasa to demand release of other monks allegedly detained for celebrating the award of the US Congress' Gold Medal the previous October. They were joined by more monks marching to protest rule by Beijing, on the 49th anniversary of the Tibetan uprising against Chinese rule.

The geopolitical game

As the Chinese government itself was clear to point out, the sudden eruption of anti-Chinese violence in Tibet, marking a new phase in the movement led by the exiled Dalai Lama, was suspiciously timed to put the spotlight on Beijing's human rights record on the eve of the coming Olympics.

The Beijing Olympics were an event seen in China as a major acknowledgement of the arrival of a prosperous new China on the world stage. The background actors in the Tibet violence confirm that Washington had been working overtime for months to prepare another of its infamous Color Revolutions, fanning public protests designed to inflict maximum embarrassment on Beijing.

The actors on the ground in and outside Tibet were all tied to the US State Department, including the National Endowment for Democracy (NED), and the CIA's Freedom House through its chairman, Bette Bao Lord, and her role in the International Campaign for Tibet.

Chinese Prime Minister Wen Jiabao accused the Dalai Lama of orchestrating the unrest to sabotage the Olympic Games "in order to achieve their unspeakable goal," Tibetan independence. Bush then telephoned his Chinese counterpart, President Hu Jintao, to press for talks between Beijing and the exiled Dalai Lama. The White House said that Bush "raised his concerns about the situation in Tibet and encouraged the Chinese government to engage in substantive dialogue with the Dalai Lama's representatives and to allow access for journalists and diplomats." President Hu reportedly told Bush the Dalai Lama must "stop his sabotage" of the Olympics before Beijing takes a decision on talks with the exiled Tibetan spiritual leader.

The Dalai Lama's odd friends

In the West the image of the Dalai Lama had been so promoted that in many circles he was deemed almost a God.

The Dalai Lama travels in what can only be called arch-conservative political circles. During the 1930's the Nazis, including Gestapo chief Heinrich Himmler and other top Nazi Party leaders, regarded Tibet as the holy site of the survivors of the lost "Atlantis" civilization, and the origin of the "Nordic pure race."

When he was 11 and already designated Dalai Lama, he was befriended by a Nazi and officer of Heinrich Himmler's feared SS, Heinrich Harrer. Harrer was an elite SS member at the time he met the 11-year-old Dalai Lama and became his tutor in "the world outside Tibet." While only the Dalai Lama knows the contents of Harrer's private lessons, the two remained friends until Harrer died in 2006 at age 93.[51]

Harrer was not the only Nazi in the Dalai Lama's circle of close friends. In April 1999, along with Margaret Thatcher, and former Beijing Ambassador, CIA Director and President, George H. W. Bush, the Dalai Lama demanded the British government release Augusto Pinochet, the former fascist dictator of Chile and a longtime CIA client who was visiting England at the time. The Dalai Lama urged that Pinochet not be extradited to Spain, where he was wanted for crimes against humanity, and would stand trial. The Dalai Lama had close ties to Miguel Serrano,[52] head of

Chile's National Socialist Party, a proponent of something called esoteric Hitlerism.[53]

The Dalai Lama had been surrounded and financed in significant part, since his flight into Indian exile in 1959, by various US and Western intelligence services and their gaggle of NGOs.

It was the agenda of the Dalai Lama's friends in Washington that was relevant. Author Michael Parenti noted in his essay, "Friendly Feudalism: The Tibet Myth," that "during the 1950s and 60s, the CIA actively backed the Tibetan cause with arms, military training, money, air support and all sorts of other help."[54]

The US-based American Society for a Free Asia, a CIA front, publicized the cause of Tibetan resistance, with the Dalai Lama's eldest brother, Thubtan Norbu, playing an active role in the group. The Dalai Lama's second-eldest brother, Gyalo Thondup, established an intelligence operation with the CIA in 1951. It was later upgraded into a CIA-trained guerrilla unit, whose recruits parachuted back into Tibet, according to Parenti.[55]

According to declassified US intelligence documents released in the late 1990s, "for much of the 1960s, the CIA provided the Tibetan exile movement with $1.7 million a year for operations against China, including an annual subsidy of $180,000 for the Dalai Lama."[56]

With the help of the CIA, the Dalai Lama fled to Dharamshala, India, in 1959, where he lives at the time of this writing. He continued to receive millions of dollars in backing up to the time of the 2008 Tibet events, not from the CIA but from the more innocuous-sounding CIA front organization, funded by the US Congress, called the National Endowment for Democracy (NED).

The NED had been instrumental in every US-backed Color Revolution destabilization from Serbia to Georgia to Ukraine to Myanmar. Its funds went to back opposition media and global public relations campaigns to popularize their pet "opposition" candidates. As in the other recent Color Revolutions, the US Government was fanning the flames of destabilization against China by funding opposition protest organizations inside and outside Tibet through its arm, the NED.

The NED was founded by the Reagan Administration in the early 1980's, on the recommendation of Bill Casey, Reagan's Director of the Central Intelligence Agency (CIA), following a series of high-publicity exposures of CIA assassinations and destabilizations of unfriendly regimes. The NED was designed to pose as an independent NGO, one step removed from the CIA and Government agencies so as to be less conspicuous, presumably. The first acting President of the NED, Allen Weinstein, commented to the Washington Post that, "A lot of what we do today was done covertly 25 years ago by the CIA."[57]

American intelligence historian William Blum wrote, "The NED played an important role in the Iran-Contra affair of the 1980s, funding key components of Oliver North's shadowy 'Project Democracy.' This network privatized US foreign policy, waged war, ran arms and drugs, and engaged in other equally charming activities. In 1987, a White House spokesman stated that those at NED 'run Project Democracy.'"[58]

The most prominent pro-Dalai Lama Tibet independence organization was the International Campaign for Tibet, founded in Washington in 1988. The ICT began receiving funds from the NED no later than 1994 . The ICT presented their annual "Light of Truth" award in 2005 to Carl Gershman, founder of the NED. The ICT Board of Directors is peopled with former US State Department officials, including Gare Smith and Julia Taft.[59]

Another very active anti-Beijing organization was the US-based Students for a Free Tibet (SFT), founded in 1994 in New York City as a project of the US Tibet Committee and the ICT. The SFT gained notoriety by unfurling a 450-foot banner atop the Great Wall in China, calling for a free Tibet and accusing Beijing of wholly unsubstantiated claims of genocide against Tibet. It made good drama to rally naive Western university students.

The SFT was among five organizations that proclaimed the start of a "Tibetan people's uprising" on January 4, 2008. SFT co-founded a temporary office in charge of coordination and financing.

Harry Wu was another prominent Dalai Lama supporter against Beijing. He became notorious for claiming falsely in a 1996 Playboy interview that he had "videotaped a prisoner whose kidneys were surgically removed while he was alive, and then the prisoner was taken out and shot. The tape was broadcast by BBC." The BBC film showed nothing of the sort, but the damage was done. How many people check old BBC archives? Wu, a retired Berkeley professor who left China after imprisonment as a dissident, is head of the Laogai Research Foundation, a tax-exempt organization funded mainly by the NED.[60]

With its US government financing, NED also supports the *Tibet Times* newspaper, run by the Dalai Lama's "government in exile" at Dharamshala, India. The NED also funds the Tibet Multimedia Center for "information dissemination that addresses the struggle for human rights and democracy in Tibet," also based in Dharamshala. And NED finances the Tibetan Center for Human Rights and Democracy.

In short, US State Department and US intelligence community fingerprints were all over the upsurge around the Free Tibet movement and the anti-Han Chinese attacks of March 2008 shortly before the Beijing Olympics. The question was why, and especially why in 2008?

Tibet's raw minerals treasure

Tibet is of strategic import to China not only for its geographical location astride the border with India, Washington's newest anti-China ally in Asia, but also because Tibet is a treasure trove of minerals and also oil. It has some of the world's largest uranium and borax deposits, one half of the world's lithium, the largest copper deposits in Asia, enormous iron deposits, and over 80,000 gold mines. Tibet's forests are the largest timber reserve at China's disposal; as of 1980, an estimated $54 billion worth of trees had been felled and taken by China. Tibet also has some of the largest oil reserves in the region.[61]

On the Tibet Autonomous Region's border with the Xinjiang Uyghur Autonomous Region is also a vast oil and mineral region in the Qaidam Basin, known as the "treasure basin." The Basin has 57 different types of mineral resources with proven reserves including petroleum, natural gas, coal, crude salt, potassium, magnesium, lead, zinc and gold. Those mineral resources have a potential economic value of 15 trillion yuan or US$1.8 trillion. Proven reserves of potassium, lithium and crude salt in the basin are the biggest in China. And situated as it is, on the "roof of the world," Tibet is perhaps the world's most valuable water source. Tibet is the source of seven of Asia's greatest rivers. which provide water for two billion people." Whoever controls Tibet's water has a powerful geopolitical lever over all Asia. Washington's prime interest in Tibet, however, was for its potential to act as a lever to destabilize and blackmail the Beijing Government.

Washington's "nonviolence as a form of warfare"

The March 2008 events in Tibet and other regions of China were played in Western media with little regard to accuracy or independent verification. Most of the enlarged pictures in European and US newspapers and TV had not shown Chinese military oppression of Tibetan lamas or monks. They were in most cases either Reuters or AFP pictures of Han Chinese being beaten by Tibetan monks belonging to paramilitary organizations. In some instances, German TV stations ran video pictures of beatings that were not even from Tibet, but rather by Nepalese police in Kathmandu.[62]

The western media's complicity simply further confirmed that the actions around Tibet were part of a well-orchestrated destabilization effort on the part of Washington. What few people realized was that the National Endowment for Democracy (NED) was also instrumental, along with Gene Sharp's misnamed Albert Einstein Institution through Colonel Robert Helvey, in encouraging the student protests at Tiananmen Square in June 1989. The Albert Einstein Institution, as it describes itself, specialized in "nonviolence as a form of warfare."[63]

Colonel Helvey was formerly with the Pentagon's Defense Intelligence Agency stationed in Myanmar. In early 1989 in Hong Kong, Helvey trained several student leaders from Beijing in mass demonstration techniques which they were to use in the Tiananmen Square incident of June 1989. He was reported also acting as an adviser to the Falun Gong in similar civil disobedience techniques. Helvey nominally retired from the army in 1991, but had been working with Albert Einstein and George Soros long before then. In its annual report for 2004 Helvey's Albert Einstein Institution admitted to advising people in Tibet.[64]

With the emergence of the Internet and mobile telephone use including social networking tools such as Twitter or Facebook or Google, the US Pentagon had refined an entirely new form of regime change and political destabilization. As researcher Jonathan Mowat described the phenomenon behind the wave of color revolutions:

> "...What we are seeing is civilian application of Secretary Donald Rumsfeld's 'Revolution in Military Affairs' doctrine, which depends on highly mobile small group

deployments 'enabled' by 'real time' intelligence and communications. Squads of soldiers taking over city blocks with the aid of 'intelligence helmet' video screens that give them an instantaneous overview of their environment, constitute the military side. Bands of youth converging on targeted intersections in constant dialogue on cell phones constitute the doctrine's civilian application. This parallel should not be surprising since the US military and National Security Agency subsidized the development of the Internet, cellular phones, and software platforms. From their inception, these technologies were studied and experimented with in order to find the optimal use in a new kind of warfare. The 'revolution' in warfare that such new instruments permit has been pushed to the extreme by several specialists in psychological warfare. Although these military utopians have been working in high places, (for example the RAND Corporation), for a very long time, to a large extent they only took over some of the most important command structures of the US military apparatus with the victory of the neoconservatives in the Pentagon of Donald Rumsfeld.[65]

Washington policy used and refined these techniques of "revolutionary nonviolence." NED operations embodied a series of "democratic" or soft coup projects as part of a larger strategy which would strategically cut China off from access to its vital external oil and gas reserves.

The 1970's quote attributed to then-Secretary of State Henry Kissinger, a proponent of British geopolitics in an American context comes to mind: "If you control the oil you control entire nations..."

The destabilization attempt by Washington using Tibet, no doubt with quiet "help" from its friends in British and other pro-NATO intelligence services, was part of a clear pattern. It included Washington's "Saffron revolution" attempts to destabilize Myanmar. It included the effort to get NATO troops into Darfur to block China's access to strategically vital oil resources there and elsewhere in Africa. It included attempts to foment problems in Uzbekistan and Kyrgyzstan, and to disrupt China's vital new energy pipeline projects to Kazakhstan. The earlier Asian Great Silk Road trade routes went through Tashkent in Uzbekistan and Almaty in Kazakhstan for geographically obvious reasons, in a region surrounded by major mountain ranges. Geopolitical control of Uzbekistan, Kyrgyzstan, Kazakhstan would enable control of any potential pipeline routes between China and Central Asia just as the encirclement of Russia controls pipeline and other ties between it and western Europe, China, India and the Middle East, where China depends on uninterrupted oil flows from Iran, Saudi Arabia and other OPEC countries.

A revealing New York Council on Foreign Relations analysis in their *Foreign Affairs* magazine from Zbigniew Brzezinski, dated September/October 1997 is worth quoting. Brzezinski, a protégé of David Rockefeller and a follower of the founder of British geopolitics, Sir Halford Mackinder, was foreign policy adviser to Presidential candidate Barack Obama in 2008. In 1997 he revealingly wrote:

> Eurasia is home to most of the world's politically assertive and dynamic states. All the historical pretenders to global power originated in Eurasia. The world's most populous aspirants to regional hegemony, China and India, are in Eurasia, as are all the potential political or economic challengers to American primacy. After the United States, the next six largest economies and military spenders are there, as are all but one of the world's overt nuclear powers, and all but one of the covert ones. Eurasia accounts for 75 percent of the world's population; 60 percent of its GNP, and 75 percent of its energy resources. Collectively, Eurasia's potential power overshadows even America's.

> Eurasia is the world's axial supercontinent. A power that dominated Eurasia would exercise decisive influence over two of the world's three most economically productive regions, Western Europe and East Asia. A glance at the map also suggests that a country dominant in Eurasia would almost automatically control the Middle East and Africa. With Eurasia now serving as the decisive geopolitical chessboard, it no longer suffices to fashion one policy for Europe and another for Asia. What happens with the distribution of power on the Eurasian landmass will be of decisive importance to America's global primacy....[66]

That statement, written well before the 1999 US-led bombing of former Yugoslavia and the 2001-2003 US military occupations in Afghanistan and Iraq, or its support of the Baku-Tbilisi-Ceyhan

Pipeline, put Washington pronouncements about "ridding the world of tyranny" and about spreading democracy, into a somewhat different context from the one usually mentioned by George W. Bush or Barack Obama. It was about global hegemony, not democracy. It should be no surprise when China was not convinced that giving Washington such overwhelming power was in China's national interest, any more than Russia thinks that it would be a step towards peace to let NATO gobble up Ukraine and Georgia and put US missiles on Russia's doorstep "to defend against threat of Iranian nuclear attack on the United States."

The US-led destabilization in Tibet was part of a strategic shift of great significance. It came at a time when the US economy and the US dollar, still the world's reserve currency, were in the worst crisis since the 1930's. It was significant that the US Administration in 2008 sent Wall Street banker and former Goldman Sachs chairman Henry Paulson to Beijing in the midst of its efforts to embarrass Beijing in Tibet. Washington was literally "playing with fire." China had long before 2008 surpassed Japan as the world's largest holder of foreign currency reserves, now in the range of $1.5 trillions, most of which were invested in US Treasury debt instruments. China was America's largest lender, its creditor.

Soon after the risky Tibet intervention Washington escalated pressure on China's oil resources by an attempt at fomenting unrest in China's oil-rich and strategic province, Xinjiang.

Washington meddles in Xinjiang

In July, 2009 in Xinjiang Uyghur Autonomous Region in China, the US Government's "independent" NGO, the National Endowment for Democracy (NED), was complicit in massive intervention to cause riots in one of China's most sensitive energy and ethnic regions.

The reasons for Washington's intervention into Xinjiang affairs had nothing to do with concerns over alleged human rights abuses by Beijing authorities against Uyghur people. It was about the strategic geopolitical location of Xinjiang on the Eurasian landmass and its strategic importance for China's future economic and energy cooperation with Russia, Kazakhastan and other Central Asia states of the Shanghai Cooperation Organization.

The major organization internationally calling for protests in front of Chinese embassies around the world was the Washington, D.C.-based World Uyghur Congress (WUC).

The WUC managed to finance a staff and a very fancy website in English, and to develop a very close relation to the US Congress-funded NED. According to published reports by the NED itself, the World Uyghur Congress received $215,000 annually from the National Endowment for Democracy for "human rights research and advocacy projects." Rebiya Kadeer, the president of the WUC was an exile Uyghur who described herself as a "laundress turned millionaire," also served as president of the Washington D.C.-based Uyghur American Association, another Uyghur "human rights" organization which received significant funding from the US Government via the National Endowment for Democracy.[67]

The NED, which masquerades as a private, non-government, non-profit foundation, receives a yearly appropriation for its international work from the US Congress. The NED money is channelled through four "core foundations". These are the National Democratic Institute for International Affairs, linked to the Democratic Party; the International Republican Institute tied to the Republican Party; the American Center for International Labor Solidarity linked to the AFL-CIO labor federation as well as the US State Department; and the Center for International Private Enterprise linked to the US Chamber of Commerce.

How then did the NED encourage the unrest in Xinjiang Uyghur Autonomous Region? Significantly, the Uyghur riots took place only days following the historic meeting of the Shanghai Cooperation Organization.

On May 18, 2009, the US-government's NED, according to the official WUC website, hosted a seminal human rights conference entitled *East Turkestan: 60 Years under Communist Chinese Rule,* along with a curious NGO with the name, the Unrepresented Nations and Peoples Organisation (UNPO).[68]

The Honorary President and founder of the UNPO was Erkin Alptekin, an exile Uyghur who founded UNPO while working for the US Information Agency's official propaganda organization, Radio Free Europe/Radio Liberty as Director of their Uyghur Division and Assistant Director of the Nationalities Services.

Alptekin also founded the World Uyghur Congress at the same time, in 1991, while he was with the US Information Agency. The official mission of the USIA at that time was "to understand, inform, and influence foreign publics in promotion of the [USA] national interest..." Alptekin was the first president of WUC, and, according to the official WUC website, is a "close friend of the Dalai Lama."[69]

UNPO was formed in 1991 as the Soviet Union was collapsing and most of the land area of Eurasia was in political and economic chaos. Since 2002 its Director General has been Archduke Karl von Habsburg of Austria who lists his title (unrecognized by Austria or Hungary) as "Prince Imperial of Austria and Royal Prince of Hungary."

Among the UNPO principles was the right to "self-determination" for the 57 diverse population groups – with a total population of some 150 million – who, by some opaque process not made public, have been admitted as official UNPO members with their own distinct flags, and headquarters in the Hague, Netherlands.

UNPO members range from Kosovo which "joined" when it was still part of then-Yugoslavia in 1991. UNPO also included the "Aboriginals of Australia" who were listed as founding members along with Kosovo. It even included the Buffalo River Dene Nation Indians of northern Canada.

The select UNPO members also included "Tibet" which is listed as a founding member. It included other explosive geopolitical groups, such as the Crimean Tartars, the Greek Minority in Romania, the Chechen Republic of Ichkeria (in Russia), and the Democratic Movement of Burma. UNPO includes the gulf enclave adjacent to Angola and the Democratic Republic of the Congo – which holds rights to some of the world's largest offshore oil fields leased to Condi Rice's old firm, Chevron Oil. Two additional geopolitical movements that were granted elite recognition by UNPO membership, and that operate in critical "hotspots," included the Southern Azerbaijan National Awakening Movement, and the Democratic Party of Iranian Kurdistan.

In April 2008 according to the website of the UNPO, the US Congress' NED sponsored a "leadership training" seminar for the World Uyghur Congress (WUC) together with the Unrepresented

Nations and Peoples Organization. Over 50 Uyghurs from around the world together with prominent academics, government representatives and members of the civil society gathered in Berlin, Germany to discuss "Self-Determination under International Law." What they discussed privately is not known. Rebiya Kadeer gave the keynote address.[70]

Timing of the Xinjiang riots

The outbreak of riots and unrest in Urumqi, the capital of Xinjiang province in the northwest part of China, exploded on July 5, 2009.

According to the website of the World Uyghur Congress, the "trigger" for the riots was an alleged violent attack on June 26 at a toy factory in China's southern Guangdong Province, where the WUC alleges that Chinese workers attacked and beat to death two Uyghur workers for allegedly raping or sexually molesting two Chinese women workers in the factory. On July 1, the Munich arm of the WUC issued a worldwide call for protest demonstrations against Chinese embassies and consulates for the alleged Guangdong attack, yet admitted the details of the incident were unsubstantiated and filled with allegations and dubious reports.

According to a press release they issued, it was the alleged attack on June 26 that gave the WUC the grounds to issue their worldwide call to action.

On July 5, a Sunday in Xinjiang but still July 4, the US Independence Day holiday in Washington, the WUC in Washington claimed that Han Chinese armed soldiers seized any Uyghur they found on the streets in Urumqi. According to official Chinese news reports, widespread riots and burning of cars along the streets of Urumqi broke out, resulting in over 140 deaths during the following three days.

China's official Xinhua News Agency said that protesters from the Uyghur Muslim ethnic minority group began attacking ethnic Han pedestrians, burning vehicles and attacking buses with batons and rocks. "They took to the street... carrying knives, wooden batons, bricks and stones," an eyewitness was quoted as saying. The French AFP news agency quoted Alim Seytoff, general secretary of the Uyghur American Association in

Washington, saying that according to his information, police had begun shooting "indiscriminately" at protesting crowds.

Two different versions of the same events: The Chinese government and pictures of the riots indicate it was Uyghur rioting and attacks on Han Chinese residents that resulted in deaths and destruction. French official reports put the blame on Chinese police "shooting indiscriminately." The French AFP report relied on the NED-funded Uyghur American Association of Rebiya Kadeer for its information. The AFP account was clearly motivated by a US geopolitical agenda, a deep game by the Obama Administration concerning China's economic future.

Nor was it merely coincidence that the riots in Xinjiang by Uyghur organizations broke out only days after the meeting in Yekaterinburg, Russia attended by member nations of the Shanghai Cooperation Organization (SCO), as well as Iran as official observer guest, represented by President Ahmadinejad.

Over the past few years, in the face of what is seen as an increasingly hostile and incalculable United States foreign policy, the major nations of Eurasia – China, Russia, Kazakhstan, Uzbekistan, Kyrgyzstan, Tajikistan – have increasingly sought means of direct and more effective cooperation in economic as well as security areas. In addition, formal observer status within SCO has been given to Iran, Pakistan, India and Mongolia. The SCO defence ministers are in regular and growing consultation on mutual defence needs, as NATO and the US military command continue provocatively to expand across the region wherever they can.

Xinjiang in Eurasian energy

There was another reason – a vital security factor – for the nations of the SCO to desire peace and stability in China's Xinjiang region. Some of China's most important oil and gas pipeline routes pass directly through Xinjiang. The energy trade between Kazakhstan and China is of enormous strategic importance for both countries, and allows China to become less dependent on oil supply sources that could be cut off by US interdiction, should relations deteriorate to that point.

Kazakh President Nursultan Nazarbayev paid a state visit to Beijing in April 2009. The talks concerned deepening economic cooperation, above all in the energy area, where Kazakhstan holds huge reserves of oil, and likely of natural gas as well. After the talks in Beijing, Chinese media carried articles with such titles as "Kazakhstani oil to fill the Great Chinese pipe."

The Atasu-Alashankou pipeline was completed in July 2009, to transport gas from the Caspian Sea in Kazakhstan to the Chinese border area of Xinjiang. Chinese energy companies also worked on infrastructure projects in Kazakhstan: the construction of a gas processing plant in the Zhanazhol field; the Pavlodar electrolysis works; and completion of the Moynakskaya hydro-electric power station.

According to the US Government's Energy Information Administration, Kazakhstan's Kashagan field is the largest oil field outside the Middle East, and the fifth largest in the world in terms of reserves. It is located off the northern shore of the Caspian Sea, near the city of Atyrau. China has built a 613-mile-long pipeline from Atasu, in northwestern Kazakhstan, to Alashankou at the border of China's Xinjiang region which is exporting Caspian oil to China. The entire length of the pipeline route from Atyrau to Alashankou is 2,228 km or 1,384 miles.

PetroChina's China Oil is the exclusive buyer of the crude oil on the Chinese side. The pipeline is a joint venture of China National Petroleum Corporation (CNPC) and Kazakhstan's pipeline operator, Kaztransoil. Some 85,000 barrels per day of Kazakh crude oil flowed through the pipeline during 2007. CNPC is also involved in other major oil exploration and extraction projects with Kazakhstan. They all depend on transit to China via Xinjiang.

In 2007 CNPC signed an agreement to invest more than $2 billion to construct a natural gas pipeline from Turkmenistan through Uzbekistan and Kazakhstan to China. That pipeline would start at Gedaim on the border of Turkmenistan and Uzbekistan, and extend 1,100 miles through Uzbekistan and Kazakhstan to Khorgos in China's Xinjiang region. Turkmenistan and China signed a 30-year supply agreement for the gas that would fill the pipeline. CNPC has set up two entities to oversee the Turkmen upstream project and the development of a second pipeline that will cross China from the Xinjiang region to southeast China at a cost of some $7 billion.

Russia and China were also discussing major natural gas pipelines from eastern Siberia through Xinjiang into China at the time of the US-instigated Xinjiang riots of 2009. Eastern Siberia contains around 135 trillion cubic feet of proven plus probable natural gas reserves. Russia's Kovykta natural gas field in Irkutsk could supply China with natural gas via Xinjiang or Manchuria. In May 2014, due to the US coup d'état in Ukraine and subsequent proxy war on Russia, President Vladimir Putin finally signed a 30-year gas pipeline deal in Beijing, worth an estimated $400 billion or more.

During the post-2008 global economic crisis, Kazakhstan received a major credit from China of $10 billion, half of which was for the oil and gas sector. The oil pipeline Atasu-Alashankou and the gas pipeline China-Central Asia were instruments of strategic "linkage" of central Asian countries to China's economy. Eurasian cohesion, from Russia to China across Central Asia, was the geopolitical force Washington most feared. Sowing instability in Xinjiang was how Washington tried, unsuccessfully that time, to upset the Shanghai Cooperation Organization and China's energy supplies.

The US-led Cold War over China's oil security is being waged on a global scale. With the world's largest growth market for oil imports, China is vulnerable to US-engineered coups, Arab Spring destabilizations, AFRICOM interventions such as in Libya, and the ongoing effort to topple the Al-Assad regime in Syria and with it, Iran, a major source of China's oil.

As the US put pressure on China's oil supplies, it moved on another front to exploit China's need for energy, by pushing the environmentally disastrous shale gas "fracking" technology on China.

Chapter Three:
Environmental Wars:
Shale Gas – Energy Independence or Environmental Threat?

In early 2012 the Government of China and Chinese state oil companies joined the US shale gas bandwagon. They began to use highly controversial methods to literally break pockets of embedded natural gas free from formations of so-called shale rock, a clay-rich rock embedded with other minerals.

In June 2012,

> state-owned oil giant Sinopec started drilling the first of nine planned shale gas wells in Chongqing, expecting by year's end to produce 11 billion to 18 billion cubic feet (300 to 500 million cubic meters) of natural gas – about the amount China consumes in a single day. It's a small start, but China's ambitions are large; by 2020, the nation's goal is for shale gas to provide 6 percent of its massive energy needs.[71]

The technology to exploit shale gas is made in America. Chinese oil companies and the Chinese Government have invited American and British oil giants to help share know-how in hopes that China can find a domestic solution to its rising energy requirements. In March, 2012, the Anglo-Dutch Royal Dutch Shell Company

> signed the first shale gas production-sharing agreement ever in China, with state-owned China National Petroleum Corporation (CNPC), also known as PetroChina. ExxonMobil, BP, Chevron, and the French company Total also have embarked on shale gas partnerships in China.[72]

The Beijing Government has received geologic estimates from the US Department of Energy's Energy Information Administration (EIA).

> A preliminary EIA assessment of world shale reserves last year indicated that China has the world's largest "technically recoverable" resources – with an estimated 1,275 trillion cubic feet (36 trillion cubic meters). That's 20

percent of world resources, and far more than the 862 trillion cubic feet (24 trillion cubic meters) in estimated U.S. shale gas stores.[73]

The EIA US study claimed that in addition to Chongqing, Tarim Basin in Xinjiang holds the most promising prospects for shale gas.

It should be noted that in recent years, some of the most highly-classified US intelligence operations have been run through the Department of Energy. Disinformation and intelligence services go hand in glove. Was the EIA report deliberately "spiked" to promote a Chinese rush to exploit its shale gas without exploring alternative proposals offering clean, safe new sources of oil and gas? If so, it would not be the first US Government intelligence report that was altered to accomplish a political aim.

It's interesting that US oil companies and agencies recommend Sichuan and Xinjiang as prime areas to extract shale gas. Significantly, the shale deposits in Sichuan and in Xinjiang Provinces are very deep compared with the US deposits. Shale in Sichuan is 1.2 to 3.7 miles (2 to 6 kilometers) below ground, and the mountainous terrain above ground increases the difficulty and cost of drilling.[74]

It is important to bear in mind that America's shale gas boom began through pressure from US Vice President Dick Cheney. The technology that makes modern shale gas extraction possible in large volumes was developed by Halliburton, Cheney's former company before he became President George W. Bush's Vice President, and the man who was responsible for the Bush Administration's energy policy. Cheney was rarely known to show any concern about harm to human life, either in Iraq or in the US, where shale gas extraction has ruined the lives and health of countless American citizens.

Interestingly, China's shale gas adviser, Dr. Julio Friedmann, is from the US Department of Energy's highly-secretive nuclear weapons lab, the Lawrence Livermore National Laboratory in California.[75]

US oil industry executives openly state that they expect China will be very "relaxed" in enforcing strict environmental rules against pollution by the shale gas exploiting companies, meaning they do not plan to make any special precautions against damage their drilling and fracking operations will cause.[76]

The following facts about the real dangers of shale gas extraction have led several EU countries to ban shale gas fracturing entirely, pending thorough safety studies.

Dangers of hydraulic "fracking"

The US Government's Department of Energy, together with a Washington energy consultancy in April 2012, released a major report estimating global resources of shale gas. Significantly, the report estimated that the largest untapped shale gas reserves worldwide were in China.[77]

In the US, oil and gas industry people have quickly forgotten the recent propaganda scare about oil and gas depletion, popularly known as the Peak Oil theory, in their new euphoria over huge new volumes of gas and also oil to be obtained by "fracking" or hydraulic fracturing of shale and coal beds. The Obama Administration speaks about a renaissance in domestic oil production.

Toxins and the Halliburton Loophole

Fracking techniques have been around since the end of World War II. Why then is the world suddenly going crazy over shale gas hydraulic fracking? One answer is that the record high oil and gas prices of recent years have made inefficient and costly processes such fracking – or extracting oil from Canada's tar sands – very profitable to the oil industry. Another reason is the advance of various horizontal underground drilling techniques, that allow companies like Halliburton or Schlumberger to pierce a large shale rock formation and inject substances to "free" the trapped gas.

However, the major reason for the recent explosion of fracking in the United States was passage of legislation in 2005 by the US Congress that exempted the oil industry's hydraulic fracking activity from regulatory supervision by the US Environmental Protection Agency (EPA) under the Safe Drinking Water Act (SDWA). "The oil and gas industry is the only industry in America that is allowed by EPA to inject known hazardous materials – unchecked – directly into or adjacent to underground drinking water supplies."[78] Little wonder they can reap huge profits.

The exemption of fracking from the SDWA is known as the "Halliburton Loophole," because it was introduced thanks to lobbying efforts by the company that produces the lion's share of chemical hydraulic fracking fluids – Dick Cheney's old company, Halliburton.

When Cheney became Vice President under George W. Bush in early 2001, Bush immediately gave him responsibility for a major Energy Task Force to devise a comprehensive national energy strategy for America. Aside from designing plans to grab Iraq's oil, as documents later revealed, the Energy Task Force used Cheney's considerable political muscle and industry-lobbying money to win EPA exemption from the Safe Drinking Water Act.[79]

During Cheney's term as Vice President, he made sure the Government's Environmental Protection Agency (EPA) would give a green light to a major expansion of shale gas drilling in the US. In 2004 the EPA issued a study of the environmental effects of fracking.

That "study has been called 'scientifically unsound' by EPA whistle-blower Weston Wilson," who risked his job to make the warning public. "In March of 2005, EPA Inspector General Nikki Tinsley found enough evidence of potential mishandling of the EPA hydraulic fracturing study to justify a review of Wilson's complaints."[80]

The US Oil and Gas Accountability Project conducted an independent review of the EPA study. They found that EPA deleted information from earlier drafts that indicated that unregulated fracturing poses a threat to human health. Even more disturbing, they found that the Agency did not include information that indicated, "fracturing fluids may pose a threat to drinking water long after drilling operations are completed."[81] All such warnings were simply ignored by the EPA and the Bush Administration.

The Halliburton Loophole was no minor affair. The process of hydraulic fracking to extract gas involves staggering volumes of water and some of the most toxic chemicals known. During the uproar over the BP Deepwater Horizon Gulf of Mexico oil spill, the Obama Administration and the Energy Department formed an advisory commission on shale gas. Their report was released in November 2011. It was a "whitewash" of the dangers of shale gas.

One did not have to look far to understand that the report would give shale gas high support. The commission was headed by former CIA director John Deutch. Deutch also sat on the board of Citigroup, one of the world's most active energy industry banks, tied to the Rockefeller family. He also sat on the board of Schlumberger which, along with Halliburton, is one of the major companies doing hydraulic fracking. In fact, of the seven advisory panel members, six had ties to the energy industry. Little surprise that the Deutch report called shale gas "the best piece of news about energy in the last 50 years." Deutch added, "Over the long term it has the potential to displace liquid fuels in the United States."[82]

Attempts by citizen organizations and individual litigants to force oil companies to disclose the composition of chemicals used in hydraulic fracking have met a stone wall of official and corporate silence in America. The companies argue that the chemicals are proprietary secrets, and that disclosing them would hurt their competitiveness. They also insist the process is "basically safe and that regulating it would deter domestic production."[83]

That piece of legal trickery allowed the fracking lobby to have its cake and eat it too. They claimed it was safe, refused to say what chemicals are used, and insisted that it must be free from the Environmental Protection Administration rules under the Safe Drinking Water Act. If they were right about how safe their chemical fracking fluids are, why were they afraid of being regulated for water safety like other chemical companies?

Shale gas and poisoned water

In a typical shale gas fracturing operation, a company drills a hole several thousand meters below surface; then they drill a horizontal branch perhaps one kilometer in length. According to one expert on fracking, after the horizontal drilling into the shale formation is done:

> ...[Y]ou send down a kind of subterranean pipe bomb, a small package of ball-bearing-like shrapnel and light explosives. The package is detonated, and the shrapnel pierces the bore hole, opening up small perforations in the pipe. They then pump up to seven million gallons of a substance known as slick water to fracture the shale and release the gas. It blasts through those perforations in the

pipe into the shale at such force – more than nine thousand pounds of pressure per square inch – that it shatters the shale for a few yards on either side of the pipe, allowing the gas embedded in it to rise under its own pressure and escape.[84]

The shale rock in which the gas is trapped is so tight that it has to be broken up to let the gas escape. Then come the real problems. A combination of sand and water laced with chemicals – including benzene – is pumped into the well bore at high pressure, shattering the rock and opening millions of tiny fissures, enabling the shale gas to seep into the pipeline.

Not only does it liberate gas – or, in the case of Bakken in North Dakota, oil – it also floods the shale formation with millions of gallons of very toxic fluids. A study conducted by Theo Colburn, director of the Endocrine Disruption Exchange in Paonia, Colorado, identified 65 chemicals that are probable components of the fracking fluids used by shale gas drillers. Those chemicals included benzene, glycol-ethers, toluene, 2-(2-methoxyethoxy) ethanol, and nonylphenols. All of the chemicals are linked to health disorders when human exposure is too high.[85]

Dr. Anthony Ingraffea, Professor of Engineering at Cornell University, who has researched fracture mechanics for more than 30 years, has said that drilling and hydraulic fracking "can liberate biogenic natural gas into a fresh water aquifer."[86] In other words the chemicals and gas can pollute water aquifers that supply drinking water.

A new study authorized by two New York State organizations, Catskill Mountainkeeper and the Park Foundation, analyzed the effects of fracking in the Marcellus Shale in New York and Pennsylvania. The study puts the lie to the gas industry's claims that fracking is harmless to ground water. Their report, published in the journal *Ground Water*, concluded, "More than 5,000 wells were drilled in the Marcellus between mid-2009 and mid-2010...Operators inject up to 4 million gallons of fluid, under more than 10,000 pounds of pressure, to drill and frack each well." To date, little sampling has been done to analyze where fracking fluids go after being injected underground.[87]

Contrary to the industry's assertion that fracking takes place in shale rocks that are impermeable, thereby preventing leaking of toxins into ground water, the scientists concluded, in their peer-reviewed article, that natural faults and fractures in the Marcellus, exacerbated by the effects of fracking itself, could allow chemicals to reach the surface in as little as "just a few years." Tom Myers, the study head who was an independent hydrologist with clients including the US Government and environmental groups, stated, "Simply put, the rock layers are not impermeable. The Marcellus shale is being fracked into a very high permeability. Fluids could move from most any injection process."[88]

Inducing Earthquakes by Fracking

Not only does hydraulic fracking risk poisoning the fresh water underground aquifers, it is done with such force that it has been also known to cause earthquakes. In the UK, the Cuadrilla Company was doing shale gas drilling in Lancashire. They suspended their shale gas test drilling in June 2011. following two earthquakes – one tremor of magnitude 2.3 hit the Fylde coast on April 1, 2011, followed by a second of magnitude 1.4 on May 27, 2011.[89] A UK Government study of the earthquakes, released April, 2012 concluded that fracking drilling operations had caused the quakes.[90]

The highly-respected US National Geographic magazine reported in January 2012, "The most recent dramatic example came on New Year's Eve outside of Youngstown, Ohio. A 4.0 earthquake was the last and largest of a series of temblors that prompted state officials to halt nearby underground disposal of wastewater from hydraulic fracturing for natural gas. Since fracking for natural gas requires typically about 4 million gallons or 15 million liters of water, a large volume of which will return to the surface at well completion, with more coming up over the life of the well, dealing with its disposal is a major environmental and health problem."[91] There have been numerous other instances where the connection between fracking and earthquakes has been established.

The new technique of hydraulic fracking was first used successfully in the late 1990s in the Barnett Shale in Texas, and is now being used to liberate oil from beneath the Bakken Shale in North Dakota. But the largest shale gas fracking activity in the US has been a literal gas bonanza drilling boom in the Marcellus Shale that runs from West Virginia into upstate New York, estimated to hold as much gas as the United States consumes in a century.[92] More recent estimates put the figure at half that or lower, suggesting the energy industry is using hype about huge reserve potentials to promote its methods.

But control of China's energy security and the attempt to manipulate China's economy through currency wars were only part of the escalating Washington hidden war against the emergence of China as a Great Power. One of the most destructive and least understood weapons of the Washington and Wall Street US elites against China was its increasing control over China's food security.

Chapter Four:
Food Wars – "Control the Food, you Control the People"

Over the past thirty or more years the most dramatic change in the food consumption in the history of China has taken place. The change has occurred slowly, such that most Chinese consumers greeted new products from mostly American food outlets as a tasty modern alternative to traditional Chinese food. Today this subtle destruction of the nutritional content of the Chinese diet has manifested in a crisis of explosive dimension.

Food as a weapon

Using food as a weapon to starve enemy populations or otherwise control peoples is an ancient practice of warfare. In the past several decades, the use of food as a weapon has been raised to a new level of sophistication by powerful agribusiness corporations tied to political and financial elites in the United States and Britain. The "weaponization" of the human and animal food chain over the past two decades by Washington has been refined into one of the most insidious threats to the future of the Peoples' Republic of China.

The main source of the problem has been the spread of US fast food chains such as McDonalds, KFC (Kentucky Fried Chicken), Pizza Hut and other large US corporations. The longer-term problem arises from the incursions of US-led agribusiness giants into the agricultural structures of the Peoples' Republic to the point where it has become an unrecognized national security crisis.

Fast Food Dangers – Destroying nutrition

The prevalence of industrial fast food, especially for Chinese youth, represents a major threat to the health and vitality of the next generation. Already, an epidemic rise in the number of cases of diabetes in China in recent years has been reported. In just twenty years, China has gone from a land where diabetes was almost unknown, to what is called the "diabetes capital of the world." What changed among young Chinese in those thirty years? Primarily what has changed is their consumption of Western-based junk food and industrialized, processed food containing huge amounts of sugars.

One recent study found the rate of diabetes among Chinese teenagers to be four times that of US teenagers – and the US itself has undergone a severe rise in diabetes. This diabetes epidemic will bring a huge burden for the Chinese health system and a dramatic weakening of China's labor power in the next several years, barring emergency action by the Beijing authorities.[93]

The ingredients in the mass-produced industrialized fast food from the United States have now been shown to be responsible for the recent epidemics of obesity and diabetes. In 2004, the respected British medical journal *The Lancet*,[94] published the results of a long-term, fifteen-year scientific study involving more than 3,000 subjects, showing a strong connection between fast-food consumption, obesity, and risk for type 2 diabetes. Called the Coronary Artery Risk Development in Young Adults (CARDIA) study, it was conducted by Mark Pereira, Ph.D., assistant professor in epidemiology, University of Minnesota School of Public Health, and David Ludwig, M.D., Ph.D., director of the Obesity Program at Children's Hospital Boston, Massachusetts.

The results showed that fast food increases the risk of obesity and type 2 diabetes.

> Participants who consumed fast food two or more times a week gained approximately 10 pounds and had twice as great an increase in insulin resistance over the 15-year period than participants who consumed fast food less than once per week.[95]

> "Fast-food consumption has increased in the United States during the past three decades," said Pereira. "While there have been many discussions about fast-food's effects on obesity, this appears to be the first scientific, comprehensive long-term study to show a strong connection between fast-food consumption, obesity, and risk for type 2 diabetes," he noted. "The CARDIA study factored in and monitored lifestyle factors including television viewing, physical activity, alcohol consumption, and smoking, but determined that increase in body weight and insulin resistance from fast-food intake seemed to be largely independent of these other lifestyle factors," said Ludwig.[96]

Another scientific study showed that fast-food diets can actually damage the brain.[97] The study in the *Journal of Clinical Investigation*, showed that fast food could actually scar the human brain. Researchers from the Diabetes and Obesity Center of Excellence at the University of Washington, who led the study, fed rats and mice a high-fat diet (HFD) similar to the classic American fast food diet. After just one day, the rodents showed inflammation in the hypothalamus – the area that produces the hormones that control hunger, thirst, sleep, moods and the rhythms of the body.[98]

The study concluded that, "In summary, we report that, in rats and mice that are susceptible to DIO [diet-induced obesity], consumption of a HFD rapidly induces neuron injury in a brain area critical for energy homeostasis... Extending these findings is MRI [magnetic resonance imaging] evidence for gliosis [scar tissue] in the hypothalamus of obese humans. Collectively, this work identifies a potential link between obesity and hypothalamic injury in humans as well as animal models."[99]

More and more young Chinese are becoming obese as a result of changes in their diet, introducing these harmful elements. What is little discussed is the fact that the reason younger Chinese keep eating American "junk food," such as that turned out by global chains like KFC or McDonalds, is the fact that the producers have deliberately laced their chicken, burgers and other fast food with addictive chemicals. Junk food in a real sense is becoming China's new Opium War. In this Opium War, the warships are not waiting outside Canton harbor. They are largely invisible.

Junk food as new Opium War?

Most alarming is that the high-fat/high-sugar junk food that is being spread across China has been proven to be as addictive as heroin. In effect, the spread of McDonalds or KFC and similar foods in China is a new Opium War every bit as destructive, or more so, than the 1840's Opium War.

A study by the American Scripps Research Institute in Florida found that the ingredients in typical junk food, especially the high-fructose corn syrup and other sugars, trigger the same center in the brain as hard drugs like opium or cocaine. In controlled experiments feeding rats junk food, the researchers found the alarming results that "Pleasure centers in the brains of those fed high-fat, high-calorie food became less responsive over time – a signal that the rats were becoming addicted. The rats started to eat more and more. They even went for the junk food when they had to endure an electric shock to get it." According to Dr. Louis J. Aronne, professor at Weill Cornell Medical School and former president of The Obesity Society, the human "brain reacts almost identically to that of a cocaine addict looking at cocaine. And the interesting thing is that someone who is obese has even more similarity to the cocaine addict. ... In many ways, they can be addicted to junk food."[100]

If there is not a dramatic cut in consumption of so-called junk food in the American diet, it is estimated that 50% of the entire US population will be obese in 28 years.

Flavor enhancers like monosodium glutamate (MSG) are another common type of industrial food ingredient whose serious danger has been covered over or disregarded by the US Food and Drug Administration (FDA). Among the dangers of excessive MSG consumption is dementia. One scientific study noted recently, "The excitatory neurotransmitter glutamate plays an important part in the development of neuro-degenerative diseases like dementia. About 70 % of all excitatory synapses in the central nervous system are stimulated by the neurotransmitter glutamate. Dysfunction of glutamatergic neuro-transmission is involved in patho-mechanism of neuro-degenerative dementia. The excitatory effect of chronically released glutamate effects the degeneration of cortical and subcortical neurons, thus leading to the occurrence of dementia symptoms."[101]

Other commonly used substances include artificial sweeteners such as Monsanto's *aspartame*, marketed under the trade name NutraSweet, Equal, Canderel, or AminoSweet, widely used as a sugar substitute in drinks like Diet CocaCola. Monsanto sold its aspartame business to the Japanese company Ajinomoto in 2000, and today Ajinomoto is the world's largest supplier of aspartame, with over 40% market share.[102]

Promoted as a "low sugar" diet substance, aspartame actually induces weight gain with constant use. Among ill effects of regular aspartame use are such symptoms as seizures and convulsions, dizziness, migraines, memory loss, chronic fatigue, depression, and panic attacks.[103]

However, the infestation of China's food supply with junk food is but one part of a conscious, concerted Washington campaign to weaken the independent will and fighting spirit of China. No US Government regulator, including the agency entrusted to ensure the safety of what Americans eat, the Food and Drug Administration, has deemed the ingredients in fast food unfit for human or animal consumption, a fact that merely reflects corruption at the very highest levels of the US Government.

The top Obama Administration official responsible for food safety today is Michael R. Taylor, Deputy Commissioner for Foods at the United States Food and Drug Administration (FDA). Taylor is a former Monsanto executive who has influenced US Government policies to overlook the dangers of genetically modified organisms (GMO) under four US presidents. His ties to Monsanto go back to 1981. From 1994 to 1996 Taylor was at the United States Department of Agriculture (USDA), where he was Administrator of the Food Safety & Inspection Service, approving GMO crops for use and export, ignoring all contrary evidence. Before joining the Obama Administration, he did research for the Rockefeller Foundation-financed think-tank, Resources for the Future, advocating US aid for African agriculture to promote US patented GMO seeds.[104]

Indeed, the second flank of the US agribusiness assault on Chinese food security comes from the USDA in collusion with Monsanto and other agri-chemical giant companies such as Cargill, Archer-Daniels-Midland (ADM), Dow and DuPont, to name the main players. It involves the forced spread of GMOs.

The deadly role of GMOs

The first major research project funded by the powerful American Rockefeller Foundation to create a major plant modification, called GMO or Genetically Modified Organism, was ultimately aimed at controlling the future grain supplies of China and Asia.

In 1985, the Rockefeller Foundation initiated the first large-scale research into the possibility of genetically engineering plants for commercial use. At the time they termed it a "major, long-term commitment to plant genetic engineering." Rockefeller Foundation money provided the essential catalyst for the worldwide scientific research and development which would lead to the creation of genetically modified plants, the Gene Revolution. Over the following two decades, the Rockefellers would spend well over $100 million of foundation monies directly, and several hundred million indirectly, to catalyze and propagate research on the development of genetic engineering, and its application to transforming world food production. Clearly, it was a very big factor in their strategic plans.

In 1982, a group of hand-picked advisers from the Foundation urged its managers to devote future resources to the application of molecular biology for plant breeding. In December 1984, the Trustees of the Rockefeller Foundation approved what was seen at the time as a 10-15 year program to apply new molecular-biological techniques to the breeding of rice, the dietary staple of a majority of the planet's population.[105]

Already back in 1984, the Rockefeller Foundation decided to launch a comprehensive program to map the rice genome, using new molecular-based techniques and advances in computing power. At the time, there existed no experimental evidence to justify that decision. Publicly, they announced that their huge research effort was an attempt to deal with world hunger in coming decades, insisting that projected world population growth should add billions of new hungry mouths to be fed.

The research monies were channeled through a new entity they created, the International Program on Rice Biotechnology (IPRB), into some of the world's leading research labs. Over the next 17 years, the foundation spent an impressive $105 million of its own money in developing and spreading genetically modified rice around the world. Furthermore, by 1989 it was spending an additional $54 million a year – amounting to more than $540 million over the following decade – on "training and capacity building" to disseminate the new developments in rice genetic modification. The seeds of the Gene Revolution were being planted very carefully.[106]

The decision to develop a genetically-modified variety of rice was a master stroke of public relations on the part of the Rockefeller Foundation and its supporters within the scientific and political establishment. Initially, the Foundation funded 46 science labs across the industrialized world, and, by 1987, they were spending more than $5 million a year on the rice gene project, mapping the rice genome. Among the recipients of Rockefeller largesse were the Swiss Federal Institute of Technology in Zurich and the Center for Applied Biosciences at Freiburg University in Germany.

The foundation developed an elite fraternity. The top five scientific researchers at the important Rockefeller-funded Philippine International Rice Research Institute (IRRI) were all Rockefeller-funded doctors. "Without the support of the Rockefeller Foundation it would have been almost impossible for us to build this capability," remarked the IRRI's Deputy Director for Research.

Soon after the program started, the IPRB decided to concentrate efforts on the creation of a variety of rice which allegedly would address Vitamin A deficiency in undernourished children in the developing world. It was a brilliant propaganda ploy. It helped to create a public perception that genetic scientists were diligently working to solve problems of world hunger and malnourishment.[107]

The only problem was that it was a deliberate deception. The choice of rice to begin the Rockefeller's gene revolution was a careful one. As one researcher pointed out, rice was the staple food for more than 2.4 billion people. It had been domesticated and developed by local farmers over a period of at least 12,000 years to grow in a wide variety of different environments.

Rice is synonymous with food security for most of Asia, where over 90% of the global rice harvest is produced, primarily by China and India, where it provides up to 80% of people's daily calories. Rice is also a staple in West Africa, the Caribbean and tropical regions of Latin America. Rice farmers had developed varieties of rice to withstand droughts, to resist pests, and to grow in every climate imaginable, all without the help of biotechnology. They had created an incredible biological diversity, with over 140,000 varieties of rice.

The Rockefeller Foundation and the US Government has had its eyes on Asia's rice bowl well before the 1984 IPRB rice project. A prime target of the foundation's Green Revolution had been Asian rice production. That Green Revolution process had significantly destroyed the world's rich rice diversity over a period of thirty years, with the so-called High-Yielding Varieties, which drew Asia's peasantry into the vortex of the world trade system and the global market for fertilizer, high-yielding seeds, pesticides, mechanization, irrigation, credit and marketing schemes packaged for them by Western agribusiness.

The core driver of that earlier rice revolution had been the very same Philippines-based International Rice Research Institute (IRRI) created by the Rockefeller Foundation. It was not surprising then, that the IRRI, with a gene bank containing more than one-fifth of the world's rice varieties, became the prime vehicle to proliferate the Rockefeller Foundation's new gene revolution in rice. They banked every significant rice variety known.[108]

IRRI has been used to gain and secure control of the irreplaceable seed treasure of Asia's rice varieties, under the ruse that they would thereby be "protected." The IRRI was put under the umbrella of the Consultative Group of International Agricultural Research (CGIAR), after its creation in 1960 by the Rockefeller and Ford Foundations, during the Green Revolution in Asia. CGIAR was the same agency which also controlled the pre-war Iraqi seed bank. CGIAR operated out of the World Bank headquarters in Washington, also with Rockefeller Foundation funding.

In this manner, the World Bank, with its political agenda defined by Washington policy, held the key to the rice seed bank of Asia. Over three-quarters of the American rice genetic makeup or germ-plasm came originally from the IRRI seed bank. That rice was then pressed on Asian countries by the US Government demanding that Asian countries remove "unfair trade barriers" to US rice imports.[109]

IRRI then became the mechanism for allowing major international agribusiness giants like Syngenta or Monsanto to illegally take the seeds from the IRRI seed bank, initially held in trust for the native farmers of the region. In the labs of Monsanto or the other biotech giants, the seeds were modified genetically, and patented as exclusive intellectual property of the biotech company. The World Trade Organization, created in 1994 out of the GATT Uruguay Round, introduced a radical new Agreement on Trade-Related Aspects of Intellectual Property Rights (TRIPS), permitting multinationals to patent plant and other life forms for the first time.

In 1993, a Convention on Biological Diversity under the UN was agreed upon to control the theft of such seed resources of the developing world. Washington, however, made a tiny alteration in the original text. It demanded that all the genetic resources held by the CGIAR system (of which IRRI is part) remain outside the rules. That affected half a million seed accessions, or 40% of the world's unique food crop germ-plasm held in gene banks. It meant that agribusiness companies were still free to take and patent them.

Using the IRRI resources as its center, Rockefeller financing for Vitamin-A-enhanced rice became the prime focus of IPRB research by the beginning of the 1990's. The Foundation's propagandists argued that lack of Vitamin A was a major cause of blindness and death in newborn infants in developing countries. UN statistics indicated that perhaps 100 to 140 million children worldwide had some form of Vitamin A deficiency, of whom perhaps 250,000 to 500,000 went blind.

It was a human interest story of prime emotional attraction to promote acceptance of the controversial new genetically modified plants and crops. Golden Rice became the symbol, the rallying flag, and the demonstration of the promise of genetic engineering, even though the promise was based on black lies and deliberate deception.

The introduction of genetically modified rice has been designed to open the prospect for the first time of directly controlling the seed grain of rice, the basic food staple of 2.4 billion people.

GMOs cause sterility

The drastic long-term dangers of allowing any GMO crops into the animal or human diet have been clearly proven in independent tests around the world. The fact that the major establishment Western media, led by BBC, CNN, the *New York Times* and the like, have deliberately ignored the alarming results of such tests is proof in itself of the massive geopolitical power behind the spread of GMOs.

In scientific independent studies in Russia in 2010, scientists proved that GMOs are harmful for mammals. The researchers found that animals that eat GMO food lose their ability to reproduce.

The scientists used Campbell hamsters that have a fast reproduction rate. The hamsters were fed for two years with ordinary soya beans, which are widely used in agriculture and contain different percentages of GMO organisms. Another group of hamsters, the control group, was fed with pure soya, which was found with great difficulty in Serbia. Today almost all the commercially-grown soybeans in the world are GMO, including some 97% of USA soybeans, 99% in Argentina and an estimated 50% or more of Brazilian soybeans.

The experiment was carried out jointly by the National Association for Gene Security and the Institute of Ecological and Evolutional Problems. Dr. Alexei Surov led the tests. He declared their shocking findings:

> We selected several groups of hamsters, kept them in pairs in cells and gave them ordinary food as always. We did not add anything for one group but the other was fed with soya that contained no GMO components, while the third group with some content of Genetically Modified Organisms and the fourth one with increased amount of GMO. We monitored their behavior and how they gain weight and when they give birth to their cubs. Originally, everything went smoothly.

> However, we noticed quite a serious effect when we selected new pairs from their cubs and continued to feed them as before. These pairs' growth rate was slower and reached their sexual maturity slowly. When we got some of their cubs we formed the new pairs of the third generation. We failed to get cubs from these pairs, which were fed with GMO foodstuffs. It was proved that these pairs lost their ability to give birth to their cubs.[110]

Another horrifying result the scientists found was that hair grew in the mouths of the third generation GMO-fed hamsters. The only way the freak growth patterns and infertility could be neutralized was when they stopped feeding the hamsters a GMO diet.[111]

The national security implications for China are highly alarming, and warrant being treated as a health risk of the highest order of urgency. Today, by exploiting a loophole in China's GMO rules, the US-based grain cartel, led by the likes of Cargill, ADM, and Bunge, controls the import of soybeans into China. China's soybean imports in early 2012 broke all records, at over 12.5 million metric tons for the first quarter, much of it from the USA.[112]

Today more than 60% of all soybeans in China are imported, and almost 100% are GMO. In 2011 China imported 52.6 million metric tons of soybeans. Near half came from the USA, accounting for 60 percent of total US soybean exports in 2011.[113] GMO is entering the Chinese diet by its use as animal feed and by direct human consumption, such as in tofu. The above Russian tests imply that within three generations, a significant portion of the Chinese population could become sterile.

A high priority for the US Government and US agribusiness over the next several years is to break the strong resistance within China against mass-scale introduction of GMO crops to the basic Chinese diet. The use of food as a geopolitical weapon by Washington has reached an extremely sophisticated level.

Beginning around the time of the economic recession of the late 1960's into the oil shocks of the early 1970's, Washington began a strategic disengagement from its own domestic economy.

But the power elites made a careful calculation that while they would not defend their domestic basic industries – whether steel or automobiles, electronics or mining and other major industries – they would concentrate their global hegemony strategy on a core of "strategic industries." The US military defense industry – including companies like Boeing, McDonnell-Douglas, Halliburton and Bechtel – would be one of the strategic national industries to be defended at all costs.

The most strategic decision – but a far less obvious one – was the decision of the US power elites around the Rockefeller faction and their junior partners, the Bush family, to make agriculture export a priority for expanding their global hegemony. The problem was that, so long as recipient countries receiving USDA grains from Washington were able to plant new seeds and grow their own harvests, say after severe weather or crop failure, their dependency on US grains ended.

Here, the development of procedures for monopolizing seeds of life and for patenting traits of those very seeds assumed the highest national security priority. It was named Genetically Modified Organisms or GMO. After 1992 it became the heart of US grain and agriculture export strategy, using the newly created World Trade Organization (WTO) to advance US agribusiness interests.[114]

GMOs Polluting the Chinese food chain

Already, using China's recent tendency to be open to many things Western, especially American, which became common after 1979, US agribusiness giant Monsanto, the largest and most aggressive of the American GMO giants, began illegally spreading its GMO seeds in the rice-growing areas in China, apparently using a strategy of local bribery, and relying on a lack of experience with GMO.

In April 2011, a Chinese environment ministry official told the weekly Nanfang Zhoumo that a joint investigation by four government departments had found that "illegal GM seeds are present in several provinces because of weak management." According to the website for the European Union's Rapid Alert System for Food and Feed, European countries found foodstuffs from China containing GMO rice 115 times between 2006 and May of 2011. The ecologist group Greenpeace said GMO rice seeds had been in China since 2005, and were found at markets in Hubei, Hunan and Jiangxi provinces in 2010, according to Fang Lifeng, a Chinese agriculture specialist with the group.[115]

Some important Chinese government officials have been convinced by the American GMO lobby and by the US Government that GMO, or as it is also known, "transgene" technology or "agri-biotechnology," holds the key to future Chinese food security.

Since 1986, research and development in agri-biotechnology has been done in more than 100 laboratories in China. For the past sixteen years their job has been to try to integrate bio-technology, the new code name for Genetic Manipulation or GMO, into conventional agriculture, in order to improve the yield and quality of crop plants.

By 2001, GM transgenic organisms for more than 130 species were obtained, with more than 100 different trait genes that affected, among other things, resistance to insects, bacteria, fungi, viruses, and drought, as well as salt tolerance. GM was touted for nutrition enrichment, quality improvement, production of edible oral vaccines and recombinant pharmaceuticals. In 1998, one hundred and twenty thousand hectares of transgenic insect-resistant Bt cotton, mainly Monsanto's Bollguard were planted. Between 1999 and 2000, Bt cotton planting acreage, including both CAAS Bt and Monsanto Bt cotton, reached three hundred and fifty thousand hectares.[116]

That trend represents perhaps the most dangerous mistake made by Chinese officials in the period since the founding of the Peoples' Republic in 1949. GMO is the Trojan Horse that Washington and the US elites calculate can destroy China's food security over the next two decades, if Chinese officials are foolish enough to allow it. As this is being written, fortunately, a heavy open debate has erupted inside China about the advisability of allowing GMO in any form. The debate has only begun. The danger remains of the highest magnitude.

The Agriculture Ministry has already approved GMO cotton, peppers, tomatoes and papayas, and has authorized imports of GMO soya and corn for the food industry.[117]

When the National People's Congress met in 2010, around 100 researchers wrote to deputies asking them to revoke authorizations for the use of experimental GMO grains, including a strain of corn, as well as the two rice types. They also demanded a public debate and clear labeling of products containing genetically modified organisms.

The GMO rice strains developed in Chinese laboratories use the Bt gene patented by the US agribusiness giant Monsanto, which will demand royalties and compensation from China if that variety is commercialized. If allowed to spread across China, even with a Chinese company selling the GMO rice seeds, the US agribusiness and agrochemical giant Monsanto and the Washington government will have control over China's rice production within a few short years.[118]

George H.W. Bush and the Hidden Danger of GMOs

In 1986, then-Vice President George H. W. Bush, former Ambassador to Beijing and former CIA Director, hosted a group of executives from the giant agribusiness and chemical company, Monsanto Corporation, of St. Louis, Missouri, for a special White House strategy meeting. The purpose of the unpublicized meeting, according to former US Department of Agriculture official, Claire Hope Cummings, was to discuss the "deregulation" of the emerging biotech industry. Monsanto had a long history of involvement with the US Government and even with Bush's CIA. It had developed the deadly herbicide Agent

Orange for defoliation of jungle areas in Vietnam during the 1960's. It also had a long record of fraud, cover-up and bribery.[119]

When he finally became President in 1988, Bush and his Vice President Dan Quayle moved swiftly to implement an agenda giving unregulated free rein to Monsanto and other major GMO companies. Bush decided it was time to make public the regulatory framework which he had negotiated a few years earlier behind closed doors.

On May 26, 1992, Vice President Quayle, as head of Bush's Council on Competitiveness, announced the Bush administration's new policy on bio-engineered or GMO food: "The reforms we announce today will speed up and simplify the process of bringing better agricultural products, developed through biotech, to consumers, food processors and farmers." Quayle told assembled executives and reporters, "We will ensure that biotech products will receive the same oversight as other products, instead of being hampered by unnecessary regulation." Pandora's Box had been opened by the Bush-Quayle Administration.[120]

Not one single new regulatory law governing biotech GMO products was passed, then or later, up to today, despite repeated efforts by concerned Congressmen and citizens, scientists, health officials and others that such laws were urgently needed to regulate unknown risks and possible health dangers from the genetic engineering of foods.

The framework that then-President Bush put in place was simple. In line with the expressed wishes of the biotech industry, the US Government would regard genetic engineering of plants and foods or animals as merely a simple extension of traditional animal or plant breeding.

Further clearing the path for Monsanto and company, the Bush Administration decided that traditional agencies, such as the US Department of Agriculture, the EPA, the Food and Drug Administration (FDA), and the National Institutes of Health (NIH), were competent to evaluate the risks of GMO products. They determined that no special agency was needed to oversee the revolutionary new field. Furthermore, the responsibilities of the four different agencies were kept intentionally vague.

That vagueness ensured overlap and regulatory confusion, allowing Monsanto and the other GMO operators maximum leeway to introduce their new genetically engineered crops. Yet, to the outside world, it appeared that the new GMO products were being carefully screened. The general public naturally assumed that the Food and Drug Administration or the National Institutes of Health were concerned about their well-being.[121]

Despite serious warnings from research scientists about the dangers of recombinant DNA based on their research and biotechnology work with viruses, the US Government opted for a system in which the industry and private scientific laboratories would "voluntarily" police themselves in the new field of genetically engineered plants and animals.

Senior US government scientists also warned repeatedly of the potential dangers of the Bush-Quayle "no regulation" decision.

Dr. Louis J. Pribyl of the FDA, one of 17 government scientists working on a policy for genetically engineered food at the time, knew from studies that toxins could be unintentionally created when new genes were introduced into a plant's cells. Pribyl wrote a heated warning memo to the FDA's Chief Scientist declaring, "This is the industry's pet idea, namely that there are no unintended effects… But time and time again, there is no data to back up their contention."[122]

Other government scientists have concluded there is "ample scientific justification" to require tests and a government review of each genetically engineered food before it is sold. "The possibility of unexpected, accidental changes in genetically engineered plants justifies a limited traditional toxicological study," they declared. Yet despite the serious warnings from scientists, such warnings went unheeded by the Bush Administration.

The White House had made their deal with Monsanto and the emerging biotech agribusiness industry. It was a geopolitical deal, even though few realized at the time. It was about the potential for the US Government to control the heart of the world's food crops. Genetic warfare had begun. USAID, an agency of the US State Department advancing the US strategic foreign policy agenda, at one point declared openly on its website, "… the principal beneficiary of America's foreign assistance programs has always been the United States. Close to 80% of the USAID contracts and grants go directly to American firms."[123]

There is seamless integration between the private GMO companies and the US government to push GMO on the world. Promoting GMO is an official part of USAID's mission. One of its roles is to "integrate GMO into local food systems." USAID even years ago launched a $100 million program for bringing "biotechnology," i.e. GMO, to developing countries. USAID's "training" and "awareness raising programs" will, its website reveals, provide companies such as "Syngenta, Pioneer Hi-Bred and Monsanto" with opportunities for "technology transfer." Monsanto, in turn, provides financial support for USAID.[124]

China Stops GMO Rice in New Blow against Monsanto

In August, 2014, the Government of the Peoples' Republic of China dealt a staggering blow to Monsanto and the US-dominated GMO agribusiness industry. In a completely unexpected development, the China Ministry of Agriculture decided not to continue with a program which developed genetically-modified rice and corn.

In stark contrast to the pro-GMO actions of the United States Government, on August 17 when licenses for a domestic variety of Chinese GMO rice and corn came up for what was assumed would be a routine renewal, the Chinese Ministry of Agriculture decided not to extend them.

The history goes back to the previous government when in 2009, the ministry's Biosafety Committee issued approval certificates to develop the two crops, GMO rice and corn. The certificates were to be renewed after five years. The conditions were that the rice and corn GMO crops only be used for research purposes, not for commercial sale. [125]

In 2009, the Chinese Agriculture Ministry announced their experimental GMO rice and corn program. I was told by Chinese agriculture scientists during a visit in late 2009 on the occasion of the release of my book, *Seeds of Destruction: The Hidden Agenda of Genetic Manipulation,* that the government wished to be sure it did not miss out on what promised to be a major new Western technology to reduce chemical herbicides as well as increasing harvest yields per hectare.

The experiment was done by the Huazhong Agricultural University, near Wuhan. There Chinese researchers, taking the rosy Monsanto and US Department of Agriculture propaganda at face value, hoped that the GMO strains would help to reduce pesticide use by 80 percent, while raising yields by as much as 8 percent, according to Huang Jikun, the chief scientist with the Chinese Academy of Sciences, in 2009.[126] The Chinese GMO rice and corn tests apparently showed no such positive results.

But because of a growing popular distrust of GMO among Chinese people, the government made it illegal to sell genetically-modified rice on the open market in China. However in July, samples of the Chinese GMO rice were found on sale in a large supermarket in Wuhan, just across the Yangtze River from the Huazhong Agricultural University, where the product was developed, which caused a public outcry. Then a team from China's state tv, CCTV, commissioned tests on five packets of rice, which were picked at random, and found three contained Chinese genetically-modified rice. The Chinese public was alarmed to put it mildly. The origins of rice cultivation can be traced to the valleys of China's Yangtze River, over 7,000 years ago.

US GMO Corn Sent Back

2014 has not been at all a good year for Monsanto and the Western GMO companies in China. At the end of 2013 and up to the present the Chinese government has repeatedly rejected import shipments of corn, claiming it had been tested and contained non-licensed GMO corn mixed with the normal corn. Since late November, China repeatedly refused shipments of US corn, saying officials detected that some contained a genetic modification developed by Syngenta AG of Basle, which Beijing had not approved. The government simply sent tankers back fully loaded. China also allows its port officials to reject an entire cargo of corn if even one kernel has an unapproved gene, exporters say.[127]

The rejections have severely hurt US farmers and grain-trading companies such as Cargill Inc., the world's largest grain trading company. China is the world's fastest-growing market for corn. In 2008 China imported a mere 47,000 tons of corn, mostly from USA, the world's largest corn exporter. In 2013 China imported 5 million tons, a staggering rise and making China a key factor to the world corn and grains market. As China's middle class prosperity has risen in the recent period, demand for beef and other animal meat, which is fed on corn and soybean meal, has exploded.

China, long a significant importer of soybeans, suddenly has become a major corn buyer. It purchased an estimated 5 million tons of foreign corn last year, up from 47,000 tons in 2008, according to the USDA.

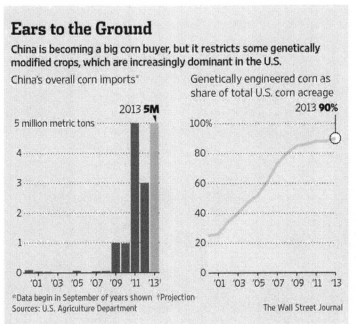

Chinese imports of corn, most US corn, have exploded since 2008. More than 90% of US corn is GMO.
Source: *Wall Street Journal*

According to an April report by the US National Grain and Feed Association (NGFA), as of then as much as $2.9 billion in economic losses had been sustained by the US corn, distillers, grains and soy sectors in the wake of the Chinese enforcement of a zero-tolerance policy on Syngenta's Agrisure Viptera™ MIR 162 GMO corn in US export shipments to China, where the GMO trait has not been approved yet for import into China as food or feed.[128]

Losses will likely be worse. This season, the US, owing to optimal weather in US corn-growing states such as Iowa or

Illinois, the USA will harvest a record large corn crop. The NGFA estimates US agriculture could have losses of up to $3.4 billion during the 2014/15 marketing year that starts Sept. 1, 2014. [129]

Falling out among thieves?

In what can only be likened to a kind of falling out among grain cartel thieves, a major brawl has already broken out between the GMO seed producers like Syngenta, Monsanto or DuPont Pioneer Hi-Bred and the giant grain shippers, the so-called grain cartel – Cargill, ADM and Bunge.

The North American Export Grain Association, which includes ADM and Cargill, has demanded that the seed companies like Monsanto or Syngenta fully bear the risks and liabilities from selling their products. It also has objected to introducing seeds with genetic modifications that haven't secured approvals in major markets. Grain groups have called on Syngenta to stop selling such seeds until China grants approval. Syngenta has rejected those calls. [130]

Suddenly American farmers who had been seduced into using Monsanto or Syngenta GMO seeds on promises of huge profit gains from higher yields (a lie) and less chemical herbicide need (another lie), are facing economic catastrophe because their GMO corn they had been convinced to grow for economic reasons, is suddenly an albatross.

China's growing administrative decisions against GMO domestically and in imports could deal a death blow to Monsanto and allies.

US Agribusiness targets China – the WTO

It should not come as a surprise then that taking long-term control over China's national food security is a strategic priority not only of private agribusiness companies such as Monsanto, but of the Pentagon and the US government. It is part of the war for control of food. As then-Secretary of State Henry Kissinger said in the 1970's, "If you control the food, you control the people." To this end, US government and agribusiness designed the agriculture trade rules of the WTO in 1995, laying the basis for the attack on China's food sovereignty. WTO definitions of "agriculture fair trade" became more important than a national decision to impose restrictions on GMO out of concern for public health and safety.

This new multinational organization, the World Trade Organization, came into being in 1995 in Geneva, Switzerland. The primary international institution pushing forward the genetically engineered seed scheme of Monsanto and other agribusiness seed multinationals is the World Trade Organization. Without the WTO, most nations that have reluctantly surrendered to international pressure and allowed GMO seeds within their borders would have resisted.

The WTO is a policeman, a global free trade enforcer. It is in effect a battering ram for the trillion-dollar annual world agribusiness trade, with the agenda to advance the interests of private agribusiness companies. For that reason, the WTO has been designed as a *supranational* entity, above the laws of nations, not answerable to any public body beyond its own walls.

Under the preceding General Agreement on Tariffs and Trade (GATT) there were no enforceable sanctions or penalties for violating agreed trade rules. The WTO does have such punitive leverage. It has power to levy heavy financial penalties or other sanctions on member countries for violations of its rules. The WTO is a new weapon which can force open various national barriers and speed the proliferation of genetically modified crops.

The idea of a WTO, as with most major post-war free trade initiatives, came from Washington. It was the outcome of the GATT Uruguay Round of trade liberalization talks.

Since the 1948 founding of the GATT, Washington had fiercely resisted including agriculture in world trade talks, fearing any common international rules would open US markets to foreign food imports and would damage American agriculture's competitiveness. Since the 1950's, US agricultural export had been a strategic national priority, tied to Cold War geopolitics.

Unlike all previous GATT trade rounds, the Uruguay Round made trade in agriculture a main priority. The reason was simple. By the mid-1980's, backed by the aggressive policies of deregulation and free market support from the Reagan Administration, American agribusiness was powerful enough to launch its global trade offensive, and in a big way.

The Washington position on the Uruguay Round agricultural agenda had been drafted by Cargill Corporation of Minneapolis, Minnesota. Daniel Amstutz, a former Cargill executive, as Special Ambassador for the Reagan Administration at the GATT, drew up the four-point Amstutz Plan.[131]

It was, in fact, the Cargill Plan. Cargill is the dominant US private agribusiness giant, with global sales of well over $56 billion, and plants in 66 countries around the world. It built its mighty global empire working with the Rockefeller interests in Latin America, as well as with Henry Kissinger in the 1970's Great Grain Robbery sales of US wheat to the Soviet Union at huge profit. Its influence on Washington, and especially on US Department of Agriculture policy, was immense.

The four Amstutz demands at the GATT talks worked uniquely to the gain of US agribusiness and their growing global position. The points included a ban on all government farm programs and price supports worldwide; a prohibition on countries who seek to impose import controls to defend their national agricultural production; and a ban on all government export controls on agriculture, even in time of famine. Cargill wanted to control the world grain export trade.

The final Amstutz demand, presented to the GATT Uruguay Round participants in July 1987, was that GATT trade rules limit the right of countries to enforce strict food safety laws![132]

The global "free market" is more important to Cargill and their agribusiness allies than human life. National food safety laws are seen by US agribusiness as a major barrier to unfettered pursuit of high profit from low-wage, low-quality industrial farm operations in developing countries, as well as in the USA. Furthermore, agribusiness wanted an unrestricted ability to market the new genetically engineered crops, with no national concerns about health and safety getting in their way.

Amstutz was a dedicated champion of agribusiness interests, so effective that he was named as the special liaison of the Bush Administration Department of Agriculture to Iraq in 2003, to direct the transformation of Iraqi farming into US-led, "market oriented" export agribusiness with GMO crops, described above.

US demands at the Uruguay Round centered on the call for a mandatory end to state agriculture export subsidies, a move aimed squarely at the European Community's Common Agriculture Program (CAP). Washington called the process "agriculture trade liberalization." The beneficiaries were US agribusiness, i.e. – the dominant players, in a scenario reminiscent of how British free trade demands in the late 1870's served the interests of British international business and banking, then the dominant world players.

Cargill created the Consumers for World Trade (CWT), a "pro-GATT" lobby which, curiously enough, represented not consumers but only agribusiness and multinational interests, including Cargill. Corporate membership cost $65,000. Cargill also formed an Emergency Committee for American Trade, to convince Congress to accept the new WTO radical agriculture agenda.

The international lobby working with Cargill and US agribusiness to push through the radical GATT agriculture agenda is named The International Food and Agricultural Trade Policy Council or IPC, as they call themselves. The IPC was founded in 1987 to promote the liberalization of agricultural trade, and in particular, the Amstutz Plan for agribusiness. IPC board members include executives from Cargill, from GMO giant Syngenta (then Novartis), from groups like the world's largest food manufacturer Nestlé; Kraft Foods; the world's largest manufacturer of GMO seeds, Monsanto; the world's largest trader of GMO soybeans, ADM; grain giant Bunge Ltd.; Winthrop Rockefeller's Winrock International foundation; the US Department of Agriculture; and Japan's largest trading group, Mitsui & Co. The IPC is an interest group that few politicians – whether in Brussels, Paris or Tokyo or elsewhere – can afford to ignore.

Cargill and the IPC worked closely with Clinton Administration US Trade Representative and later Commerce Secretary, Mickey Kantor. By presenting the WTO's operations as being substantially similar to GATT consensus rules – thus, essentially by lying – Kantor got the Uruguay Round's WTO proposal through the US Congress.

WTO Agreement on Agriculture

The WTO Agreement on Agriculture was written by Cargill, ADM, DuPont, Nestlé, Unilever, Monsanto and other agribusiness corporations. It was designed to allow the nullification of national laws and other safeguards against the powerful pricing power of the agribusiness giants.

As the WTO was being established, Washington policy was to give full backing to the development of genetically-modified plants as a major US "strategic" priority. The Clinton Administration had made "biotechnology," along with the Internet, a strategic priority, with full US Government backing, formal as well as informal. Clinton gave full support to Mickey Kantor, his chief negotiator for the WTO ratification process.

When Kantor left Washington in 2001, he was rewarded for his service to US agribusiness during the GATT negotiations. Monsanto Company, the world's most aggressive promoter of genetically modified crops and related herbicides, named Kantor to their Board of Directors. The revolving door between government and the private sector was well oiled.

Monsanto, DuPont, Dow Chemical and other agricultural chemical giants had transformed themselves into controllers of patented genetically-modified seeds for the world's major staple crops. The time was ripe to establish a police agency that could force the new GMO crops on a skeptical world. The WTO Agreement on Agriculture was to be the vehicle for that, along with the WTO rules enforcing TRIPS – Trade Related Intellectual Property Rights.

The WTO is the parallel agency to promote the globalization of world agriculture under terms defined by US agribusiness. WTO rules open the legal and political path to the creation of a global "market" in food commodities, similar to that created by the oil cartel under the Rockefeller Standard Oil group a century before. Never before the advent of agribusiness had agriculture crops been viewed as a pure commodity with a global market price. Crops had always been local along with their markets, the basis of human existence and of national economic security.

Washington's Amstutz Plan became the WTO's Agreement on Agriculture, or AoA, as it is known. The policy goal of the AoA is to realize the first priority of agribusiness – a free and integrated global market for its products. While talking rhetorically about "food security," AoA mandates that such security is only possible under a regime of free trade, an agenda uniquely beneficial to the giant global grain traders such as Cargill, Bunge and ADM.[133]

In 1992 the senior Bush Administration made the ruling, without public debate, that genetically engineered or modified food or plants were "substantially equivalent" to ordinary seeds and crops and hence needed no special government regulation.

That principle was enshrined into the WTO's "Sanitary and Phytosanitary Agreement," or the SPS. Phytosanitary is a fancy scientific term which simply means it deals with plant sanitation, i.e., with GMO plant issues.

The crafty formulation of the SPS rule stipulated that "food standards and measures aimed at protecting people from pests or animals can be potentially used as a deliberate barrier to trade," and hence, must be forbidden under WTO rules. Under the guise of appearing to enshrine plant and human health safety into WTO standards, the IPC and the powerful GMO interests within it, ensured just the opposite. Few politicians in WTO member countries bothered to even read past the formidable term, "phytosanitary." They listened to their own agribusiness lobby and approved.

Under the WTO's SPS rule, national laws banning genetically modified organisms from the human food chain, because of national health concerns regarding potential threat to human or animal life, were not fair. They were indeed termed "unfair trade practices." Other WTO rules prohibited national laws that required labeling of genetically engineered foods, declaring them to be "Technical Barriers to Trade." Under the WTO, "trade" was deemed a higher concern than the citizen's right to know what he or she was eating. Which trade and to whose benefit was left unspoken.

Terminator

The GMO agenda is one of covert warfare. Monsanto and the US Government are very careful not to reveal what they are up to. Hopefully the Chinese Government takes these words of warning seriously and initiates its own independent investigation into the accuracy of what is written here.

If China opens its doors to Monsanto or other GMO crops and chemical herbicides such as Monsanto Roundup, it is not only allowing its non-GMO crops to be contaminated by windblown seeds and chemicals, and other means. China is opening itself to eventual bondage worse than during the Opium Wars, this time by Monsanto seeds that once planted, commit suicide – so-called Genetic Use Restriction Technology seeds (GURTs), popularly known as "Terminator" seeds after the Hollywood movies of Arnold Schwarzenegger.

In 2007, Monsanto quietly bought the company that together with the US Government held the "Terminator" patent. Since 1983 the United States Government has been financing research on a genetic engineering technology which, when commercialized, will give its owners the power to control the food seed of entire nations or regions. A little-known company named Delta & Pine Land has been working quietly with the US Department of Agriculture on genetic technology. Now, that little-known company is part of the world's largest supplier of patented genetically-modified seeds (GMO): Monsanto Corporation of St. Louis, Missouri.[134]

In March 1998 the US Patent Office granted Patent No. 5,723,765 to Delta & Pine Land for a patent titled, "Control of Plant Gene Expression." The patent is owned jointly, according to Delta & Pine's US Security & Exchange Commission 10K filing, "by D&PL and the United States of America, as represented by the Secretary of Agriculture."[135] That means it is the officially stated US Government policy to promote GMO Terminator technology and export it to China and other countries. They know very well what they are doing. They are engaging in the ultimate food wars by preparing technologies that can, for the first time in human history, arbitrarily cut off seeds for essential staple crops like rice.

The patent has global coverage. To quote from the official D&PL SEC filing: "The patent broadly covers all species of plant and seed, both transgenic (GMO-ed) and conventional, for a system designed to allow control of progeny seed viability without harming the crop" (sic).

Then, D&PL boasts, "One application of the technology could be to control unauthorized planting of seed of proprietary varieties... by making such a practice non-economic since non-authorized saved seed will not germinate, and, therefore, would be useless for planting." D&PL calls the thousand-year-old tradition of farmer-saved seed by the pejorative term "brown bagging," as though it were something dirty and corrupt.

Translated into lay language, D&PL officially declares that the purpose of its Patent No. 5,723,765, Control of Plant Gene Expression, is to prevent farmers – once they get trapped into buying transgenic or GMO seeds from a company such as Monsanto or Syngenta – from "brown bagging" or being able to break free of control of their future crops by Monsanto and friends. As D&PL puts it, their patent gives them "the prospect of opening significant worldwide seed markets to the sale of transgenic technology in varietal crops in which crop seed currently is saved and used in subsequent seasons as planting seed."[136]

The key scientific member on the Delta & Pine Land board since 1993 has been Dr. Nam-Hai Chua. Chua, 62, has also headed the Rockefeller University Plant Molecular Biology Laboratory in New York for over 25 years. These labs are at the heart of the Rockefeller Foundation's decades-long development and investment of more than $100 million in research grants to create their Gene Revolution. Until 1995, Chua was also a scientific consultant to Monsanto Corporation, as well as to DuPont's Pioneer Hi-Bred International. Chua is at the heart of Rockefeller's Gene Revolution. And, clearly, Delta & Pine Land and their research on Terminator have been in the center of that work.

The giant Monsanto group, with its enormous corporate and financial clout, is well-placed globally to proliferate the suicide seeds of Delta & Pine Land, now that it owns the company. Delta & Pine already has subsidiaries, including several in China. They include D&PL Argentina, D&PL China, D&PL China PTE in Singapore, Deltapine Paraguay, Delta Pine de Mexico, Deltapine Australia, Hebei Ji Dai Cottonseed Technology Company in China, CDM Mandiyu in Argentina, Delta and Pine Land Hellas in Greece, D&M Brazil Algodao of Brazil, D&PL India, and D&PL Mauritius Ltd.[137]

This vast global network, combined with Monsanto's dominant position in the GMO seeds and agri-chemicals market, along with the unique DP&L Patent No. 5,723,765, Control of Plant Gene Expression, now give Monsanto and its close friends in Washington an enormous leap forward in their plans to dominate world food and plant seed use.

China's GMO seed serfdom to US agribusiness is a national security threat to China even greater than US military threats because it is largely unrecognized.

Chapter Five:
Chemical Warfare: Herbicides and Pesticides

Just as dangerous as the GMO seeds for rice, corn, soybeans and other crops are the specially paired chemical herbicides that the GMO seeds are specifically manipulated to resist. The most toxic of chemicals are used in the GMO-tied herbicides and pesticides.

Monsanto's Bid to Round Up the World's Farmers

The most widely sold herbicide or weed-killer in the world is Roundup, a chemical cocktail produced originally by Monsanto of St. Louis in the USA. Monsanto is the world's largest seller of Genetically Modified Organisms, GMO seeds for such crops as soybeans, corn, rice or cotton.

Monsanto's seeds are exclusively sold in a contract that forces the farmer to also buy Monsanto's herbicide Roundup. No Roundup means no Roundup Ready GMO seeds. It is the ultimate trap for the farmer, as Roundup has been repeatedly proven to be less effective at killing weeds over time. Across North America in recent years, new Roundup-resistant "super-weeds" have grown up which no herbicide is able to kill, a true Frankenstein monster. The GMO seed companies have made great efforts to hide this reality.

Glyphosates Kill More than Weeds: New Studies Show Tumors in GMO-fed Rats

New independent scientific research demonstrates conclusively that Roundup, whose main active chemical is glyphosate, is alarmingly toxic, even to human embryo cells in what the US Government deems to be "safe" doses.

On September 19, 2012, French scientists at the University of Caen published the world's first long-term, peer-reviewed scientific study of rats fed a diet of GMO.[138] Until the study appeared, Monsanto and the biochemical GMO cartel had succeeded, through numerous legal and other pressures, in preventing such a long-term independent study from being made.

The Caen results created a major new debate about the dangers of GMO across Europe, the United States, Russia and beyond. The EU Commission in Brussels ordered an immediate review of the study by the European Food Safety Agency (EFSA), and the Russian Government and other governments imposed an import ban on Monsanto GMO corn. Countries across the globe began to re-examine their entire GMO policies in light of the study.[139] The Caen study, led by Prof. Gilles-Eric Seralini, noted the following:

> The health effects of a Roundup-tolerant genetically modified maize (from 11% in the diet), cultivated with or without Roundup, and Roundup alone (from 0.1 ppb in water), were studied 2 years in rats. In females, all treated groups died 2-3 times more than controls, and more rapidly... Females developed large mammary tumors almost always more often than and before controls, the pituitary was the second most disabled organ; the sex hormonal balance was modified by GMO and Roundup treatments. In treated males, liver congestions and necrosis were 2.5-5.5 times higher. This pathology was confirmed by optic and transmission electron microscopy.

> Marked and severe kidney nephropathies were also generally 1.3-2.3 greater. Males presented 4 times more large palpable tumors than controls which occurred up to 600 days earlier. Biochemistry data confirmed very significant kidney chronic deficiencies; for all treatments and both sexes, 76% of the altered parameters were kidney related. These results can be explained by the non-linear endocrine-disrupting effects of Roundup, but also by the over-expression of the transgene in the GMO and its metabolic consequences.[140]

It was a study of ten groups of rats carried out over a span of two years, the average life-span of a healthy non-GMO-fed rat. Until this study the GMO industry had been able to limit tests to three months or less. Among the highlights and findings of the alarming research were:

► Roundup provoked chronic hormone and sex dependent pathologies in the rats.

► Female mortality was 2-3 times increased mostly due to large mammary tumors and disabled pituitary.

▶ Male rats had liver congestions, necrosis, severe kidney nephropathies and large palpable tumors.

▶ This may be due to an endocrine disruption linked to Roundup and a new metabolism due to the transgene.

▶ GMOs and formulated pesticides must be evaluated by long- term studies to measure toxic effects.[141]

Because rats are also mammals, their systems react to these chemicals in a way similar to those of a human test subject. That suggests that humans or animals such as pigs or cattle, fed a diet of GMO sprayed with Roundup herbicide, should be susceptible to the same high mortality, growth of new tumors, and early death as the rats.

No laboratory in the world at present dares to test the effect on humans, testing that would require significant financing and government support to do accurately.

A German group tested and found traces of glyphosate in human urine samples. In searching for the cause of serious diseases of entire herds of animals in northern Germany, especially cattle, glyphosate has repeatedly been detected in the urine, faeces, milk and feed of the animals. Even more alarming, glyphosate was detected in the urine of the farmers. To date approximately half of the 800,000 tons of glyphosate produced annually worldwide is produced in China since the Monsanto patent on its Roundup expired.[142]

According to a report published by the Delinat-Institute for Ecology and Climate Farming in Switzerland:

> Pesticide and insecticide use is associated with considerable waiting periods before harvest. However, the waiting period for glyphosate [and similar drugs such as glufosinate-ammonium (Basta/Liberty Link), deiquat or diquat (Reglone), carfentzarone (Shark, cyanamide (Azodef), cinidon-ethyl (Lotus) and pyraflufen (Quickdown)], is completely inadequate because it is classified as a herbicide. While in viticulture, for example, a waiting period of 8 weeks before harvest is mandated for the usage of purely mineral sulphide; grains can be sprayed with glyphosate a mere 7 days before harvest. There is an urgent need for action. Regardless of all the other risks associated with glyphosate, an immediate ban

of desiccation must be enforced. Desiccation can be considered nothing less than negligent physical injury and is irreconcilable with current animal welfare laws.[143]

In 1992, the US Government, using its scientifically fraudulent Doctrine of Substantial Equivalence, in fact, turned the entire American population into human guinea pigs for GMO and Roundup with glyphosate, but still refuses to allow any serious scientific study of the effects despite alarming such tests from around the world.

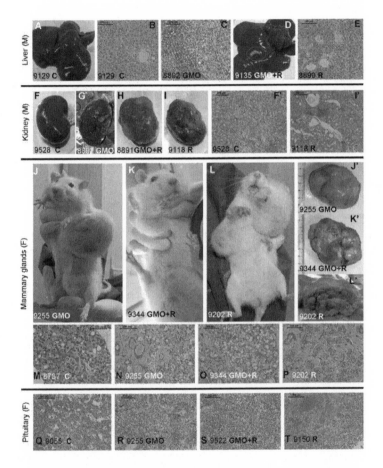

Photographic evidence from Seralini study of rat tumors from GMO diet coupled with Roundup herbicide. Source: Seralini et al, *Journal of Food and Chemical Toxicology.*

What the Seralini study in France demonstrated to an alarming degree was that rats fed a diet of Monsanto GMO maize developed pathological symptoms – including premature death – directly because of the combination of GMO corn together with its paired Monsanto herbicide, Roundup, with glyphosate and other chemicals which Monsanto refuses to reveal, claiming "trade secret" protection under WTO rules.

Evidence of pathological or toxic effects of glyphosate, the herbicide used in virtually every GMO seed sold in the world, is not restricted to the Seralini study cited.

In 2011, Prof. Dr. Don M. Huber, coordinator of the Emergent Diseases and Pathogens Committee of the American Phytopathological Society, as part of the US Department of Agriculture (USDA) National Plant Disease Recovery System, warned the USDA of a new, self-replicating, micro-fungal organism which he believes is causing spontaneous abortions in livestock, sudden death syndrome in Monsanto's Roundup Ready soybeans, and wilt in Monsanto's Roundup Ready GMO corn.[144]

Prof. Huber, one of America's most respected plant pathologists and authorities on GMOs, has studied plant pathogens for over 50 years and glyphosates for over 20 years. He warned: "I believe we've reached the tipping point toward a potential disaster with the safety of our food supply. The abuse, or call it over use if you will, of Roundup, is having profoundly bad consequences in the soil. We've seen that for years. The appearance of this new pathogen may be a signal that we've gone too far."

In an interview with the *Organic and Non-GMO Report*, veteran plant pathologist Huber discussed his team's conclusions that glyphosate can "significantly increase the severity of various plant diseases, impair plant defense to pathogens and diseases, and immobilize soil and plant nutrients, rendering them unavailable for plant use."[145]

In a letter to US Secretary of Agriculture Tom Vilsack, Prof. Huber noted, "many growers/producers are experiencing severe increases in disease of both crops and animals that are threatening their economic viability."[146]

Based on wide research across US farm areas sprayed with glyphosate, Huber had earlier warned that glyphosates "significantly increase the severity of various plant diseases, impair plant defense to pathogens and diseases, and immobilize soil and plant nutrients rendering them unavailable for plant use."[147]

Sudden Death Syndrome in soy where the right field was sprayed the previous year with glyphosate. Iowa, 2010. (Photo by Don Huber)

Professor Huber added, "glyphosate stimulates the growth of fungi and enhances the virulence of pathogens." In the last 15 to 18 years, the precise time widespread planting of GMO crops was allowed in the USA, Huber noted, "There are more than 40 diseases reported with use of glyphosate, and that number keeps growing as people recognize the association between glyphosate and disease."[148]

In other tests carried out in 2011 by the US Government Geological Survey Office of the Interior Department, Roundup glyphosate was found in air and water samples from two US farm states. Paul Capel, environmental chemist and head of the agricultural chemicals team at the US Geological Survey Office, stated, "It is out there in significant levels. It is out there consistently." According to Capel glyphosate, the key ingredient in Roundup herbicide, was found in every stream sample examined in Mississippi in a two-year period and in most air samples taken. Tests were also done in Iowa. "So people are exposed to it through inhalation," Capel said.[149]

Similar independent tests of the effects of glyphosate have produced equally alarming results. The Committee of Independent Research and Information on Genetic Engineering (CRIIGEN) and Universities of Caen and Rouen were able to obtain Monsanto's confidential raw data of its 2002 feeding trials on rats after a European court made it public in 2005. The data "clearly underlines adverse impacts on kidneys and liver, the dietary detoxifying organs, as well as different levels of damages to heart, adrenal glands, spleen and haematopoietic system," reported Gilles-Eric Séralini, who reviewed the data with the group.[150]

In 2010 Argentine scientists found that Roundup causes birth defects in frogs and chickens. Publishing their paper, "Glyphosate-Based Herbicides Produce Teratogenic Effects on Vertebrates by Impairing Retinoic Acid Signaling," in the scientific journal, *Chemical Research in Toxicology*, Professor Andrés Carrasco, Alejandra Paganelli and other researchers noted:

> In Argentina and Paraguay, doctors and residents living in GM soy producing areas have reported serious health effects from glyphosate spraying, including high rates of birth defects as well as infertility, stillbirths, miscarriages, and cancers. Scientific studies collected in the new report confirm links between exposure to glyphosate and premature births, miscarriages, cancer, and damage to DNA and reproductive organ cells.

Researcher Andrés Carrasco, stated, "The findings in the lab are compatible with malformations observed in humans exposed to glyphosate during pregnancy."[151]

> Carrasco said people living in soy-producing areas of Argentina began reporting problems in 2002, two years after the first big harvests of GM Roundup Ready soy. He said, "I suspect the toxicity classification of glyphosate is too low ... in some cases this can be a powerful poison."
>
> Residents also reported environmental damage from glyphosate, including damage to food crops and streams strewn with dead fish. These accounts are backed by studies in the report that show glyphosate is toxic to the environment.[152]

In a 2005 paper published in the scientific journal, Environmental Health Perspectives, Sophie Richard and her group of research scientists compared the toxicity of Roundup with that of glyphosate alone, the active ingredient in Roundup. They found Roundup to be more toxic. The reason was because of undisclosed chemical adjuvants Monsanto adds to the glyphosate. It refuses to disclose details claiming trade secret protection. Richard's group also found that endocrine disruption increased over time so that only ten percent of the amount prescribed for agriculture caused cell deformation. Citing other research, they also reported that Roundup adjuvants bond with DNA.[153]

An alarming article about the dangers of the herbicide chemical used for the world's GMO crops has appeared in *Scientific American*, one of the most widely respected US scientific journals. It reported that recent independent studies have shown conclusively that so-called "inert" chemicals added to Monsanto herbicide, Roundup, actually combine actively with the main chemical present to develop a highly toxic mix that is deadly to human cells. Roundup is the most-used herbicide in the world, and is essential to every GMO plant patented by Monsanto.

The article reports on a recent study conducted at France's University of Caen by a team led by molecular biologist, Gilles-Eric Seralini. One specific "inert" ingredient, polyethoxylated tallowamine, or POEA, their study showed, was more deadly to human embryonic, placental and umbilical cord cells than the herbicide itself – a finding the researchers call "astonishing."

Until now, most health studies have focused on the safety of glyphosate, rather than the mixture of ingredients found in Roundup. But in the new study, scientists found that Roundup's inert ingredients actually *amplified* the toxic effect on human cells – even at concentrations much more diluted than those used on farms and lawns! The French team studied multiple concentrations of Roundup, from the typical agricultural or lawn dose down to concentrations 100,000 times more dilute than the products sold on shelves. The researchers saw cell damage at all concentrations.[154]

"This clearly confirms that the [inert ingredients] in Roundup formulations are not inert," they reported. "Moreover, the proprietary mixtures available on the market could cause cell damage and even death [at the] residual levels" found on Roundup-treated crops, such as soybeans, alfalfa and corn, or lawns and gardens.

The French research team suspects that Roundup might cause pregnancy problems by interfering with hormone production, possibly leading to abnormal fetal development, low birth weights or miscarriages.

In the French study, researchers tested four different Roundup formulations, all containing POEA and glyphosate at concentrations below the recommended lawn and agricultural dose. They also tested POEA and glyphosate separately to determine which caused more damage to embryonic, placental and umbilical cord cells.[155]

Glyphosate, POEA and all four Roundup formulations damaged all three cell types. Umbilical cord cells were especially sensitive to POEA. Glyphosate became more harmful when combined with POEA, and POEA alone was more deadly to cells than glyphosate.

Until this alarming study, Monsanto, the creator of Roundup, maintained that the main ingredient in the herbicide, glyphosate, had low toxicity when used at the recommended doses. It also claimed their private tests had shown that the various inert ingredients such as POEA were not active. The US Government until now had accepted Monsanto's claims as valid without independent testing.

Many allegedly inert ingredients in herbicides amplify the effects of active ingredients by helping them penetrate clothing, protective equipment and cell membranes, or by increasing their toxicity. A Croatian team recently found that a herbicide formulation containing atrazine caused DNA damage, which can lead to cancer, while atrazine alone did not.

POEA was recognized as a common inert ingredient in herbicides in the 1980s, when researchers linked it to a group of poisonings in Japan. Doctors there examined patients who drank Roundup, either intentionally or accidentally, and determined that their sicknesses and deaths were due to POEA, not glyphosate. POEA is a surfactant, or detergent, derived from animal fat. It is added to Roundup and other herbicides to help them penetrate plants' surfaces, making the weed killer more effective.

The new Caen University study raises severe questions as to the safety not only of GMO plants which have been explicitly patented to be used in conjunction with Monsanto's Roundup, but also of Roundup itself. It suggests that the entire GMO commercial project as it now exists is so scientifically unsound, and also unsafe in terms of human and animal risk, as to warrant an immediate "moratorium" on all GMO planting. In fact, this has been called for recently by the American Academy of Environmental Medicine. All GMOs are by definition "unnatural" combinations which are inherently unstable, constantly mutating, and dangerous to human and animal health.

In 2009 the American Academy of Environmental Medicine issued a position paper on GMO plants in which they state clearly:

> ...several animal studies indicate serious health risks associated with GM food consumption including infertility, immune dysregulation, accelerated aging, dysregulation of genes associated with cholesterol synthesis, insulin regulation, cell signaling, and protein formation, and changes in the liver, kidney, spleen and gastrointestinal system.

> There is more than a casual association between GM foods and adverse health effects. There is causation as defined by Hill's Criteria in the areas of strength of association, consistency, specificity, biological gradient, and biological plausibility. The strength of association and consistency between GM foods and disease is confirmed in several animal studies.

> Specificity of the association of GM foods and specific disease processes is also supported. Multiple animal studies show significant immune dysregulation, including upregulation of cytokines associated with asthma, allergy, and inflammation. Animal studies also show altered structure and function of the liver, including altered lipid and carbohydrate metabolism as well as cellular changes that could lead to accelerated aging and possibly lead to the accumulation of reactive oxygen species (ROS). Changes in the kidney, pancreas and spleen have also been documented. A recent 2008 study links GM corn with infertility, showing a significant decrease in offspring over time and significantly lower litter weight in mice fed GM corn.[156]

Suspiciously, what is believed to be due to the powerful lobby influence of Monsanto and the agri-chemical cartel of companies, since 2007 the pro-GMO US Department of Agriculture refuses to update its database of USA pesticide and herbicide use. The glyphosate use is estimated to be more than double EPA estimates for 2000.[157]

When the alarming results of the September 2012 University of Caen studies by Professor Seralini are placed in the context of the earlier studies of the effects of glyphosate, and the more toxic Roundup on plants, animals, the air and water quality, the conclusion is inescapable: glyphosate is a chemical which should not be classified as an agricultural herbicide but rather as a toxic chemical warfare agent. Glyphosate should, therefore, be summarily banned just as DDT was banned in most industrialized countries in the 1970s. The responsibility of the Chinese Government to help end this crisis is real – because Chinese chemical companies today produce almost half of all glyphosates in the world.

Death of the Birds and the Bees[158]

Birds and bees contribute to the essence of life on our planet. A study by the US Department of Agriculture estimated that "...perhaps one-third of our total diet is dependent, directly or indirectly, upon insect-pollinated plants."

Neonicotinoids and the agrochemical toxins

One of the least understood aspects of the destruction of China's food chain, ever so slowly at first, but in recent years with a dramatic acceleration in volume and tempo, is the use of highly toxic agrochemicals in conjunction not only with GMO crops like corn or soybeans or GMO cotton, but also with non-GMO varieties of the same.

The dangers of Monsanto glyphosate, marketed under the brand name Roundup® has been cited already. Far more toxic perhaps, and far less understood are a range of new pesticides called neonicotinoids. The FDA has given these highly toxic chemicals a green light despite overwhelming evidence from neutral scientific tests that they are toxic not only to bee and songbird populations, but also to humans.

This is yet another vehicle by which US elites have calculated to bring China to its knees by contaminating the essential food chain. The neonicotinoid insecticides, derived from nicotine, are gaining larger and larger market shares in the global crop protection market.[159]

In 1990, the global crop protection market of insecticide products consisted of organic phosphorus (43%), pyrethroids (18%) and carbamates (16%). However, since the launch of the first neonicotinoid, imidacloprid, jointly developed by Bayer CropScience and Nihon Tokushu Noyaku in 1991, these toxic new pesticides have been used by 89 countries and regions on over 60 kinds of crops. In 2005 the neonicotionoids gained 16% of the global pesticide market. With annual sales of $1.941, billion the neonicotinoids overtook the pyrethroids and become the fastest-growing agricultural pesticide. Therein lies the alarming danger to China's food supply and food security. Developed in the 1990's by Bayer, neonicotinoids have rapidly grown to become the best-selling type of insecticide in the world.[160]

They work on the central nervous system of insects, including bees and small birds and, most alarmingly, in cumulative doses, on humans according to some research. Nerve cells in the body send messages using chemicals called "neurotransmitters," crucial to both the central nervous system (brain and spinal cord) and involuntary bodily functions within the peripheral nervous system. Neurotransmitters play a role in brain plasticity, arousal and reward. Crucially, they activate muscles. Opposite in effect, Neonicotinoids behave similarly to nicotine. At toxic levels, they block the pathways that allow for the breakdown of acetylcholine and lead to muscle contractions, respiratory paralysis, and death.[161]

In China, a significant manufacturer of neonicotinoids under license to Bayer AG and Japanese agrochemical concerns is Shandong Sino-agri United Biotechnology Co., Ltd. ("Sino-agri Union"), a subsidiary of CNAMPGC, which wholly owns Shandong United Pesticide Industry Co., Ltd. and Taian United Biochemistry Technology Co., Ltd. Sino-Agri Union is at present the largest and most active Chinese producer of licensed neonicotinoids. The company cooperates with the Japan Pesticide Industry Association and especially Japan's leading neonicotinoid producers, Sumitomo and Shimadzu.[162]

What is so alarming for China about the spread of a chemical that is praised for so effectively killing insect pests which damage food crops? The problem is that neonicotinoids not only kill off tiny crop pests effectively, but they also kill entire bee colonies and songbirds, and their widespread spraying on food crops threatens the human brain and other organs.

The honey bee, Apis mellifera, is the most important pollinator of agricultural crops. Honey bees pollinate over 70 out of 100 crops that in turn provide 90% of the world's food. They pollinate most fruits and vegetables – including apples, oranges, strawberries, onions and carrots.[163] But while managed honey bee populations have increased over the last 50 years, bee colony populations have decreased significantly in many European and North American regions. Simultaneously, crops that are dependent on insects for pollination have increased. The phenomenon has received the curious designation of Colony Collapse Disorder (CCD), implying it could be caused by any number of factors. Serious recent scientific studies, however, point to a major cause: massive use of new, highly toxic, systemic pesticides – neonicotinoids – used in global agriculture since about 2004, including on a large scale in China.

If governments in China, the EU, USA and other countries fail to impose a total ban on these new chemical insecticides, not only could bees become a thing of the past, but the human species could face staggering new challenges merely to survive. The immediate threat comes from the widespread proliferation of the neonicotinoid insecticides. Chemically similar to nicotine, they act on the central nervous system of insects, bees, and small songbirds. Alarmingly, recent evidence suggests that they could also affect brain development in human newborns.[164]

In recent years, reports began to circulate from around the world, especially from the United States, and then increasingly from around the EU, especially in the UK, that entire bee colonies were disappearing. Since 2004 over a million beehives have died across the United States, and beekeepers in 25 states report what is called Colony Collapse Disorder. In the winter of 2009 an estimated one fifth of bee hives in the UK were lost, double the natural rate.[165] Government authorities claimed it was a mystery.

In the USA, a fact sheet from the Environmental Protection Agency (EPA) on Bayer AG's clothianidin, a widely used neonicotinoid, warned:

Available data indicate that clothianidin on corn and canola should result in minimal acute toxic risk to birds. However, assessments show that exposure to treated seeds through ingestion may result in chronic toxic risk to non-endangered and endangered small birds (e.g., songbirds) and acute/chronic toxicity risk to non-endangered and endangered mammals."[166]

Alarming UK results

Two British environmental organizations, Buglife and the Soil Association, undertook tests to try to determine the cause of the bee die-offs. They found that the decline was caused in part by neonicotinoids.[167] They are "systemic" chemicals that kill insects by getting into the cells of the plant. In Britain they are widely used for crops like oilseed rape and for the production of potted plants.

Neonicotinoids are found in the UK in various products, including Chinook, used on oilseed rape, and Bayer UK 720, used in the production of potted plants, which then end up in gardens and homes around the country. The new study examined in detail the most comprehensive array of peer-reviewed research into possible long-term effects of neonicotinoid use. They concluded that the pesticides damage the health and life cycle of bees over the long term by affecting the nervous system. The report noted, "Neonicotinoids may be a significant factor contributing to current bee declines and could also contribute to declines in other non-target invertebrate species."[168] The organization called for a total ban on pesticides containing any neonicotinoids.

The president of the UK Soil Association, Peter Melchett, told the press that pesticides were causing a continued decline in pollinating insects, putting the entire farming sector at risk. "The UK is notorious for taking the most relaxed approach to pesticide safety in the EU; Buglife's report shows that this puts at risk pollination services vital for UK agriculture," he warned.[169]

In March 2012, Sir Robert Watson, Chief Scientist at the British Government's Department for Environment, announced that his government was reconsidering its allowance of neonicotinoid use in the UK. Watson told a British newspaper, "We will absolutely look at the University of Stirling work, the French work, and the American work that came out a couple of months ago. We must look at this in real detail to see whether or not the current British position is correct or is incorrect. I want this all reassessed, very, very carefully."[170] To date no policy change has ensued however. Given the seriousness of the scientific studies, and the resulting claims of danger, a prudent policy would have been to provisionally suspend further use of neonicotinoids pending further research.

EPA Corruption

In the United States the government agency responsible for approving or banning chemicals deemed dangerous to the environment is the Environmental Protection Agency (EPA). In 2003, over the clear warnings of its own scientists, the EPA licensed the neonicotinoid clothianidin, patented by Germany's Bayer AG, together with the Japanese company Takeda. It is sold under the brand name Poncho. It was immediately used on over 88 million acres of US corn in the 2004 crop, and since that time, the shocking die-off of more than one million beehives across the corn prairies of the Midwest has been reported.[171]

The political appointees at EPA allowed Bayer to license Poncho despite the official judgment of EPA scientists that clothianidin is "highly toxic to bees by contact and oral exposure," and that it is "highly mobile in soil and groundwater – very likely to migrate into streams, ponds and other fields, where it would be absorbed by wildflowers" – and go on to kill more bees and non-target insects, such as butterflies and bumblebees. The warning, from a leaked EPA memo dated September 28, 2005, summarizes the Environmental Fate and Effects Division's Environmental Risk Assessment for clothianidin, which it said "will remain toxic to bees for days after a spray application. In honey bees, the effects of this toxic exposure may include lethal and/or sub-lethal effects in the larvae and reproductive effects to the queen."[172]

The EPA scientists judged it to be many times more toxic than Bayer's other neonicotinoid, Imidacloprid, sold under the brand name Gaucho, which itself is "7,000 times more toxic to bees than DDT."[173] DDT was banned in the USA in 1972 after numerous studies proved its toxic effects on both animals and humans.

Then in January 2012 another US Government agency, the US Department of Agriculture, published a significant new report from scientists under the direction of Jeffrey Pettis of the USDA

Bee Research Laboratory. The findings, published in the German scientific journal, Naturwissenschaften, were explosive.

The Pettis study found that careful experiments – with control groups of bees exposed and not exposed to neonicotinoids – clearly demonstrated that there was "an interaction between sublethal exposure to imidacloprid [Bayer's Gaucho] at the colony level and the spore production in individual bees of honey bee gut parasite Nosema." Moreover, the study went on:

> Our results suggest that the current methods used to evaluate the potential negative effect of pesticides are inadequate. This is not the first study to note a complex and unexpected interaction between low pesticide exposure and pathogen loads... We suggest new pesticide testing standards be devised that incorporate increased pathogen susceptibility into the test protocols. Lastly, we believe that subtle interactions between pesticides and pathogens, such as demonstrated here, could be a major contributor to increased mortality of honey bee colonies worldwide.[174]

Contrary to claims by Bayer and other neonicotinoid manufacturers, the renowned Dutch toxicologist Dr. Henk Tennekes reported that bees living near corn fields sprayed with neonicotinoids are exposed to them throughout the entire growing season, and the toxicity is cumulative. Tennekes noted, "Bees are exposed to these compounds and several other agricultural pesticides in several ways throughout the foraging period. During spring, extremely high levels of clothianidin and thiamethoxam were found in planter exhaust material produced during the planting of treated maize seed. We also found neonicotinoids in the soil of each field we sampled, including unplanted fields."[175]

Effect on the Human Brain?

The most alarming of all is the evidence that exposure to neonicotinoids has horrific possible effects on humans, as well as on birds and bees.

Professor Henk Tennekes describes the effects:

> Today the major illnesses confronting children in the United States include a number of psychosocial and behavioral conditions. Neurodevelopmental disorders –

including learning disabilities, dyslexia, mental retardation, attention deficit disorder, and autism – occurrence is more prevalent than previously thought, affecting 5 percent to 10 percent of the 4 million children born in the United States annually. Beyond childhood, incidence rates of chronic neurodegenerative diseases of adult life such as Parkinson's disease and dementia have increased markedly. These trends raise the possibility that exposures in early life act as triggers of later illness, perhaps by reducing the numbers of cells in essential regions of the brain to below the level needed to maintain function in the face of advancing age. Prenatal and childhood exposures to pesticides have emerged as a significant risk factor explaining impacts on brain structure and health that can increase the risk of neurological disease later in life.[176]

There is also growing evidence suggesting persistent exposure to plants sprayed with neonicotinoids could be responsible for damage to the human brain, including the recent sharp rise in incidents of autism in children. (Emphasis added by author.)

Referring to recent studies of the effects of various exposures of neonicotinoids on rats, Tennekes noted,

Accumulating evidence suggests that chronic exposure to nicotine causes many adverse effects on the normal development of a child. Perinatal exposure to nicotine is a known risk factor for sudden infant death syndrome, low-birth-weight infants, and attention deficit/hyperactivity disorder. Therefore, the neonicotinoids may adversely affect human health, especially the developing brain."[177]

Referring to studies recently published in the magazine, *Science,* Brian Moench noted:

The brain of insects is the intended target of these insecticides. They disrupt the bees homing behavior and their ability to return to the hive, kind of like "bee autism." But insects are different from humans, right? Human and insect nerve cells share the same basic biological infrastructure. Chemicals that interrupt electrical impulses in insect nerves will do the same in humans. But humans are much bigger than insects and the doses to humans are miniscule, right?

During critical first trimester development, a human is no bigger than an insect, so there is every reason to believe that pesticides could wreak havoc with the developing brain of a human embryo. But human embryos aren't out in corn fields being sprayed with insecticides, are they? A recent study showed that every human tested had the world's best-selling pesticide, Roundup, detectable in their urine at concentrations between five and twenty times the level considered safe for drinking water.[178]

The most alarming part of the neonicotinoid story is that governments and the EU to date are content to take little or no precautionary steps to stop even suspected contamination from neonicotinoids pending thorough long-term tests that would determine conclusively whether they are as dangerous as indicated by the considerable and growing scientific evidence.

Bayer AG and Neonicotinoids

In early 2011 the UN Environment Programme (UNEP) published a report on bee mortalities around the world. The Bayer neonicotinoids, Poncho and Gaucho, are cited there as a threat to numerous animals.

According to the UN report,

Systemic insecticides such as those used as seed coatings, which migrate from the roots through the entire plant, all the way to the flowers, can potentially cause toxic chronic exposure to non-target pollinators. Various studies revealed the high toxicity of chemicals such as Imidacloprid, Clothianidin, Thiamethoxam and associated ingredients for animals such as cats, fish, rats, rabbits, birds and earthworms. Laboratory studies have shown that such chemicals can cause losses of sense of direction, impair memory and brain metabolism, and cause mortality.[179]

Yet Bayer AG shows no signs of voluntarily stopping production and distribution of its toxic neonicotinoids.

The German pharmaceutical giant counts among its historic achievements one it prefers today to forget – the first synthesis of something it marketed as cough medicine in 1898 under the trade name Heroin, taken from the "heroic" feeling it gave to Bayer workers on whom it was tested.[180] If Bayer AG is allowed to persist in the sale of its range of deadly neonicotinoids, they may far surpass the collective death, suffering and destruction wrought by heroin over the past century.

According to the German citizen watchdog group, Coalition against BAYER Dangers, Gaucho and Poncho are among Bayer's top-selling pesticides: "In 2010, Gaucho sales were valued at US$ 820 million, while Poncho sales were valued at US$ 260 million. Gaucho ranked first among Bayer's best-selling pesticides, while Poncho ranked seventh. It is striking that in the 2011 Annual Report, no sales figures for Gaucho and Poncho are shown."[181]

Banned in many EU Countries

Unlike the United States, several EU countries have banned the use of neonicotinoids, refusing to accept test and safety reports from the chemical manufacturers as adequate. This again suggests that there is a geopolitical agenda to the promotion and export of highly toxic chemicals by the US Government. China is a major target of this strategy.

In Europe, one case in point was in Germany where the Julius Kühn Federal Research Centre for Cultivated Plants, a state-run crop research institute, collected samples of dead honeybees and determined that clothianidin had caused the deaths.

Bayer CropScience provided an unconvincing counter-claim, blaming "defective seed corn batches." The company claimed that the chemical coating came off as the seeds were sown, which allowed unusually high amounts of toxic dust to spread to adjacent areas where bees collected pollen and nectar. The attorney for a coalition of groups filing the suit, Harro Schultze, stated, "We're suspecting that Bayer submitted flawed studies to play down the risks of pesticide residues in treated plants. Bayer's ... management has to be called to account, since the risks ... have now been known for more than 10 years."[182]

Significantly, in Bayer's home country, Germany, the government has banned Bayer's neonicotinoids since 2009. France and Italy have imposed similar bans. In Italy, the government found that after the ban, bee populations returned, helping to uphold the ban despite strong chemical industry pressure.[183]

Despite the alarming evidence of links between neonicotinoids and bee colony collapse disorder, as well as possible impacts on human fetal cells and brains, the reaction so far in the European

Union Commission has been scandalously slow. Brussels has been so weak in responding that European Union Ombudsman Nikiforos Diamandou opened an investigation, after a complaint from the Austrian Ombudsman Board that the European Commission had failed to take account of the new evidence on the role of neonicotinoids in bee mortality. "In its view, the Commission should take new scientific evidence into account and take appropriate measures, such as reviewing the authorization of relevant substances," said a statement from the EU Ombudsman's office. The Commission in response asked the European Food Safety Agency (EFSA) to carry out a full review of all neonicotinoid insecticides.[184]

Giving EFSA the final say on food safety for Europe's consumers and honeybees is tantamount to asking the foxes to guard the hen house. EFSA is heavily influenced by members with conflicts of interest and dubious ties to agribusiness interests like Bayer AG and other agrochemical multinationals.[185]

Bayer is one of six global companies tied to the development of patented GMO seeds and related chemicals, controlling inputs into the entire food chain. As a tightly inter-linked group, Monsanto, Dow, BASF, Bayer, Syngenta and DuPont control the global seed, pesticide and agricultural biotechnology markets. This concentration of power over world agriculture is unprecedented. As one observer noted, it enables them to "control the agricultural research agenda; dictate trade agreements and agricultural policies; position their technologies as the 'science-based' solution to increase crop yields, feed the hungry and save the planet; escape democratic and regulatory controls; subvert competitive markets."[186]

Dutch toxicologist Tennekes and Alex Lu, Associate Professor of Environmental Exposure Biology at Harvard's Department of Environmental Health, are among a growing number of scientists around the world calling for an immediate and global ban on the use of the new neonicotinoid pesticides.[187] Professor Lu calls for a very simple test: "I would suggest removing all neonicotinoids from use globally for a period of five to six years. If the bee population is going back up after the ban, I think we will have the answer."

The fact that despite glaring proof of the dangers of neonicotinoids, the United States Government continues to promote the toxic chemicals worldwide, is prima facie proof of a sinister agenda. China is being targeted as a major focus of those efforts now.

We have seen how China is increasingly under attack in the areas of currency stability, access to oil, and the safety of her food supply. The attacks are manifold and often covert. One of the most covert and most threatening is the assault on China from American-dominated pharmaceutical companies pushing a vast array of harmful and life-damaging drugs and vaccines, a new Opium War with licensed "drugs" instead of illegal heroin.

Chapter Six:
Health Wars: Drugs and Vaccines: America's New Opium War

The deadly, often crippling Anglo-American pharmaceutical drug system has been developed over decades, using medical drugs to literally weaken whole populations, referred to by them as "herds." The entire vaccine and drug industry almost without exception in the US, UK and Switzerland and Japan has been developed since World War II as a vital part of the eugenics agenda of the Rockefeller family circles of the Anglo-American establishment. Responsible persons concerned with the future health of the Chinese people would do well to examine this highly strategic form of warfare.

CIA, drugs and social control

The introduction of Western medicine and most especially western-conceived vaccines and medical drugs is one of the most dangerous subversions facing China today from Anglo-American power elites. This is all the more so because so few people in positions of responsibility in today's China have even the slightest idea how Anglo-American power elites have weaponized the distribution of pharmaceutical vaccines and drugs in recent years to achieve unprecedented control over entire populations.

For those who might believe that the claim is exaggerated, it is instructive to read a 1961 statement by one of the members of the Anglo-American inner circle, Aldous Huxley, author of *Brave New World*. The book is not so much about life under communism, as it was characterized in the west, as it is a blueprint for how leading Western elites planned to control their own and other societies. Aldous Huxley's brother, Sir Julian Huxley, a rabid eugenicist and population reduction advocate, was the first head of UNESCO after World War II.

Aldous Huxley stated back in 1961:

> There will be, in the next generation or so, a pharmacological method of making people love their

servitude, and producing dictatorship without tears, so to speak, producing a kind of painless concentration camp for entire societies, so that people will in fact have their liberties taken away from them, but will rather enjoy it, because they will be distracted from any desire to rebel by propaganda or brainwashing, or brainwashing enhanced by pharmacological methods. And this seems to be the final revolution.[188]

Today the West is fully in that "next generation or so." It must be understood that Huxley was not merely a writer. He was part of a tight-knit group working secretly with CIA director Allen Dulles and President Eisenhower's Special Advisor for Cold War Strategy, Nelson Rockefeller,[189] sponsored by the private Ford Foundation, on a top secret "mind-control" project called MK-Ultra, which created the 1960's drug LSD and its "hippie revolution" in the US as a project of ultimate social control experimentation. Dr. Humphrey Osmond, Timothy Leary, author Ken Kesey, and others were involved in the secret CIA experiments, together with leading pharmaceutical companies.[190]

The CIA techniques of using various drugs to control people's minds and bodies have been quietly transferred into the everyday "anti-depressant" drugs, typically given to young children supposedly diagnosed with so-called hyperkinesis, given the more frightening name, "Attention Deficit Disorder" (ADD) or "Attention Deficit Hyperactivity Disorder" (ADHD), as but one of hundreds of examples. Drugs typically used for children who are ADHD-diagnosed include: Amphetamine-dextroamphetamine (Adderall); Dexmethylphenidate (Focalin); Dextroamphetamine (Dexedrine, Dextrostat); Lisdexamfetamine (Vyvanse); and Methylphenidate (Ritalin, Concerta, Metadate, Daytrana).[191]

For Chinese authorities to continue to permit Anglo-American or European pharmaceutical companies to market and even produce their drugs in China and be consumed by Chinese people is a national security danger of the highest order, again even more so than the 1840's Opium War.

Drugs designed to control people have many names and many disguises.

In 2010 a series of vaccine scandals and resulting deaths from them became the subject of a heated debate in the Chinese media, after China was hit by several vaccination scandals.

Disease control and prevention authorities in Guangzhou found after an initial investigation that some children became ill or paralyzed after receiving an H1N1 flu vaccine. According to the Hong Kong-based Mingpao magazine, one of Jiangsu province's top vaccine producers, Jiangsu Yanshen Biological Stock Co Ltd, later bought by Simcere Group Ltd., had produced contaminated vaccines that over the years had sickened over one million people. The company halted production and seven top executives were arrested on charges of producing and selling fake vaccines. In Changzhi city, three-year-old Jia Xiaonu fell ill with a mysterious case of necrotising fasciitis after receiving a vaccine for mumps in July 2008.[192]

The scandals were promptly the subject of intense accusations and investigations, while "faulty preparation measures" were blamed for the deaths and vaccine-related illnesses. What escaped notice is the fact that the trillion-dollar, US-led pharmaceutical industry is integrated into a global system of producing drugs and also licensing them to countries like China.

Indicative of the insidious nature of this new drug war is a new and deadly vaccine which is being pushed ruthlessly around the world, allegedly to "protect" young pre-teen girls at age 11 or 12 years or before puberty, from possible cancer of the cervix, which they have named HPV (Human Papillomavirus). The largest purveyors of these deadly new vaccines are GlaxoSmithKline of the UK, makers of Cervarix, and Merck in the USA, the maker of Gardasil. The pharmaceutical industry is pushing to make HPV vaccinations mandatory for children in the US and UK, even without knowledge of their parents. There are countless reports of severe injuries, including in some cases death, immediately after HPV vaccination.[193]

The entire scientific basis of vaccinating with a given toxin to make someone "immune" to that toxin is based on highly suspicious scientific "evidence." As medical researcher Eustace Mullins noted, "Edward Jenner (1796-1839) 'discovered' that cowpox vaccine would supposedly inoculate persons against the eighteenth century scourge of smallpox. In fact, smallpox was already on the wane, and some authorities believe it would have vanished by the end of the century, due to a number of contributing factors. After the use of cowpox vaccine became widespread in England, a smallpox epidemic broke out which killed 22,081 people. The smallpox epidemics became worse each year that the vaccine was used. In 1872, 44,480 people were killed by it. England finally banned the vaccine in 1948, despite the fact that it was one of the most widely heralded 'contributions' which that country had made to modern medicine. This action came after many years of compulsory vaccination, during which period those who refused to submit to its dangers were hurried off to jail." Mullins added, "Japan initiated compulsory vaccination in 1872. In 1892, there were 165,774 cases of smallpox there, which resulted in 29,979 deaths."[194]

He further noted, "Medical historians have finally come to the reluctant conclusion that the great flu 'epidemic' of 1918 was solely attributable to the widespread use of vaccines. It was the first war in which vaccination was compulsory for all servicemen. The *Boston Herald* reported that forty-seven soldiers had been killed by vaccination in one month. As a result, the military hospitals were filled, not with wounded combat casualties, but with casualties of the vaccine. The epidemic was called 'the Spanish Influenza,' a deliberately misleading appellation, which was intended to conceal its origin. This flu epidemic claimed twenty million victims..."[195]

It is not at all hard to imagine that a massive wave of deliberate vaccine-induced illness will target China in coming months or years, when Anglo-American elites determine that China is becoming too powerful or influential in world affairs. Take the example of India to understand how this might be done.

In India in 2011-2012 there was a massive outbreak of poliomyelitis. Cases of non-polio acute flaccid paralysis (NPAFP), a much more serious condition than polio, skyrocketed as a result of widespread polio vaccination. A report published in the *Indian Journal of Medical Ethics* (IJME) explained that, clinically, NPAFP is indistinguishable from polio paralysis. But according to the Office of Medical & Scientific Justice (OMSJ), NPAFP is twice as deadly as polio paralysis, yet it was not even an issue in India prior to the rollout of the massive polio vaccine campaigns.[196]

In 2011, the year India was declared to be polio-free, there were 47,500 known cases of NPAFP, a shockingly high figure. Based on data collected from India's National Polio Surveillance Project, cases of NPAFP across India rose dramatically in direct proportion to the number of polio vaccines administered, which suggests that the vaccines were responsible for spurring the rapid spread of this deadly condition.[197]

Similarly, cases of vaccine-associated polio paralysis (VAPP), a condition in which paralytic symptoms similar or identical to those of ordinary polio appear after vaccination, are also on the rise. Not only are the paralysis symptoms associated with NPAFP and VAPP far worse than those brought about by wild-type polio, but they may be accompanied by other negative side effects, including neurological damage.

India's polio vaccine campaign induced a new epidemic of a much worse type of polio-related paralysis that was more deadly than the first one. Overall rates of NPAFP in particular were 12 times higher in India following the polio vaccine campaigns, with some areas of the country reporting rates as much as 35 times higher.[198]

Not accidentally, the entire polio vaccine scam in India was spawned from grants made by the Bill & Melinda Gates Foundation.[199] The Gates Foundation today is massively targeting Africa for vaccination campaigns. Gates has admitted he is supporting vaccines that reduce population.

Bill Gates and "The Good Club"

In May 2009, at the home of Sir Paul Nurse, Nobel Prize winning biologist and President of The Rockefeller University, a highly influential group of select guests arrived to discuss world events. The guests were selected personally by David Rockefeller, former chairman of Chase Manhattan Bank and head of the family dynasty: Bill Gates of the pro-eugenics Gates Foundation, George Soros, Warren Buffett, CNN founder Ted Turner, among others. According to reports leaked from the meeting, a central theme of the secret meeting of the plutocrats was how to advance more effectively their agenda of birth control and global population reduction.

Gates and Buffett are major funders of global population reduction programs, as is Ted Turner. The programs in Africa and elsewhere are masked as philanthropy and as providing health services for poor Africans. In reality they involve population sterilization via vaccination and other medicines that make women of child-bearing age infertile. Buffett, considered the world's richest man with a fortune of over $60 billion, has made gifts of almost half that amount. The primary beneficiary is The Gates Foundation, which is also backing the introduction of GMO seeds into Africa under the cloak of a "Second Green Revolution."[200]

For those who doubt that the long-term agenda of the Anglo-Saxon elites is a drastic population reduction, especially of the Asiatic peoples, in particular China and India, the world's two most populous nations, a quick look at a video presentation at a select California conference make it clear.

Bill Gates, founder of Microsoft and one of the world's wealthiest men, boasts of using his billions, via his tax exempt Bill & Melinda Gates Foundation, to "tackle diseases, solve food shortages in Africa and alleviate poverty." But at the conference in California, Gates revealed the true hidden agenda of his philanthropy – reducing the population of yellow, brown and dark-skinned peoples.

At the Long Beach, California TED-2010 Conference, a private $6,000 a head, invitation-only event, Gates gave a speech titled "Innovating to Zero!," in which he presented a scientifically inane diatribe about reducing man-made CO_2 emissions worldwide to zero by 2050. Four-and-a-half minutes into his remarks, Gates said:

> "The world today has 6.8 billion people. That's headed up to about 9 billion. Now if we do a really great job on new vaccines, health care, reproductive health services, we lower that by perhaps 10 or 15 percent."[201]

That's right: Gates said, "if we do a great job on new vaccines," his crowd could lower world population by 10-15%.

The Bill and Melinda Gates Foundation, the world's largest private foundation, is a major shareholder in GMO producer Monsanto. The Foundation is promoting universal vaccination in Africa at the same time it backs Kofi Annan's "Association for a Green Revolution in Africa" (AGRA), which attempts to bring the incomparable agricultural riches of the African continent under the control of GMO giant Monsanto and the US-controlled agribusiness cartels. As with everything else that the Gates Foundation does, its ultimate goal is eugenics and genocide.

Africa and the CIA's "anti-AIDS' war

One of the clearest and most brutal examples of the US elites' weaponization of drugs was the fraudulent US and World Bank "anti-AIDS" campaign in Africa during the Clinton Administration. Conveniently, the campaign focused on the very African countries which hold invaluable strategic raw materials, which US Pentagon interests and private corporate interests want to control and deny to China and other potential rivals.

As the prominent AIDS critic, Dr. P.H. Duesberg noted,

> "One of the great oddities of AIDS is its definition. If a person has antibodies for HIV, and also has one or more of 30 "AIDS defining illnesses," such as tuberculosis, the patient is diagnosed as having AIDS. However, if he has one or more of the same 30 illnesses, but tests negative for HIV antibodies, then he does not have AIDS – just ordinary tuberculosis, etc. Thus, the correlation between AIDS and HIV is an artificial byproduct of the definition itself, and not scientific reality." [202]

Dr. Robert Gallo made millions of dollars designing and patenting the arbitrary HIV "test."

On April 17, 2000, in Washington, D., the former Wall Street banker and World Bank President James D. Wolfensohn announced that his bank would commit "unlimited money" to fight HIV/AIDS in poor countries. The plan was to impose Zidovudine (AZT) Retrovir made by GlaxoSmithKline, the first drug approved by the FDA for the treatment of HIV, and other expensive new and highly-toxic pharmaceutical drugs on the estimated 34 to 50 million people who were presumed to have HIV in underdeveloped nations, mainly in Africa, India, China, and the Caribbean, all of them major World Bank clients then. At least 70%-80% of those "AIDS" victims, according to United Nations figures, lived in mineral-rich Sub-Saharan Africa, the same countries which today are the focus of major investment and diplomatic activity by China. [203]

As medical researcher Robert Herron noted:

> On April 30, 2000, the Clinton Administration formally designated the HIV/AIDS epidemic as a major threat to United States security. This declaration was based mainly on a recent Central Intelligence Agency report, *The Global*

Infectious Disease Threat and Its Implications for the United States.[204] This report was declassified in record speed to share with the public earlier this year. The CIA claimed that the HIV epidemic would destabilize governments throughout the world. Therefore, drastic intervention was needed.[205]

President Clinton then did something under the cover of "national security." He assigned the National Security Council and the CIA to supervise the US government's global campaign against AIDS, rather than the agencies qualified to fight disease, the US Public Health Service and Centers for Disease Control.[206] Herron continued:

> At Clinton's request, the National Security Council, which has never before been involved in combating disease, has been coordinating the US government's international efforts to combat HIV/AIDS. On April 30th, the Clinton Administration also doubled the budget to battle AIDS overseas to $254 million per year. Most of this money will be used to buy anti-HIV medications from American and British drug companies for administering to people in underdeveloped nations... May 3, 2000, in Washington, D.C., David Gordon of the US Government's National Intelligence Council held a press conference to expand the scope of dire predictions. He said urgent action is needed now because in the future the HIV epidemic could be sweeping like a plague through Asian and Pacific Rim countries even faster than it is going through Sub-Saharan Africa today.[207]

The Clinton Administration launched this "anti-AIDS" campaign not to help sick Africans or others. Numerous studies, including several funded by the US government, had found that *HIV does not cause AIDS.* In fact, HIV is relatively harmless. Dr. Charles Thomas, molecular biologist and former Harvard Professor of Biochemistry, explained, "The HIV-causes-AIDS dogma represents the grandest and perhaps the most morally destructive fraud that has ever been perpetrated on the young men and women of the Western world (Sunday Times, London, 3 April, 1994).[208]

In the 1990's as Clinton was launching the massive AIDS attack, numerous prominent scientists, including Nobel Prize winners,

spoke out against the HIV/AIDS theory. Some of their comments
are worth citing:

Dr. Kary Mullis, Biochemist, 1993 Nobel Prize for
Chemistry:

"If there is evidence that HIV causes AIDS, there should be
scientific documents which either singly or collectively
demonstrate that fact, at least with a high probability.
There is no such document." (*London Sunday Times*, 28
Nov., 1993)

Dr. Heinz Ludwig Sänger, Emeritus Professor of Molecular
Biology and Virology, Max-Planck-Institutes for
Biochemistry, München, Robert Koch Award 1978:

"Up to today there is actually no single scientifically really
convincing evidence for the existence of HIV. Not even
once has such a retrovirus been isolated and purified by
the methods of classical virology." (Letter to *Süddeutsche
Zeitung*, 2000)

Dr. Serge Lang, Professor of Mathematics, Yale University:

"I do not regard the causal relationship between HIV and
any disease as settled. I have seen considerable evidence
that highly improper statistics concerning HIV and AIDS
have been passed off as science, and that top members of
the scientific establishment have carelessly, if not
irresponsibly, joined the media in spreading
misinformation about the nature of AIDS." (*Yale Scientific*,
Fall 1994)[209]

In the early 1990's a number of scientists formed "The Group for
the Scientific Reappraisal of the HIV/AIDS Hypothesis." They
drafted "a letter, signed by 12 people, including several scientists
with advanced medical degrees, published in *Science* (17 Feb.
1995, vol. 267, pp. 945-946), which read:"[210]

We have proposed that researchers independent of the HIV
establishment should audit the Centers for Disease
Control's records of AIDS cases, bearing in mind that the
correlation of HIV with AIDS, upon which the case for HIV
causation rests, is itself an artifact of the definition of
AIDS. Since 1985, exactly the same diseases or conditions
have been defined as "AIDS" when antibodies are present,
and as "non-AIDS" when HIV and antibodies are absent.

Independent professional groups such as the Society of Actuaries should be invited to nominate members for an independent commission to investigate the following question: How frequently do AIDS-defining diseases (or low T cell counts) occur in the absence of HIV? Until we have a definition of AIDS that is independent of HIV, the supposed correlation of HIV and AIDS is mere tautology. Other independent researchers should examine the validity of the so-called "AIDS tests," especially when these tests are used in Africa and Southern Asia, to see if they reliably record the presence of antibodies, let alone live and replicating virus.[211]

Since that letter was published, over 2,600 people signed their names in agreement to the founding statement. The list comprised "The Group for the Scientific Reappraisal of the HIV/AIDS Hypothesis."[212]

To kill harmless HIV, the US government, World Bank, and other organizations spent billions of dollars purchasing and distributing hazardous anti-HIV medications to the estimated 36 to 50 million people who are presumed to have HIV worldwide. But those drugs such as Zidovudine (AZT) Retrovir made by GlaxoSmithKline never cured anyone said to have "AIDS." Nor did the drug makers ever claim they did.[213]

Not one person was ever cured by the highly toxic chemicals. Not one life saved. Research indicated that virtually everyone taking these drugs was dying and, most alarming, that most of the 22 million people who were thought to have died from AIDS actually died from the adverse side effects of anti-HIV drugs. According to numerous studies, AIDS patients' immune-deficiency was the result of chemicals that damaged the immune system, including recreational drugs like cocaine, nitrite inhalants, and heroin, over-use of certain medicines such as antibiotics, alcohol abuse, pesticides, industrial pollutants, other environmental toxins, *and* anti-HIV medications like ATP. In Africa, so-called AIDS victims are simply victims of prolonged malnutrition – the main cause of AIDS in Africa – repeated infections, chronic stress, and sleep deficit.[214]

Drugs "more dangerous than heroin"

Prescription painkillers are even deadlier and more damaging than many illegal drugs such as heroin. In 2008, more Americans died from pharmaceutical painkillers than illegal drugs like cocaine and heroin combined. In the USA, prescription drug deaths outnumber traffic accidents in number of fatalities. More than 12 million individuals in the United States reported taking prescription painkillers "purely for the high" that they give, rather than for the intended purpose.[215]

In fact, almost all recent USA "massacre shooters," including the "Batman shooter" James Holmes in Colorado in July 2012, were reportedly taking hardcore pharmaceutical drugs which are known to produce "altered mental states" and "unusual thoughts or behavior."[216]

The FDA in the US, and the Department of Health and the Joint Committee on Vaccination and Immunization (JCVI) in the UK, have been proven to hide the dangers of countless drugs. The FDA has refused to ban drugs for asthma which were demonstrated to cause 4,000 deaths of asthma patients annually.[217]

In the UK, in March 2012 a report published by Dr Lucija Tomljenovic found the following shocking situation:

> The JCVI made continuous efforts to withhold critical data on severe adverse reactions and contra-indications to vaccinations from both parents and health practitioners in order to reach overall vaccination rates which they deemed were necessary for "herd immunity," a concept which with regards to vaccination, and contrary to prevalent beliefs, does not rest on solid scientific evidence, as will be explained. As a result of such vaccination policy promoted by the JCVI and the DH, many children have been vaccinated without their parents being disclosed the critical information about demonstrated risks of serious adverse reactions, one that the JCVI appeared to have been fully aware of. It would also appear that, by withholding this information, the JCVI/DH neglected the right of individuals to make an informed consent concerning vaccination. By doing so, the JCVI/DH may have violated not only International Guidelines for Medical Ethics (i.e., Helsinki Declaration and the International Code of Medical Ethics) but also, their own Code of Practice.

Tomljenovic's 45-page report concluded that:

Transcripts of the JCVI/DH meetings from the period from 1983 to 2010 appear to show that:

1) Instead of reacting appropriately by re-examining existing vaccination policies when safety concerns over specific vaccines were identified by their own investigations, the JCVI either a) took no action, b) skewed or selectively removed unfavourable safety data from public reports and c) made intensive efforts to reassure both the public and the authorities of the safety of respective vaccines;

2) Significantly restricted contraindication to vaccination criteria in order to increase vaccination rates despite outstanding and unresolved safety issues;

3) On multiple occasions requested from vaccine manufacturers to make specific amendments to their data sheets, when these were in conflict with JCVI's official advices on immunisations;

4) Persistently relied on methodologically dubious studies, while dismissing independent research, to promote vaccine policies;

5) Persistently and categorically downplayed safety concerns while over-inflating vaccine benefits;

6) Promoted and elaborated a plan for introducing new vaccines of questionable efficacy and safety into the routine pediatric schedule, on the assumption that the licenses would eventually be granted;

7) Actively discouraged research on vaccine safety issues;

8) Deliberately took advantage of parents' trust and lack of relevant knowledge on vaccinations in order to promote a scientifically unsupported immunisation program which could put certain children at risk of severe long-term neurological damage;

Notably, all of these actions appear to violate the JCVI's own Code of Practice.[218]

This deadly or crippling Anglo-American pharmaceutical drug system has been developed over decades to use medical drugs to literally weaken whole populations, referred to by them as "herds." The entire vaccine and drug industry almost without exception in the US, UK and Switzerland and Japan has been developed since World War II as a vital part of the eugenics agenda of the Rockefeller family circles of the Anglo-American establishment.

Responsible persons concerned with the future health of the Chinese people would do well to examine this highly strategic form of warfare.

Margaret Chan, WHO and Swine Flu

A central agency in the promotion of Washington and London's drug agenda for China is the World Health Organization in Geneva. In the past several years the leadership of the WHO has been *de facto* "weaponized" as an instrumentality of US strategic military policy. A key role in this weaponization is being played by Dr. Margaret Chan, the Hong Kong-born Director General of WHO. Chan has been in the center of three crucial Pentagon-orchestrated phony epidemic and pandemic scenarios – the 1997 H5N1 avian influenza or "bird flu" scare, the 2003 SARS scare in Hong Kong, and the fraudulent declaration of a global H1N1 swine flu "pandemic."[219]

Chan follows orders. Her orders come from an elite cabal of pharmaceutical giants who control every aspect of WHO vaccine and health policy worldwide. In the swine flu or H1N1 instance, WHO actually changed their definition of what constituted a "global Pandemic Emergency, Phase 6" some weeks before the fraudulent swine flu scare hit major media. New WHO Pandemic guidelines were made public on April 20, 2009, conveniently enough just in time to affect the May-June 2009 world pandemic scare. According to a WHO official responsible for the report, the revision of 2005 WHO Pandemic guidelines was begun "well before the Mexican flu cases were first reported." The official spoke off the record.[220]

Even more curious was the fact that new April 2009 WHO pandemic response guidelines crucially redefined what constituted "pandemic." No longer was it required that a disease cause "enormous numbers of deaths and illness."

The previous definition of a pandemic stated:

"An influenza pandemic occurs when a new influenza virus appears against which the human population has no immunity, resulting in several, simultaneous epidemics worldwide with enormous numbers of deaths and illness."[221]

WHO issued its pandemic declaration – the first in 40 years – just as 74 countries had reported a total 144 deaths from the novel H1N1 infection, hardly alarming even if all 144 were directly caused by something called H1N1 virus, which was highly doubtful. The world was gripped with fears of swine flu as the alert increased from Phase 5 to Phase 6, the highest level. Immediately, pharmaceutical companies began working to develop vaccines, and countries tailored their responses to address the situation. Dr. Thomas Frieden, head of the US Centers for Disease Control and Prevention, or CDC, announced on June 8, 2009, that the US would respond "aggressively" to the virus.[222]

Billions of dollars were spent on untested vaccines. President Obama exempted the major drug makers from possible liability resulting from the untested new vaccines.

The new, looser definition made it easy for Chan and the WHO to declare "Phase 6, Pandemic" for what was to be the mildest ordinary flu outbreak in recent history.

For the WHO H1N1 "pandemic," the symptoms were the same as for a severe common cold, no more. The new rule that WHO may declare an official Pandemic global alert practically at any time is all the more bizarre when the "global wave" of cases reportedly have been so mild as to be indistinguishable from the symptoms of ordinary flu.

The entire hoax was orchestrated from the corrupt WHO Scientific Advisory Committee of Experts or SAGE. The WHO's SAGE Chairman since 2005 was the UK Director of Immunization at the British Department of Health, Dr David Salisbury. In the 1980's Salisbury reportedly drew major criticism for backing a massive vaccination of children with a multiple MMR vaccine manufactured by the predecessor company of GlaxoSmithKline. That vaccine was pulled off the market in Japan, after significant numbers of children developed adverse reactions, and the Japanese government was forced to pay significant compensation to the victims. In Sweden, the MMR vaccine was removed after scientists linked it to outbreaks of Crohn's disease. Apparently that had little impact on WHO SAGE chairman Salisbury.[223]

According to one independent UK investigator, Alan Golding, who obtained Freedom of Information documents on the case:

...in 1986 Trivirix, an MMR compound containing the Mumps Urabe strain AM-9, was introduced in Canada to replace MMR I. Concerns regarding the introduction of MMR in the UK are recorded in the minutes of the Joint Working Party of the British Paediatric Association and the Joint Committee on Vaccination and Immunization (JCVI) Liaison Group on June 26th of that year. Such concerns were soon to prove well grounded, as reports began to come in of an increased incidence of aseptic meningitis in vaccinated individuals. Ultimately, all MMR vaccines containing the Urabe strain of mumps were withdrawn in Canada in early 1988. This was before Urabe-containing vaccines were licensed by the Department of Health for use in the UK...[224]

The report adds,

Smith-Kline-French, the pharmaceutical company who became Smith-Kline-Beecham [today GlaxoSmithKline] and were involved in UK manufacture at that time, were concerned about these safety issues and were reluctant to obtain a UK license for their Urabe-containing vaccines. As a result of their "concern" that children might be seriously damaged by one of their products, they requested that the UK government indemnify them against possible legal action that might be taken as a result of "losses" associated with the vaccine, which by then was known to carry significant risk to health. The UK government, advised by Professor Salisbury and representatives from the Department of Health, in its enthusiasm to get a cheap MMR onto the market, agreed to this request."[225]

The same Dr Salisbury was advocating global proliferation of untested H1N1 vaccines manufactured by the same firm. In hearings after the pandemic swine flu scare passed, it came out that the major pharmaceutical giants had deliberately pressured Chan's WHO to soften the definition of "pandemic" weeks before the H1N1 scare of 2009. Dr. Wolfgang Wodarg, former head of health at the Council of Europe, the Strasbourg-based body responsible for the European Court of Human Rights, concluded in hearings that drug companies manipulated the WHO into downgrading its definition of a pandemic, and declaring a H1N1 flu "pandemic."[226]

The new "soft" definition of pandemic remains WHO policy today. It is not clear whether Chinese government health authorities are aware of the massive political manipulations by big drug companies and WHO. Hopefully they are.

CDC Autism Vaccine Study Whistleblower In Grave Danger

26 August, 2014. The sensational and explosive scandal that is erupting over a whistleblower inside the US Government Centers for Disease Control (CDC) in Atlanta is dramatically escalating. The whistleblower is known. His name is William W. Thompson, PhD, a scientist at CDC's National Center for Immunizations and Respiratory Diseases who was just fired by the CDC and escorted by guards from his office.[227]

Some brief background is needed for those not familiar. On August 8, 2014, Dr Brian Hooker of the Focus Autism Foundation published in the peer-reviewed scientific journal, Translational Neurodegeneration, that he was in contact with a then-anonymous CDC whistleblower who said he had a guilty conscience, and decided to reveal the fraud in a CDC study of possible correlation between MMR (measles, mumps, rubella) vaccines and autism. According to the whistleblower, the true study of the CDC revealed that young Afro-American boys who got their first MMR vaccine *before 3 years of age* (36 months) had a 340% greater chance of becoming autistic than comparable Afro-Americans of the same age and social status vaccinated after age three.

CDC researchers took data on 2,583 children living in Atlanta, Georgia born between 1986 and 1993. However, according to the whistleblower, William W. Thompson, who was involved in the study, the CDC researchers arbitrarily excluded children that did not have a valid State of Georgia birth certificate. That simple trick cut the sample size being studied by 41% and masked the significance of the link between autism and MMR vaccine.[228]

According to fired CDC scientist Thompson, the CDC, under pressure from the vaccine makers, told its scientists to arbitrarily alter the data sample to erase the clear link between autism and MMR.

Thompson, who played a key role in studies of various vaccines and his life, some believe, is now in grave danger because he did not immediately go public with his charges and instead tried to first work from the shadows through others. Now, according to sources close to the situation, the CDC discovered Thompson's identity and escorted him off the CDC premises under guard on August 20.[229] In other words they got him before he could decide to go public and make it far more difficult for the Government or others to "destroy the evidence."

> In 2007, he [Thompson] published a study on the effects of mercury (thimerosal) on babies and very young children – and he concluded that there were both positive and negative effects, but the effects on both sides were very small.
>
> The study was used by the press and the government to trumpet the idea (the lie) that everybody could rest easy; vaccines containing mercury weren't harming anyone.
>
> Now, this, too, comes under scrutiny. If Thompson was lying about the MMR vaccine, did he also lie about mercury and its toxic effects? Did he intentionally underplay those effects? Did he cook the data in that study, too?[230]

In brief, Thompson has the potential to blow the lid off the entire pharmaceutical industry vaccine corruption.

Autism: a historical note

The notable thing about autism is that it is a disorder that has grown dramatically in recent years, curiously enough, in parallel to the growth of the number of vaccinations and the earlier age doctors recommend giving them. Harris Coulter, the co-author of "DPT: A Shot in the Dark," wrote a revealing little-known fact about the rise of autism. DPT refers to the combination vaccine Diptheria, Pertussis (whooping cough), Tetanus:

> Vaccination programs were instituted in the late 1930s... In the 1940s a new mental syndrome, which Dr. Leo Kanner called autism, was noted. It appeared in the wake of the U.S. pertussis vaccine schemes. [Pertussis is one component of the DPT vaccine.]

When vaccination programs were expanded after the war, the number of autistic children increased greatly... (When) the U.S. occupied Japan and forcibly vaccinated the children: their first case of autism was diagnosed in 1945.

In England the [pertussis] shot was subject to large scale promotion in the late fifties: a society for autistic children was founded in 1962.

In the U.S. at first the malady [autism] was noticed in higher income families. This was before the free or forced pertussis vaccine programmes; only the better-off parents could afford the 'latest medical advance'...later parents from across the socio-economic spectrum gained equal access... Thus, autistic children were now being discovered within every kind of family and in dreadfully greater numbers than ever before imagined.[231]

The dramatic breaking story around Thompson has the potential to deal a devastating blow to the pharmaceutical industry just as they are on the verge, with the complicity of Dr. Margaret Chan of the WHO, to impose untested new vaccines against "ebola."

Source: "Are We Poisoning Our Kids in the Name of Protecting their Health?", flyer produced by GenerationRescue.org, http://njvaccinationchoice.org/docs/genrescue.pdf

The USA's corrupt pro-vaccine lobby

In the USA there is a strong lobby of pediatricians and non-profit organizations that advocate every child be thoroughly and repeatedly vaccinated before age two. CBS News investigative correspondent Sharyl Attkisson reported:

They're some of the most trusted voices in the defense of vaccine safety: the American Academy of Pediatrics, Every Child By Two, and pediatrician Dr. Paul Offit.

But CBS News has found these three have something more in common - strong financial ties to the industry whose products they promote and defend.

The vaccine industry gives millions to the Academy of Pediatrics for conferences, grants, medical education classes and even helped build their headquarters. The totals are kept secret, but public documents reveal bits and pieces.

COMPARISON OF CDC MANDATORY SCHEDULE
Children birth to six years (recommended month)

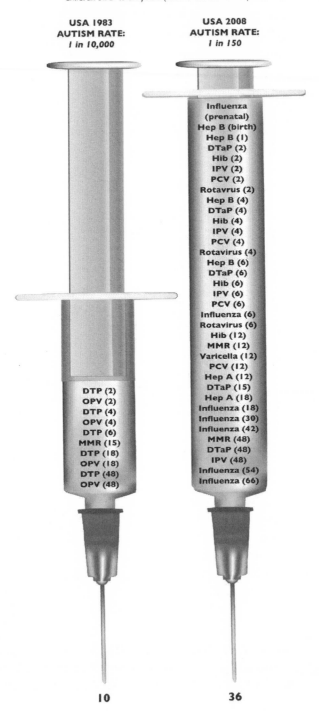

**USA 1983
AUTISM RATE:**
1 in 10,000

**USA 2008
AUTISM RATE:**
1 in 150

DTP (2)
OPV (2)
DTP (4)
OPV (4)
DTP (6)
MMR (15)
DTP (18)
OPV (18)
DTP (48)
OPV (48)

Influenza
(prenatal)
Hep B (birth)
Hep B (1)
DTaP (2)
Hib (2)
IPV (2)
PCV (2)
Rotavrus (2)
Hep B (4)
DTaP (4)
Hib (4)
IPV (4)
PCV (4)
Rotavirus (4)
Hep B (6)
DTaP (6)
Hib (6)
IPV (6)
PCV (6)
Influenza (6)
Rotavirus (6)
Hib (12)
MMR (12)
Varicella (12)
PCV (12)
Hep A (12)
DTaP (15)
Hep A (18)
Influenza (18)
Influenza (30)
Influenza (42)
MMR (48)
DTaP (48)
IPV (48)
Influenza (54)
Influenza (66)

10   36

A $342,000 payment from Wyeth, maker of the pneumococcal vaccine - which makes $2 billion a year in sales.

A $433,000 contribution from Merck, the same year the academy endorsed Merck's HPV vaccine - which made $1.5 billion a year in sales.

Another top donor: Sanofi Aventis, maker of 17 vaccines and a new five-in-one combo shot just added to the childhood vaccine schedule last month.[232]

Notably, in 2012 Attkisson, a courageous award-winning investigative journalist, was severely attacked in the media for "promoting pseudoscientific theories about an alleged link between autism and vaccines." She had reported on a groundbreaking scientific review by a retired drug industry scientist, Dr Helen Ratajczak.

In another exposé on CBS, Attkisson reported,

> The article in the Journal of Immunotoxicology is entitled "Theoretical aspects of autism: Causes – A review." The author is Helen Ratajczak, surprisingly herself a former senior scientist at a pharmaceutical firm. Ratajczak did what nobody else apparently has bothered to do: she reviewed the body of published science since autism was first described in 1943. Not just one theory suggested by research such as the role of MMR shots, or the mercury preservative thimerosal; but all of them...

> Ratajczak reports that about the same time vaccine makers took most thimerosal out of most vaccines (with the exception of flu shots which still widely contain thimerosal), they began making some vaccines using human tissue. Ratajczak says human tissue is currently used in 23 vaccines. She discusses the increase in autism incidences corresponding with the introduction of human DNA to MMR vaccine, and suggests the two could be linked. Ratajczak also says an additional increased spike in autism occurred in 1995 when chicken pox vaccine was grown in human fetal tissue.

> Why could human DNA potentially cause brain damage? The way Ratajczak explained it to me: "Because it's human DNA and recipients are humans, there's homologous

recombination... That DNA is incorporated into the host DNA. Now it's changed, altered itself and the body kills it. Where is this most expressed? The neurons of the brain. Now you have body killing the brain cells and it's an ongoing inflammation. It doesn't stop, it continues through the life of that individual."[233]

On March 10, 2014, Attkisson resigned from CBS News, reportedly due to frustration over the network's lack of dedication to investigative reporting.

The CDC autism study scandal is far from over. The grave danger now is that the US Government silences Thompson. One insider to the CDC and the power of the pharmaceutical industry to silence threats to its power warns,

> Threats of various kinds, at the very least, will now be applied to Thompson. Legal action, perhaps arrest, perhaps worse. When it comes to vaccines and protecting that empire, the games are very serious. Deadly serious. The gloves come off. People have to understand this, if Thompson disappears or shows up dead 'as a suicide.' Since Thompson isn't, as of this moment, stepping forward himself to provide full disclosure on his past actions, and since his name is already out there....the best protection he has is other people. Other people making his name and his dangerous situation known.[234]

Autism and Western Vaccines see Parallel Rise in China

The escalating scandal around the alleged deliberate fraud by the US Government's Centers for Disease Control (CDC) to drastically alter a major study of the possible link between MMP vaccines (Measles, Mumps, Pertussis) in children vaccinated under three years age, and incidence of autism is throwing light on one of the most criminal strategies of Western pharmaceutical vaccine makers. Now it comes to light that a major epidemic spread of cases of autism in China arose directly parallel to China's opening up to the Western drugmakers and to WTO trade rules some twenty years ago.

In the mid-1980's western drug makers introduced multiple combined vaccines and steadily lowered the recommended age at which children should receive the repeated vaccinations. They were backed by what are now provably corrupt official agencies in the US including the CDC. Organizations of US pediatricians, which received millions of dollars in favors from the same drug makers, joined the bandwagon for early and massive infant vaccination. Unknowing parents were in effect terrorized into allowing the vaccination surge in fear of being responsible for horrible disease or damage to their children were they to refuse.

China's new 'Opium War': Vaccines

By the early 1990's, as the Peoples' Republic of China continued its unprecedented opening to all things Western, the Government allowed Western drug makers to enter China in a major way.

Western pharmaceutical companies have moved in, establishing production facilities and using their immense financial and PR skills to promote the same vaccine agenda that the CDC in the United States promote for Americans. There has been a considerable effort to discredit thousand-year-old natural healing techniques of Traditional Chinese Medicine (TCM) in the process to open the door of a vast new market for Western drug companies.

China's membership in the WTO in 2001 opened the door for a considerable increased presence of Western drugmakers in China including GlaxoSmithKline, Bayer, Bristol-Myers Squibb, Merck & Co and Eli Lilly & Company. GSK, Roche, Novo Nordisk, and others, have come to China to set up R&D centers. The leading pharmaceutical companies have established joint venture manufactories in China. Some have set up sole propriety manufactories. As of 2004, amongst the largest 500 overseas enterprises, 14 of them are pharmaceutical companies.

Parallel to the rise in distribution of vaccines produced by Merck, GSK and others in China, the country began to register for the first time a dramatic rise in children diagnosed with neurological disorders, something the WHO and CDC try to ignore because of its huge implications for vaccinations containing mercury and other adjuvants believed responsible for the neurological damage termed autism.

Before the late 1980's in China, children with symptoms the West calls autism were virtually unknown. It has since spread massively.

In 2011 at an International Autism Research Collaboration Development Conference in Shanghai, autism was ranked "Number 1" among mental disorders in China. The World Health Organization estimated China today has one million autistic children.[235] Twenty years ago the number was near zero.

The drug makers and their medical supporters claim the rise in autism in China has to do with "genetic defects" something that lets them nicely off the hook. But genetics in humans and animals do not change so dramatically in so short a time period. Dr Francis S. Collins, current Director of the National Institutes of Health, stated in evidence to US House of Representatives Committee May 2006 when he was Director of the US National Human Genome Research Institute:

> Recent increases in chronic diseases like diabetes, childhood asthma, obesity or autism cannot be due to major shifts in the human gene pool as those changes take much more time to occur. They must be due to changes in the environment including diet...[236]

Autism, to restate, cannot be due to any major shift in the human gene pool. Then what is the cause? "Environment, including diet..." would have to consider the possible effects of injection of vaccines laced with adjuvants such as mercury, with proven neuro-muscular side effects, as a possible factor, especially when the dramatic rise of autism in China is paralleled in time by the dramatic rise in child and infant vaccinations, following the recommendations of the US CDC and WHO.

Kuang Guifang, director of the psychology department at Qingdao Children's Hospital, stated when asked what he viewed as the cause of the dramatic rise of autism in modern China, "Birth defects, environmental causes such as heavy metals and pesticides, and childhood vaccines also are blamed."[237]

US data

More and more it is emerging that autism is a reaction to specific vaccines or combinations of vaccines, especially when administered to children below age three. If we were to graph the rise in CDC Mandatory Vaccine Schedules in the USA to the rise in autism there, in 1983 incidence of child autism was one in 10,000 children. Then the exposure to vaccines and their adjuvants was dramatically less. Infant vaccination at six months or earlier was almost unknown. Since then, under CDC pressure, the dosages of infant vaccines have exploded. So have incidences of autism in American children. In 2013, 1 in 150 American children were diagnosed with autism.

No less an authority than the then-Director of the US Centers for Disease Control, Dr. Julie Gerberding, admitted to CBS News, that:

> Now, we all know that vaccines can occasionally cause fevers in kids. So if a child was immunized, got a fever, had other complications from the vaccines. And if you're predisposed with the mitochondrial disorder, it can certainly set off some damage. Some of the symptoms can be symptoms that have characteristics of autism.[238]

Despite that shocking admission, which she made almost casually to CNN, Gerberding left CDC to take a well-paid job as President of Merck's Vaccines Division, where the suspect MMR vaccines are made that are implicated in the current CDC scandal of faked test results. She is also Director of MSD Wellcome Trust Hilleman Laboratories Private Limited, a joint initiative between Merck and Wellcome Trust.

MMR vaccines, invented at Merck, are ostensibly to immunize six month and older infants from the effects of Measles, Mumps and Rubella (German Measles). The Merck MMR vaccine combination is of live vaccines. The MMR vaccine is a mixture of live attenuated viruses of the three diseases, administered via injection, developed by Maurice Hilleman while at Merck.[239]

Live Rubella virus has been admitted as a cause of autism. The first known cause of autism was rubella virus, known since the 1960s. And rubella virus is one of the three live viruses in the Merck MMR vaccine. Walter Orenstein, Assistant US Surgeon General wrote in 2002, "rubella (congenital rubella syndrome) is one of the few proven causes of autism."[240]

> The explosive rise of autism in China to become today the nation's Number 1 mental health disorder, combined with the explosive rise in US cases of autism parallel to introduction of repeated early infant vaccinations including MMP, suggest the autism-vaccine link should become a highest priority research focus for genuinely independent researchers not tainted by the drug makers or their PR organizations.

The Pentagon and the "Other" Drug Cartel

This vast global killing and maiming machine of the modern pharmaceutical industry is organized in a drug cartel even more ruthless than those of Mexico, Colombia, Afghanistan or Kosovo. The activities of the private US pharmaceutical companies, the "other," more deadly drug cartel, are being coordinated today by the US Pentagon.

In July 2012, DARPA, the US Department of Defense research and development agency, issued a press release announcing that they had produced over 10 million doses of H1N1 flu vaccine in a single month.[241] They did this using techniques of genetic manipulation or GMO. The alarming point is that no one seriously questions why the Pentagon is spending taxpayer funds to create 10,000,000 H1NI flu vaccines, let alone using asking what will happen in a future US Presidential declaration of emergency or WHO declaration, again using the new watered-down definition of pandemic. Will these GMO vaccines be dispensed in such a way that hundreds of millions of innocent Chinese become human guinea pigs for the Pentagon?

Already back in the early 1970s, US National Security Memorandum 200, advanced by Mr. Nixon's National Security Adviser Henry Kissinger, called for massive "Third World" depopulation efforts in order to maintain the economic alignment of the superpowers. China was on the list of Third World countries to target even back then.

The most powerful group behind the weaponization of pharmaceutical drugs today is the Rockefeller group. In 1939 the "Drug Trust" alliance was formed by the Rockefeller group as they were moving into agribusiness, and extending their plans to use their control over oil to control the world economies after "victory" in the coming World War II. The early Rockefeller drug and chemical companies included Imperial Chemical Industries (ICI), Squibb and Sons, Bristol Meyers, Whitehall laboratories, Procter and Gamble, Roche, Hoechst and Bayer and Co. By the 1970's the Rockefeller Empire, in tandem with the family-controlled Chase Manhattan Bank then headed by David Rockefeller, owned over half of the USA's pharmaceutical interests, and was the largest drug manufacturing combine in the world.

Today this Anglo-American-controlled legal drug industry has become the second largest manufacturing industry in the world next to the arms industry, also owned by the same hegemonic circles.[242]

The Rockefeller interest in drugs and "drug-based Western medicine" is not casual. The Rockefeller Foundation began in the 1920's to completely reorganize American medical schools around their concept of using drugs and invasive surgery instead of proven, older, natural treatment methods.[243]

In 1987, the eighteen largest drug firms were ranked as follows:

1. Merck (U.S.) (Rockefeller controlled)
2. Glaxo Holdings (UK) (today, Rothschild's GlaxoSmithKline)
3. Hoffman LaRoche (Switzerland)
4. Smith Kline Beckman (U.S.) (today GlaxoSmithKline of UK)
5. Ciba-Geigy (Switzerland)
6. Pfizer (U.S.) (Rockefeller group)
7. Hoechst A. G. (Germany) (Rockefeller and Rothschild control)
8. American Home Products (U.S.)
9. Eli Lilly (U.S.) (Rockefeller group)
10. Upjohn (U.S.)
11. Squibb (U.S.) (Rockefeller ties)
12. Johnson & Johnson (U.S.) (Rockefeller group)
13. Sandoz (Switzerland)
14. Bristol Myers (U.S.) (Rockefeller group)
15. Beecham Group (United Kingdom) (today GlaxoSmithKline)
16. Bayer A. G. (Germany) (Rockefeller group links)
17. Syntex (U.S.)
18. Warner Lambert (U.S.)

Thus we find that the United States maintained an overwhelming lead in the production and sale of drugs.[244]

The number one US drug group Merck was tied to the Rockefeller group through Chase Manhattan Bank. The number two Glaxo (today GlaxoSmithKline) was tied to the London Rothschilds banking interests. Almost all the major pharmaceutical giants today are linked directly or indirectly to either or both the

Rockefeller or Rothschild Anglo-American groups which also control the four major oil giants – ExxonMobil, Chevron, BP and Shell.

The control of the global drugs industry has not substantially changed despite a wave of mergers and takeovers in recent years. The world's largest drug producer is Pfizer of the US, followed by Johnson & Johnson (US); Hoffmann-La Roche (Switzerland); Novartis (Switzerland); GlaxoSmithKline (UK); Sanofi-Aventis (France); AstraZeneca (UK/Sweden); Abbott Laboratories (US); Merck & Co. (US); Bristol-Myers Squibb (US); Eli Lilly and Company (US); Boehringer Ingelheim (Germany); Takeda Pharmaceutical Co. (Japan); Bayer (Germany); Amgen (US); Genentech (US); Baxter International (US).[245]

The global pharmaceutical cartel operates like the oil or grain cartel, with tight and total control held by powerful US and UK family interests, who are also tied to a long-term agenda of eugenics and population reduction of non-Anglo-Saxon nations, such as China and India.

Chapter Seven:
Military Wars – South China Sea, Indian Ocean and the Pentagon's "String of Pearls" Strategy

China today, because of its dynamic economic growth and its determination to pursue sovereign Chinese national interests, is a challenge merely by existing. Thus it has become the Pentagon's new "enemy image," along with Russia, and the false "enemy image" of Islam, which was used after September 2001 by the Bush-Cheney Administration to justify the Pentagon's global power pursuit. The new US military posture against China has nothing to do with any aggressive threat from the side of China. The Pentagon has decided to escalate its aggressive military posture towards China merely because China has become a strong, vibrant, independent pole in world economics and geopolitics.

The Pentagon Targets China

Since the collapse of the Soviet Union and the nominal end of the Cold War some twenty years back, rather than reducing the size of its mammoth defense spending, the US Congress and US Presidents have enormously expanded spending for new weapons systems, and increased permanent military bases around the world. The US has expanded NATO not only to former Warsaw Pact countries on Russia's borders, but also has expanded the NATO and US military presence deep into Asia, on the perimeters of China, through its conduct of the Afghan war and related campaigns.

Leaving aside the huge budgets for national security and defense-related agencies such as the Department of Energy, US Treasury and others, the US Department of Defense spent some $739 billion in 2011 on its military requirements. If all other spending on defense and national security is included, the London-based International Institute for Strategic Studies estimates US military spending at over $1 trillion annually. That is an amount *greater than the total defense-related spending of the next 42 nations combined*, and more than the Gross Domestic Product of most nations.

China officially spent barely 10% as much as the US on defense, some $90 billion, or if certain defense-related arms import and other costs are included, perhaps $111 billion a year. Even if the Chinese authorities do not publish complete data on such sensitive areas, it is clear China spends a small fraction of the US budget, and is starting from a military technology base far behind the USA.

The US defense budget is not only the world's largest by far. It also bears no relation to any perceived threat. In the nineteenth century, the British Royal Navy built the size of its fleet according to the fleets of Britain's two most powerful potential enemies; America's defense budget strategists declare it will be "doomsday" if the United States builds its navy to anything less than five times China and Russia combined.[246]

If we include the spending by Russia, China's strongest ally within the Shanghai Cooperation Organization, their combined total annual defense spending is barely $142 billion. The world's top ten defense spending nations – after the USA as largest and China as second largest – include the UK, France, Japan, Russia, Saudi Arabia, Germany, India and Brazil. In 2011 the military spending of the United States equaled a staggering 46% of total defense spending by the world's 171 governments and territories, almost half the entire world's budget.[247]

Clearly, for all its rhetoric about "peace-keeping" missions and "democracy" promotion, the Pentagon is pursuing what its planners refer to as "Full Spectrum Dominance," the total control of all global air, land, and ocean space, as well as outer space and now cyberspace.[248] It is clearly determined to use its military might to secure global domination or hegemony. No other interpretation is possible.

Because of its dynamic economic growth and its determination to pursue its sovereign national interests, China's very existence poses a challenge. Thus it has become the Pentagon's new "enemy image," along with Russia, and the false "enemy image" of Islam, which was used after September 2001 by the Bush-Cheney Administration to justify the Pentagon's global power pursuit. The new US military posture against China has nothing to do with any aggressive threat from the side of China. The

Pentagon has decided to escalate its aggressive military posture towards China merely because China has become a strong, vibrant, and independent pole in world economics and geopolitics.

The Obama Doctrine: China is the New "Enemy Image"

After almost two decades of neglecting its interests in East Asia, the Obama Administration announced in 2011 that the US would make "a strategic pivot" in its foreign policy to focus its military and political attention on the Asia-Pacific region, particularly Southeast Asia, that is, China.

During the final months of 2011 the Obama Administration publicly defined a new threat doctrine for US military readiness, in the wake of US military failures in Iraq and Afghanistan. During a Presidential trip to the Far East, while in Australia, the US President unveiled what is being termed the Obama Doctrine.[249]

The following sections from Obama's speech in Australia are worth citing in detail:

> With most of the world's nuclear power and some half of humanity, Asia will largely define whether the century ahead will be marked by conflict or cooperation... As President, I have, therefore, made a deliberate and strategic decision – as a Pacific nation, the United States will play a larger and long-term role in shaping this region and its future... I have directed my national security team to make our presence and mission in the Asia Pacific a top priority... As we plan and budget for the future, we will allocate the resources necessary to maintain our strong military presence in this region. We will preserve our unique ability to project power and deter threats to peace... Our enduring interests in the region demand our enduring presence in the region.

> The United States is a Pacific power, and we are here to stay. Indeed, we are already modernizing America's defense posture across the Asia Pacific. It will be more broadly distributed – maintaining our strong presence in Japan and the Korean Peninsula, while enhancing our

presence in Southeast Asia. Our posture will be more flexible – with new capabilities to ensure that our forces can operate freely. And our posture will be more sustainable, by helping allies and partners build their capacity, with more training and exercises. We see our new posture here in Australia... I believe we can address shared challenges, such as proliferation and maritime security, including cooperation in the South China Sea.[250]

The centerpiece of Obama's visit was the announcement that at least 2,500 elite US Marines will be stationed at Darwin, in Australia's Northern Territory.

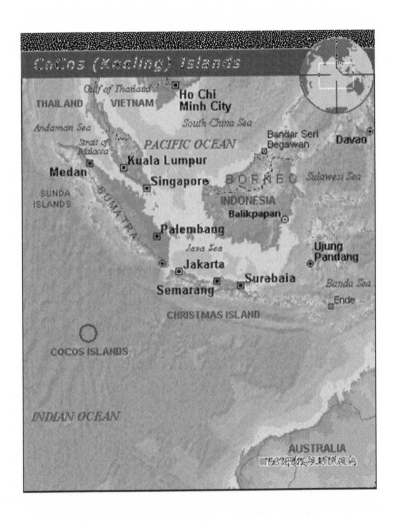

The Pentagon's Target is China.

Phillip Hammond, the UK Secretary of State for Defence, made make the point clear to fellow NATO members in July 2012. At a meeting in Washington, he explicitly declared that the new US defense shift to the Asia-Pacific region was aimed at China. Hammond said that, "the rising strategic importance of the Asia-Pacific region requires all countries, but particularly the United States, to reflect in their strategic posture the emergence of China as a global power. Far from being concerned about the tilt to Asia-Pacific, the European NATO powers should welcome the fact that the US is willing to engage in this new strategic challenge on behalf of the alliance."[251]

As with many of its operations, the Pentagon deployment is far more sinister than the relatively small number of 2,500 new US soldiers might suggest.

In August 2011 the Pentagon presented its annual report on China's military. It stated that China had closed key technological gaps. Deputy Assistant Secretary of Defense for East Asia, Michael Schiffer, said that the pace and scope of China's military investments had "allowed China to pursue capabilities that we believe are potentially destabilizing to regional military balances, increase the risk of misunderstanding and miscalculation and may contribute to regional tensions and anxieties."[252]

He cited Chinese refurbishing of a Soviet-era aircraft carrier and China's development of its J20 Stealth Fighter, as indications of the new capability requiring a more active US military response. Schiffer also cited China's space and cyber operations, saying it was "developing a multi-dimensional program to improve its capabilities to limit or prevent the use of space-based assets by adversaries during times of crisis or conflict."[253]

The Pentagon's "Air-Sea Battle"

Details of the Pentagon strategy to defeat China in a coming war, called "Air-Sea Battle," have filtered into the US press. The plan calls for an aggressive and coordinated US attack, in which American stealth bombers and submarines would knock out China's long-range surveillance radar and precision missile systems, located deep inside the country. The initial "blinding campaign" would be followed by a larger air and naval assault on China itself. Crucial to the advanced Pentagon strategy, which has already quietly begun to be deployed, is the US naval and air force presence in Japan, Taiwan, Philippines, Vietnam and across the South China Sea and Indian Ocean. Australian troop and naval deployment is aimed at accessing the strategic Chinese South China Sea as well as the Indian Ocean. The stated motive is to "protect freedom of navigation" in the Malacca Straits and the South China Sea.

Air-Sea Battle's goal is to help US forces withstand an initial Chinese assault, then counterattack to destroy sophisticated radar and missile systems that China has built to keep US ships away from its coastline.[254]

In mid-September, 2014, US Armed Forces staged a military exercise, Valiant Shield, in the western Pacific Ocean. It involved some 18,000 US soldiers, and was designed to test the Pentagon's Air-Sea Battle concept against China in a potential war situation. The Air-Sea Battle concept as tested first blinds China's "communications in space and cyberspace, then destroys land- and sea-based weapons platforms. It also aims to shoot down or otherwise defeat China's deployed weapons... At the beginning of the fight, the US aims squarely at the web of networks and satellites controlling the enemy's missiles and other weaponry in a 'blinding campaign.'"

In 2010 Air-Sea Battle became official Pentagon doctrine for a future war against China, and now had a specially-dedicated office inside the Pentagon focused on defeating China. "'Air-Sea Battle is about China – no doubt,' said Aaron Friedberg, a Princeton University professor who published a book this year on Air-Sea Battle."[255]

Notably, the exercises were carried out just days before the US State Department and CIA launched their Hong Kong "Occupy Central" civil disobedience "Color Revolution" that clearly was intended to destabilize Beijing. Washington had clearly decided time to rein in China's growing role in the world, as time was getting short.

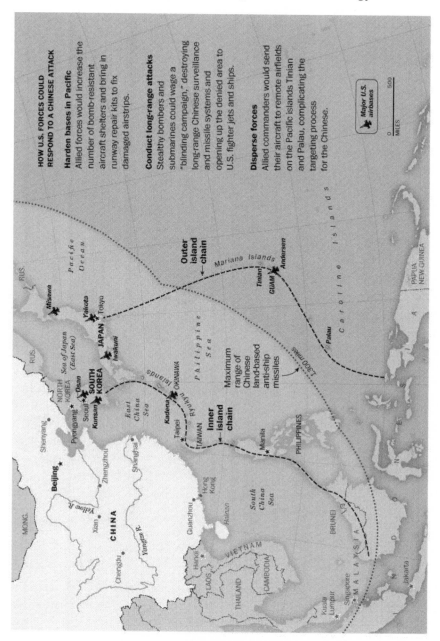

US "Air-Sea Battle" against China

In addition to stationing US Marines in northern Australia, Washington plans to fly long-range American surveillance drones from the remote Cocos Islands – an Australian territory in the strategically vital Indian Ocean. It will also have use of Australian Air Force bases for American military aircraft, and increased ship and submarine visits to the Indian Ocean through a naval base outside Perth, on Australia's west coast.[256]

The architect of "Air-Sea Battle" is Andrew Marshall, the man who has shaped Pentagon advanced warfare strategy for more than 40 years and who counts Dick Cheney and Donald Rumsfeld among his pupils.[257] Since the 1980s, Marshall has been a promoter of an idea first posited in 1982 by Marshal Nikolai Ogarkov, then chief of the Soviet general staff, called RMA, or "Revolution in Military Affairs."

The best definition of RMA was the one provided by Marshall himself: "A Revolution in Military Affairs (RMA) is a major change in the nature of warfare brought about by the innovative application of new technologies which, combined with dramatic changes in military doctrine and operational and organizational concepts, fundamentally alters the character and conduct of military operations."[258]

As head of the President's National Security Council, Henry Kissinger brought RAND Corporation nuclear expert Marshall onto the NSC. Marshall was then appointed by In 1973, President Nixon appointed Marshall to direct the Office of Net Assessment, a highly secretive internal Pentagon think tank, on the recommendation of Kissinger and Defense Secretary James R. Schlesinger. Marshall was reappointed by every president thereafter, a feat surpassed only by the late FBI Director, J. Edgar Hoover. Andrew Marshall was the only official in the Rumsfeld Pentagon who had participated in strategic war planning throughout virtually the entire Cold War, beginning in 1949 as a nuclear strategist for the RAND Corporation, until moving to the Pentagon in 1973.[259]

It was also Andrew Marshall who convinced US Defense Secretary Donald Rumsfeld and his successor Robert Gates to deploy the Ballistic Missile "Defense" (BMD) Shield in Poland, the Czech Republic, Turkey and Japan, as a strategy to minimize any potential nuclear threat from Russia and, in the case of Japan's BMD, any potential nuclear threat from China.

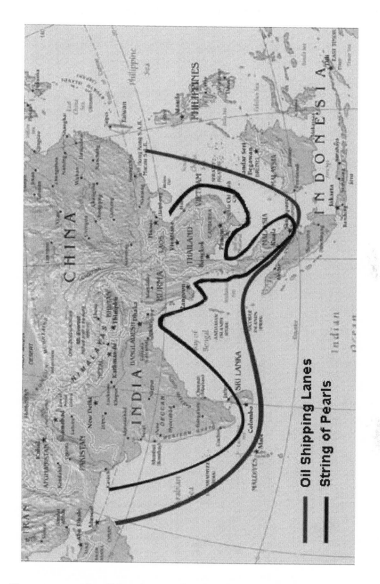

The Pentagon's "String of Pearls" Strategy

In their 2005 Annual Report to Congress, a select group of commissioners, with ties to the US intelligence community, defined their view of the emerging "danger" of China. They wrote:

> China's methodical and accelerating military modernization presents a growing threat to U.S security

interests in the Pacific. While Taiwan remains a key potential flashpoint, China's aggressive pursuit of territorial claims in the East and South China Seas points to ambitions that go beyond a Taiwan scenario and poses a growing threat to neighbors, including U.S. alliance partners, on China's periphery. Recent and planned military acquisitions by Beijing – mobile ballistic missiles, improved air and naval forces capable of extended range operations – provide China with the capability to conduct offensive strikes and military operations throughout the region...

...China wants a military that is capable of performing a variety of essential offshore missions, including protecting its eastern seaboard and ensuring the security of the sea lanes through which it receives resources essential to its continued economic development. But as Secretary of Defense Rumsfeld warned a Chinese military audience, 'expanding [Chinese] missile forces' and 'advances in Chinese strategic capability' worry China's neighbors and raise questions, 'particularly when there is an imperfect understanding of such developments on the part of others.'

China's aggressive pursuit of territorial claims arising from disputes with Japan in the East China Sea and multiple countries in the South China Sea, and its forays into the Bay of Bengal give rise to growing regional security concerns in Japan, India, and Southeast Asia. China's military threat against Taiwan is implicitly a threat to the United States as a result of both explicit and tacit assurances that have been expressed to Taiwan by every U.S. Administration since 1949. Taiwan has successfully converted from authoritarian rule to a functioning democracy, making it an even more significant symbol of American interest in the region and increasing the likelihood that a Chinese conflict with Taiwan will also involve U.S. forces.[260]

The 2005 China report to the US Congress went on to describe what the group saw as Chinese military strategy to defend her access to vital oil from the Persian Gulf and elsewhere:

In addition, a growing dependence on imported energy resources needed to sustain its economic development exposes China to new vulnerabilities and heightens its need to secure new energy sources and the sea lines of communications (SLOCs) from East Asia to the Persian Gulf and Africa needed to move energy supplies to China. With Myanmar's consent, China operates a maritime reconnaissance and electronic intelligence station on Great Coco Island and is building a base on Small Coco Island in the Bay of Bengal. According to an Asian defense analyst, China is helping Myanmar modernize several naval bases as a means of extending its power into the region. Moreover, Indian authorities claim that China has helped build radar, refit, and refuel facilities there to support further Chinese naval operations in the region in the future.[261]

In January 2005, Andrew Marshall, the man behind the Pentagon's secret "Air-Sea Strategy" against China and Director of the Office of Net Assessment, issued a classified internal report to Rumsfeld entitled "Energy Futures in Asia," prepared by the Booz Allen Hamilton think tank. The report, which was leaked in full to *The Washington Times*, used the term "China's String of Pearls Strategy" to describe what it called the growing Chinese military threat to "US strategic interests" in the Asian space.[262]

> China is building strategic relationships along the sea lanes from the Middle East to the South China Sea in ways that suggest defensive and offensive positioning to protect China's energy interests, but also to serve broad security objectives.
>
> The internal report stated that China was adopting a "string of pearls" strategy of bases and diplomatic ties stretching from the Middle East to southern China, including a new naval base under construction at the Pakistani port of Gwadar.
>
> Beijing already has set up electronic eavesdropping posts at Gwadar in the country's southwest corner, the part nearest the Persian Gulf. The post is monitoring ship traffic through the Strait of Hormuz and the Arabian Sea, the report said."[263]

"String of Pearls" was not a Chinese term, but was first coined in Marshall's report. It went on to name other "pearls" in China's sea-lane strategy:

• Bangladesh: China is strengthening its ties to the government and building a container port facility at Chittagong. The Chinese are "seeking much more extensive naval and commercial access" in Bangladesh.

• Burma: China has developed close ties to the military regime in Rangoon, and turned a nation wary of China into a "satellite" of Beijing close to the Strait of Malacca, through which 80 percent of China's imported oil passes.

China is building naval bases in Burma and has electronic intelligence gathering facilities on islands in the Bay of Bengal and near the Strait of Malacca. Beijing also supplied Burma with "billions of dollars in military assistance to support a de facto military alliance," the report said.

• Cambodia: China signed a military agreement in November 2003 to provide training and equipment. Cambodia is helping Beijing build a railway line from southern China to the sea.

The sea in question is the Gulf of Thailand. The c0mpleted network, known as the Kunming-Singapore Railway, will link China with Burma, Bangkok, Malaysia and Singapore, as well as the Indochinese nations of Vietnam, Laos and Cambodia, as originally planned by the French and British colonial powers.

- South China Sea: Chinese activities in the region are less about territorial claims than "protecting or denying the transit of tankers through the South China Sea," the report said.

China also is building up its military forces in the region to be able to "project air and sea power" from the mainland and Hainan Island. China recently upgraded a military airstrip on Woody Island and increased its presence through oil drilling platforms and ocean survey ships.

- Thailand: China is considering funding construction of a $20 billion canal across the Kra Isthmus that would allow ships to bypass the Strait of Malacca. The canal project would give China port facilities, warehouses and other infrastructure in Thailand aimed at enhancing Chinese influence in the region, the report said.

The report reflects growing fears in the Pentagon about China's long-term development. Many Pentagon analysts believe China's military buildup is taking place faster than earlier estimates, and that China will use its power to project force and undermine U.S. and regional security.

The U.S. military's Southern Command produced a similar classified report in the late 1990s that warned that China was seeking to use commercial port facilities around the world to control strategic "chokepoints."[264]

Breaking the String of Pearls

Significant Pentagon and US actions since that 2005 report have been aimed at countering China's attempts to defend its energy security via that "String of Pearls."

The US interventions since 2008 into Burma/Myanmar were of two phases. The first, as noted earlier, was the so-called Saffron Revolution, a US State Department and CIA-backed destabilization in 2007 aimed at putting the international spotlight on the Burmese military dictatorship's human rights practices. The aim was to further isolate Burma internationally from economic relations aside from China, especially threatening the China-Myanmar oil and gas pipelines.

Forcing Burma's military leaders into tighter dependency on China was one of the factors triggering the decision of the military to open up economically to the West. They declared that the tightening of US economic sanctions had done the country great harm. President Thein Sein made his major liberalization opening as well as allowing US-backed dissident, Aung San Suu Kyi, to be free and to run for elective office with her party in return for promises from US Secretary of State Hillary Clinton of US investment in the country.[265]

The US corporations approaching Burma are hand-picked by Washington to introduce the most destructive "free market" reforms that will open Burma to instability. The United States will not allow investment in entities owned by Myanmar's armed forces or its Ministry of Defense. It also is able to place sanctions on "those who undermine the reform process, engage in human rights abuses, contribute to ethnic conflict or participate in military trade with North Korea." The United States will block businesses or individuals from making transactions with any "specially designated nationals" or businesses that they control – allowing Washington, for example, to stop money from flowing to groups "disrupting the reform process." It's the classic "carrot and stick" approach, dangling the carrot of untold riches if Burma opens its economy to US corporations and punishing those who try to resist the takeover of the country's prize assets. Oil and gas, vital to China, will be a special target of US intervention. American companies and individuals will be allowed to invest in the state-owned Myanma Oil and Gas Enterprise (MOGE), but any investors will need to notify the State Department within 60 days.[266]

Mr. Obama also created a new power for the government to impose "blocking sanctions" on any individual threatening peace in Myanmar. Businesses with more than $500,000 in investment in the country will need to file an annual report with the State Department, with details on workers' rights, land acquisitions and any payments of more than $10,000 to government entities, including Myanmar's state-owned enterprises.

As well, US "human rights" NGOs, many closely associated with or believed to be associated with US State Department geopolitical designs, including Freedom House, Human Rights Watch, Institute for Asian Democracy, Open Society Foundations, U.S. Campaign for Burma, United to End Genocide – will now be allowed to operate inside Burma according to a decision by State Secretary Clinton in April 2012.[267]

Thailand, another key in China's defensive "String of Pearls" strategy, has also been the object of intense destabilization over the past several years. With the sister of the corrupt former Prime Minister in office, US-Thai relations significantly improved.

After months of bloody clashes in 2011, the US-backed billionaire, former Thai Prime Minister Thaksin Shinawatra, managed to "buy" a way to put his sister Yingluck Shinawatra in as Prime Minister, with him pulling the policy strings from abroad, comfortably ensconced in the US. After three years, however, Yingluck too ran out of luck, being deposed by a military coup in May 2014; this was welcomed by China, but "represents a slap in the face for the US." The new rulers intend to dismantle the Shinawatra machine for good before holding elections. The US quickly threatened to deploy its color revolution weapon on the Thai military again: "the US State Department declared that it would use 'every political lever, economic lever where applicable' to pressure the military regime to return Thailand to democratic rule."[268]

US relations with Thaksin's prime minister sister had been moving in direct fulfillment of the new Obama "strategic pivot" to focus on the "China threat." In June 2012, General Martin E. Dempsey, chairman of the US Joint Chiefs of Staff, visited Thailand, the Philippines and Singapore, the key "beads" in "the String of Pearls." On his return, he remarked, "We want to be out there partnered with nations and have a rotational presence that would allow us to build up common capabilities for common interests."

The Pentagon is now seeking to regain use of bases that were abandoned after the Vietnam War. It was negotiating with the Thai government to create a new "disaster relief" hub at the Royal Thai Navy Air Field at U-Tapao, 90 miles south of Bangkok. In the 1960s, the US military built the two-mile long runway there, one of Asia's longest, as a major staging and refueling base during the Vietnam War.

However, in August 2014, at the urging of the new military government, the National Council for Peace and Order (NCPO), the Thai airport authority approved a plan to upgrade U-Tapao to a full-fledged public civilian airport, over long-standing resistance by the Thai Navy.[269]

The Pentagon had also been working to secure more rights to US Navy visits to Thai ports, and joint surveillance flights to monitor trade routes and military movements. The US Navy will soon base four of its newest warships – Littoral Combat Ships, or gunboats – in Singapore, and would rotate them periodically to Thailand and other Southeast Asian countries. The Navy was also pursuing options to conduct joint airborne surveillance missions from Thailand.[270]

In addition, Deputy Defense Secretary Ashton Carter went to Thailand in July 2012, and Defense Secretary Leon Panetta toured Australia, Cambodia and Thailand in November of that year.[271]

In December 2013, the US Navy sent the first deployment of the new P-8A Poseidon reconnaissance and submarine hunter aircraft to the Pacific, replacing the P-3C Orion surveillance planes. The move came shortly after the Chinese announcement of the East China Sea Air Defense Identification Zone.

In May 2014, the Navy moved two of its new high-altitude RQ-4 Global Hawk surveillance drones forward from Guam to a base in Japan. "The long-range, unarmed drones could be used to monitor Chinese military activities."[272]

India-US Defense Department "Look East Policy"

Several years ago, during the Bush Administration, Washington made a major move to lock India in as a military ally against the emerging Chinese presence in Asia. India calls it their "Look East Policy." In reality, despite all claims to the contrary, it is a "look out for China" military policy.

In comments in August 2012, Deputy Secretary of Defense Ashton Carter stated, "India is also a key part of our rebalance to the Asia-Pacific, and, we believe, to the broader security and prosperity of the 21st century. The US-India relationship is global in scope, like the reach and influence of both countries."[273]

In remarks following a trip to New Delhi, Carter continued,

> Our security interests converge: on maritime security, across the Indian Ocean region; in Afghanistan, where India has done so much for economic development and the Afghan security forces; and on broader regional issues, where we share long-term interests. I went to India at the

request of Secretary Panetta and with a high-level delegation of U S technical and policy experts.[274]

Indian Ocean

The Pentagon's "String of Pearls" strategy against China was no beautiful necklace, but a hangman's noose around the perimeter of China, designed in the event of major conflict to completely cut off China from its access to vital raw materials, most especially oil from the Persian Gulf and Africa. As former Pentagon adviser Robert D. Kaplan noted, the Indian Ocean is becoming the world's "strategic center of gravity," and who controls that center controls Eurasia, including China. The Ocean is the vital waterway passage for energy and trade flows between the Middle East and the Far East. Strategically, it is also the heart of a developing South-South economic axis between China, Africa and Latin America.

Since 1997, trade between China and Africa has risen more than twenty-fold, and China's trade with Latin America, including Brazil, has risen fourteen-fold in only ten years. This dynamic, if allowed to continue, will eclipse the economy of the European Union, as well as the declining North American industrial economies, in less than a decade. That is a development that Washington circles and Wall Street are determined to prevent at all costs.[275]

No rival economic bloc can be allowed to challenge American hegemony. The octagenarian Zbigniew Brzezinski, geostrategic adviser to presidents Johnson, Carter, and Obama, is still today along with Henry Kissinger one of the most influential persons in the US power establishment. He summed up the US position in his 1997 book, *The Grand Chessboard: American Primacy And Its Geostrategic Imperatives:*

> It is imperative that no Eurasian challenger emerges, capable of dominating Eurasia and thus of also challenging America. The formulation of a comprehensive and integrated Eurasian geo-strategy is therefore the purpose of this book.[276]

> For America, the chief geopolitical prize is Eurasia.... Now a non-Eurasian power is preeminent in Eurasia – and America's global primacy is directly dependent on how

long and how effectively its preponderance on the
Eurasian continent is sustained.[277]

In that context, how America "manages" Eurasia is critical.
Eurasia is the world's largest continent and is geopolitically axial.
A power that dominates Eurasia would control two of the world's
three most advanced and economically productive regions. A
mere glance at the map also suggests that control over Eurasia
would almost automatically entail Africa's subordination,
rendering the Western Hemisphere and Oceania geopolitically
peripheral to the globe's main continent. About 75 per cent of the
world's people live in Eurasia, and most of the world's physical
wealth is there as well, both in its enterprises and underneath its
soil. Eurasia accounts for 60 per cent of the world's GNP and
about three-fourths of the world's known energy resources.[278]

Since the end of the Cold war in 1989, the emergence of an
economically powerful China, and other much smaller Asian
powers, has challenged US hegemony over the Indian Ocean for
the first time since World War II. Especially in recent years as
American economic influence has precipitously declined
globally, and that of China has risen spectacularly, the Pentagon
has begun to rethink its strategic presence in the Indian Ocean.
The Obama Asian Pivot was designed to assert decisive control
over the sea lanes of the Indian Ocean and the waters of the
South China Sea.

As of 2010, the US military base at Okinawa, Japan was being
rebuilt as a major center to project US military power towards
China. At the time, there were over 35,000 US military personnel
stationed in Japan, and another 5,500 American civilians
employed there by the US Department of Defense. As of this
writing, the US Seventh Fleet is based in Yokosuka, the 3rd
Marine Expeditionary Force in Okinawa, and 130 USAF fighters
are at the Misawa and Kadena air force bases.

In 2011, the Japanese government began an armament program
designed to counter the perceived growing Chinese threat. The
Japanese command has urged their leaders to petition the United
States to lift the ban on export sales of F-22A Raptor fighter jets.
The South Korean and American military have deepened their
strategic alliance, and over 45,000 American soldiers are now
stationed in South Korea. The South Koreans and Americans

claim this is due to the North Korean military's modernization. China and North Korea denounce it as needlessly provocative.[279]

Under the cover of the US "War on Terror," the US has developed major military agreements with the Philippines, as well as with Indonesia's army.

Still, the military base on the island of Diego Garcia is the lynchpin of US control over the Indian Ocean. In 1971, the US military expelled the citizens of Diego Garcia, and built a major military installation there to carry out missions against Iraq and Afghanistan. China has two Achilles heels – the Strait of Hormuz at the mouth of the Persian Gulf, and the Strait of Malacca near Singapore. Some 20% of Chinese oil imports pass through the Strait of Hormuz, and 80% through the Strait of Malacca, along with a great proportion of its freight trade.

The Indian Ocean is crowned by what some have called an Islamic Arc of Muslim countries stretching from East Africa to Indonesia by way of the Persian Gulf countries and Central Asia. To prevent China from emerging successfully as the major world economic competitor of the United States, Washington launched the so-called Arab Spring in late 2010. While the aspirations of millions of ordinary Arab citizens in Tunisia, Libya, Egypt and elsewhere for freedom and democracy were real, Washington used these movements as unwitting cannon fodder to unleash a strategy of chaos across the entire oil-rich Islamic world, from Libya in North Africa across to Syria and ultimately Iran in the Middle East.

The US strategy within the Islamic Arc countries has been carefully developed. Its goals, according to Mohamed Hassan, a strategic analyst of the Islamic world are, as follows:

> The US is therefore seeking to control these resources to prevent them reaching China. This was a major objective of the wars in Iraq and Afghanistan, but these have turned into a fiasco. The US destroyed these countries in order to set up governments there which would be docile, but they have failed. The icing on the cake is that the new Iraqi and Afghan government trade with China! Beijing has therefore not needed to spend billions of dollars on an illegal war in order to get its hands on Iraq's black gold: Chinese companies simply bought up oil concessions at auction totally within the rules.

One can see that the USA's imperialist strategy has failed all along the line. There is nevertheless one option still open to the US: maintaining chaos in order to prevent these countries from attaining stability for the benefit of China. This means continuing the war in Iraq and Afghanistan and extending it to countries such as Iran, Yemen or Somalia.[280]

South China Sea

Completion of the Pentagon's "String of Pearls" noose, to choke off China's supply lines in event of war, was centered around increased US manipulation of events in the South China Sea. China's Ministry of Geological Resources and Mining estimated that the South China Sea may contain 17.7 billion tons of crude oil (compared to Kuwait with 13 billion tons). The most optimistic estimate suggested that potential oil resources (not proven reserves) of the Spratly and Paracel Islands in the South China Sea could be as high as 105 billion barrels of oil, and that the total for the South China Sea could be as high as 213 billion barrels.[281]

The presence of such vast reserves is understandably of great importance for China's energy security. Washington has made a calculated intervention in the past several years to sabotage those Chinese interests, using Vietnam especially as a wedge against Chinese oil exploration there. In July 2012 the National Assembly of Vietnam passed a law demarcating Vietnamese sea borders to include the Spratly and Paracel islands. US influence in Vietnam has become decisive since the country opened itself to economic liberalization, i.e., to US banks and corporations.

In 2011, the US military began cooperation with Vietnam, including joint "peaceful" military exercises. Washington has backed both the Philippines and Vietnam in their territorial claims over Chinese-claimed territories in the South China Sea, emboldening those small countries not to seek a diplomatic resolution.[282]

In 2010, US and UK oil majors entered the bidding for exploration in the South China Sea. The bid by Chevron and BP added to the presence of US-based Anadarko Petroleum Corporation in the region. These moves were essential to give Washington the pretext of "defending US oil interests" in the area.[283]

In April 2012, the Philippine warship *Gregorio del Pilar* was involved in a standoff with two Chinese surveillance vessels in the Scarborough Shoal, an area claimed by both nations. The Philippine navy had been trying to arrest Chinese fishermen who were allegedly taking government-protected marine species from the area, but China's surveillance boats prevented them. On April 14, 2012, the US and the Philippines held their yearly exercises in Palawan, Philippines. On May 7, 2012, Chinese Vice Foreign Minister Fu Ying called a meeting with Alex Chua, chargé d'affaires of the Philippine Embassy in China, to make a serious representation over the incident at the Scarborough Shoal.

From South Korea to the Philippines to Vietnam, the Pentagon and US State Department are fanning the clash over rights to the South China Sea, aiming to insert a US military presence there on the pretext of "defending" Vietnamese, Japanese, Korean or Philippine interests. The military hangman's noose around China is being slowly drawn tighter.

While China's access to vast resources of offshore conventional oil and gas were being restricted, Washington was actively trying to lure China into provocations and incidents that amount to a sophisticated form of economic warfare, namely trade wars, using the US-controlled WTO as referee.

Chapter Eight:
Economic Wars – Trade Wars and the WTO

The problem from a Chinese national security standpoint was the extreme degree of dependency on foreign multinationals, especially American, for China's spectacular economic growth. The economic miracle in China over the last 33 years was made possible by the rest of the world, and China has been only a small shareholder in it. Most of the profits have gone to multinational companies from the developed countries, especially the USA. Many products have been made in China, but not so many have been designed or created or invented in China.

Threats to the Workshop of the World

Powerful figures in America's finance and banking corporations, in circles around David Rockefeller and Henry Kissinger, quietly prepared Richard Nixon's China initiative in the early 1970's, opening the doors for US corporations to turn China into what has become the "workshop of the world." China has been skillful in capitalizing on its most valuable asset, its abundant human labor power in the process, to turn the country into the world's second largest economy after the United States. This development, however, is not without certain risks.

In 2008, the EU surpassed the USA as China's largest trade partner, with some $330 billion in bilateral trade. Japan was third, and those three accounted for nearly $1 trillion of China's annual trade, about two-thirds of the total. That is a high degree of dependency on a small number of actors, all of them bound in military dependency on the United States or NATO. India, South Korea, and Australia are also major trading partners, and are the focus of Washington's "pivot" strategy of militarily and economically isolating China.[284]

Walmart

The clearest example of China's external dependency on a US corporate giant for trade and jobs is the relationship to one single

US company, Walmart. The Arkansas-based retail chain has been the single largest U.S. importer of Chinese-made consumer goods, surpassing the trade volume of major countries, such as Germany and Russia.[285]

Sam Walton, founder of the Arkansas retail giant, was closely tied to the powerful elite US families who ran Wall Street. Walton's financial banker for the phenomenal growth of Walmart was the Little Rock investment bank, Stephens & Co., founded by Jackson Stephens.[286]

Stephens Inc. is one of the biggest institutional shareholders in 30 large multinationals, including Walmart and another Arkansas-based company, Tyson Food, the world's largest industrial chicken factory operation.

Jackson Stephens evidently built his career and fortune by being connected to the "right" people. He was a US Naval Academy classmate of Jimmy Carter, and used his connection to Carter during the Georgia bank scandals of President Carter's Office of Management & Budget chief, Bert Lance. Stephens stepped in to bail Lance out of an extremely embarrassing financial debacle with National Bank of Georgia, Lance's old bank. Stephens helped by introducing Lance to a Pakistani businessman, Agha Hasan Abedi, the founder of a Luxembourg-registered, London-based bank called the Bank of Commerce and Credit International (BCCI). In 1990, BCCI was convicted of money laundering for the Columbian cocaine cartels in Miami.[287]

In October, 1992, the Senate Foreign Relations Committee released an 800-page report on the BCCI collapse. They called the BCCI scandal "the largest case of organized crime in history, spanning over some 72 nations," adding that it represented an "international financial crime on a massive and global scale," and that the bank "systematically bribed world leaders and political figures throughout the world."

The Senate report concluded that among the provable charges against BCCI were "BCCI's criminality, including fraud... involving billions of dollars; money laundering in Europe, Africa, Asia, and the Americas; BCCI's bribery of officials in most of those locations; its support of terrorism, arms trafficking, and the sale of nuclear technologies; its management of prostitution; its commission and facilitation of income tax evasion, smuggling, and illegal immigration; its illicit purchases of banks and real estate; and a panoply of financial crimes limited only by the imagination of its officers and customers."

Jackson Stephens was no casual business acquaintance of BCCI's Agha Hasan Abedi. In response to the concerns over Jackson Stephens' involvement in BCCI, the Ohio Attorney General noted in a 1993 report, "Stephens' name has been linked to securities violations that allegedly occurred when BCCI acquired stock and control over the Washington-based First American Bank." In 1991, Stephens joined BCCI investor Mochtar Riady in buying BCCI's former Hong Kong subsidiary from its liquidators.

Indeed, in addition to Abedi, The Stephens Group was well-connected to another interesting Asian banking group, the billionaire Indonesian Riady family of Mochtar and his son James Riady, who also owned the Lippo Bank in Indonesia. The Riadys were Chinese-Indonesian businessmen who moved in the 1970's to Arkansas, of all places, despite holding billions of assets in Asia. Stephens and Riady became business friends, and soon Stephens and Riady bought a bank in Hong Kong. Stephens then invited Riady to invest in a Little Rock Arkansas bank called Worthen Bank. Another Jackson Stephens protégé was former Arkansas Governor and recipient of Stephens' political funding, Bill Clinton.[288]

According to an exposé in the May 28, 2003 *Wall Street Journal*, a young lawyer named Hillary Clinton, then married to the new Arkansas governor Bill Clinton, was made a partner in 1977 in the house law firm of Stephens Inc, Rose Law Firm of Little Rock. In 1987, according to the *Wall Street Journal*:

> Officials at investment giant Stephens Inc., including longtime Clinton friend, David Edwards, take steps to rescue Harken Energy, a struggling Texas oil company with George W. Bush on its board. Over the next three years, Mr. Edwards brings BCCI-linked investors and advisers into Harken deals. One of them, Abdullah Bakhsh, purchases $10 million in shares of Stephens-dominated Worthen Bank.[289]

Walmart in China

Deng Xiaoping had opened the People's Republic of China to investment, easing restrictions on foreign businesses, and encouraging Chinese entrepreneurs to enter joint ventures with

Westerners. Deng declared the fishing village of Shenzhen, just across the border from Hong Kong, as a "special economic zone," with no taxes on foreign businesses for the first few years of operation. Across South China, the government began building roads, ports, and other infrastructure. In 1994, it devalued China's currency, from roughly 5 to 8 yuan to the dollar, further fueling the country's explosive development.

China, suddenly the cheapest workshop in Asia, attracted vast capital investment. Millions of migrant workers flooded industrial centers. Clever entrepreneurs migrated from Hong Kong and Taiwan, eager for a piece of the action. Many shut down their plants at home to set up new factories and hire mainland Chinese workers.

Shenzhen boomed. Growing at the rate of 20 percent a year, it became known as China's "Miracle City." In two decades, a fishing village mushroomed into a city of 7 million people, with high rises, miles of factories, and modern electronics headquarters. Here in Shenzhen, Walmart built its global sourcing headquarters.

David Glass, who succeeded Sam Walton as Walmart's CEO in the early '90s, advised students to learn Mandarin Chinese. Glass told Walmart executives that if they didn't think internationally, they were working for the wrong company. "The only reason [manufacturing] moved from Taiwan was China's low level of wages," said one early Walmart Hong Kong buyer.[290]

What allowed Walmart and other US and EU multinationals to dramatically increase their investment in production in China was the admittance of China into the newly-created World Trade Organization (WTO).

Luring China into the WTO

Bill Clinton, who promoted China's WTO entry in 2000, said that allowing China WTO entry would be a great deal for America. It was certainly a great deal for Clinton's Arkansas friend, Sam Walton, who became a billionaire in the process.

"We do nothing," Clinton said about Chinese WTO membership. "They have to lower tariffs. They open up telecommunications for investment. They allow us to sell cars made in America in China at much lower tariffs. They allow us to put our own distributorships there. They allow us to put our own parts there.

We don't have to transfer technology or do joint manufacturing in China any more. This a hundred-to-nothing deal for America when it comes to the economic consequences."[291]

A vital part of the long-term US hegemony strategy to maintain future control over an economically westernizing China was to make certain that China played "by the rules." This would be guaranteed by luring China to accept membership into the World Trade Organization (WTO), which would write the "rules" of world trade to suit its American patrons. The WTO had formally opened its doors in Geneva in 1995. China formally joined in December 2001.

The price of entry into what has been called the "rich nations' club" was high. China had to relax over 7,000 tariffs, quotas and other trade barriers. It uprooted Chinese farmers, owing to WTO sanctioned imports of soybeans and other products. On the surface, WTO membership opened China to huge capital investments by US and EU megacorporations, and it appeared China was the "winner." In reality, China has provided staggering rates of profit to US and Western manufacturers in return for very little.

China is being forced to play by the "rules" of the WTO, rules dominated by the interest groups linked to Washington and Brussels.

The WTO headquarters were established in Geneva, Switzerland, a nominally neutral, scenic, and peaceful location. Behind this façade, however, the WTO was anything but peaceful or neutral. The WTO had been created as a policeman, a global free trade enforcer, and, as noted elsewhere in this work, a battering ram for the trillion- dollar annual world agribusiness trade, and for a US-directed globalization which benefited US corporate and financial interests uniquely. For that reason, the WTO was designed as a supranational entity, to be above the laws of nations, answerable to no public body beyond its own walls.[292]

Earlier GATT (General Agreement on Tariffs and Trade) agreements had no enforceable sanctions or penalties for violating agreed trade rules. By contrast, the new WTO did have such punitive leverage. It had the power to levy heavy financial penalties or other sanctions on member countries found in violation of its rules. Founded in 1995, the WTO emerged as a weapon which could force open national protectionist trade barriers and force the proliferation of genetically modified crops, among other products.

The idea of a WTO, as with all major post-war free trade initiatives, came from Washington. It was the outcome of the GATT Uruguay Round of trade liberalization talks, which began in Punte del Este, Uruguay, in September 1986, and concluded in Marrakesh, Morocco, in April 1994. Ever since 1948 and the initial founding of the GATT, Washington had fiercely resisted including agriculture in world trade talks, fearing any common international rules would open US markets to foreign food imports and damage American agriculture's competitiveness. Since the 1950's, US agricultural export had been a strategic national priority, tied to Cold War geopolitics. Unlike all previous GATT trade rounds, the Uruguay Round made trade in agriculture a main priority, as well as a new category, Intellectual Property Rights (IPR).

In terms of agriculture trade – a major vulnerability for China – WTO rules were drafted by US grain cartel members, especially Cargill, ADM and Monsanto, to benefit their long-term interests.[293] WTO rules for agribusiness trade were as a result dominated by a Group of Four, the so-called QUAD countries: the USA, Canada, Japan and the EU. The QUAD could meet behind closed doors and decide policy for all 134 nations. And within the QUAD, the US-led agribusiness giants – Cargill, ADM, Bunge – controlled major policy. In effect it was a consensus, but a consensus of private agribusiness that determined WTO policy.

The WTO Agreement on Agriculture – written by Cargill, ADM, DuPont, Nestlé, Unilever, Monsanto and other members of the US and EU agribusiness corporate cartel – was explicitly designed to allow the nullification of national laws and elimination of safeguards against the powerful pricing power of the agribusiness giants.[294]

Turning the WTO against China

As Washington and Wall Street saw it, once China had been "captured" in the globalized trade system established by Washington through the WTO, then China would inevitably begin to develop its own sizeable Chinese manufactures for export, and the WTO would be turned against China to keep her economically dependent as a satrapy of the American globalized system.

By 2011, Washington was increasingly using the WTO to escalate trade and economic pressure on the Peoples' Republic. So long as China was the main outsourced cheap labor assembly site for US Fortune 500 globalized corporations, where the profits from Chinese work went to the mother companies such as KFC, Nike or Buick, the WTO was neutral. The minute China began to develop its own technology giants and patent its own inventions that competed with US rivals, Washington used the WTO as a weapon to police and penalize China, in a sophisticated new form of trade war in essence no different from the Opium Wars of the Dutch and British East India companies of the 1840s.

In early 2010, WTO Director General Pascal Lamy held a press conference to state that there would be increasing trade friction between the United States and China over everything from cars to chemicals.[295] The United States and China were engaged now in a series of trade battles over products as diverse as steel, poultry, patents and Hollywood films.

Google's decision to pull out of China over "concerns about censorship and security" also was used by Washington to sour relations between the two countries.

In 2010, US Secretary of State Hillary Clinton intervened into what should have been no matter for the US Government. She demanded that the Chinese government answer Google's allegations of interference, alleging China had committed "politically motivated censorship."[296]

Google founder, Russian-born Sergey Brin, told the *New York Times* the company's reason for leaving China: "Our objection is to those forces of totalitarianism," referring in his remarks to his past in the Soviet Union. Brin was the son of professor parents who had lived for six years a privileged life under the Soviet system.

There was another agenda with Google, which the US government was intimately involved in. Clinton's defense of Google against Chinese charges of possible covert spying on Chinese in China got a blow when a former US intelligence officer exposed the name of the CIA contact person who initially gave Google its seed money, and who is the CIA liaison to Google. In short, the Chinese government had every reason to distrust Google activities inside China.[297]

In late 2011, Claire Reade, the US trade official in charge of China affairs, said to Congress that restrictions and "interventionist policies" on issues such as intellectual property rights remain a "concern" for American companies operating in China. "Trade frictions with China can be traced to China's pursuit of industrial policies that rely on trade-distorting actions to promote or protect China's state-owned enterprises." Translated into clear English, Reade accused China of pursuing a national economic agenda, not the globalization agenda being pushed in Washington to extend American global economic hegemony.[298]

The Solar Wars

One of the most significant trade war frictions between China and Washington involves a genuine Chinese breakthrough technology in building solar energy or photovoltaic systems far more effective and far cheaper than any Western company's comparable product, including a US company that was personally tied to President Obama before it was forced into bankruptcy by the superior Chinese solar systems.

In May 2012, the US Department of Commerce issued a preliminary anti-dumping ruling against the three leading Chinese solar panel manufacturers.[299] Washington knew that China is in a difficult position to enact a trade counter-attack against the USA.

By July 2012, Washington had recruited the EU to join its attack on China's solar exports. In the last three years, China has bankrupted leading US and EU solar companies simply by building a more advanced and far more inexpensive Chinese-patented alternative, and capturing 60% of the world solar market. The three leading Chinese solar companies under pressure from Washington were Suntech, Yingli and Trina. Their "crime" was that they had applied science to technology and come up with a superior, Chinese-owned product.

ACTA: New Trade Danger

In March 2010, documents were leaked on the Internet, exposing an extraordinary new level of Washington's preemptive trade war, directed mainly against the Peoples' Republic of China. It went by the name ACTA, short for Anti-Counterfeiting Trade Agreement.

The ACTA was a multinational treaty allegedly for the purpose of establishing international standards for intellectual property rights enforcement. The agreement's sponsors in the US Trade Representative's Office in Washington claimed it aimed to establish an international legal framework for targeting counterfeit goods, generic medicines and copyright infringement on the Internet, and would create a new governing body outside existing forums, such as the World Trade Organization, the World Intellectual Property Organization, or the United Nations.

In reality, as investigations by multiple governments and parliamentary bodies and other organizations revealed, ACTA was an attempted coup d'etat. It was a move to side-step even the WTO or other established international arbitration bodies, and create a false pretext for seizing Chinese or Indian or any other developing country's products, even without verifiable proof of counterfeiting, if on a claim of "probable cause" to suspect.

The most revealing aspect of ACTA was the fact that its negotiators worked in complete secrecy, until an Internet leak of its secret protocols exposed Washington's attempt to create a worldwide trade war coup d'etat. ACTA was a rogue agreement in terms of international law. ACTA was due to come into force in 2013, after ratification by only six countries. By October 2011, Washington had lined up some of its closest trade partners to sign, including Australia, Canada, Japan, Morocco, New Zealand, Singapore, and South Korea. In 2012, Mexico, the European Union and 22 countries which are member states of the European Union signed as well. Mexico later withdrew and the European Parliament of the EU refused to approve or ratify the EU Commission's decision to join.

When details of the treaty were leaked on the Internet, a hornet's nest was stirred. According to Wikipedia,

> Opponents say the convention adversely affects fundamental rights including freedom of expression and privacy. ACTA has also been criticized by Doctors Without Borders for endangering access to medicines in developing countries.[300]

ACTA was sponsored by the US-dominated pharmaceutical industry, US trade unions, and the Motion Picture Association of America. In addition to these lobbies, it later became known that a select handful of the most powerful US mega-corporations were privy to the secret talks drafting ACTA. The list included Google, eBay, Intel, Dell, News Corporation, Sony Pictures, Time Warner, and Verizon. All were given advance copies of the ACTA for comment, and sworn to secrecy. Other members of the advisory group to the US Trade Representative on ACTA were the US representative of the US-China Business Council; Walmart; Citigroup; Boeing Corporation; the GMO giants Monsanto, Dow Chemical and DuPont; US drug giants Eli Lilly, Abbott Labs, Merck & Co, and Johnson & Johnson. Also included were General Motors, Cisco Systems, Sun Microsystems; IBM; and the US Semiconductor Industry Association.

> The secret negotiations excluded civil society groups, developing countries [including China and India], and the general public from the agreement's negotiation process and it has been described as "policy laundering" by critics, including the Electronic Frontier Foundation and the Entertainment Consumers Association."[301]

The signature of the EU and many of its member states resulted in the resignation in protest of the European Parliament's appointed chief investigator, rapporteur Kader Arif, as well as widespread protests across Europe. Anti-ACTA street demonstrations erupted across the EU.

In 2012, the newly-appointed rapporteur, British MEP David Martin, recommended against the treaty, stating: "The intended benefits of this international agreement are far outweighed by the potential threats to civil liberties." On 4 July 2012, the European Parliament rejected the agreement in plenary session.[302]

In a remarkable indication of the massive pressure on the EU to ram through ACTA, despite the rejection of ACTA by an overwhelming majority of the European Parliament, EU Trade Commissioner Karel De Gucht said in a speech that the Commission would nevertheless press ahead with the treaty should it fail to pass the European Parliament. De Gucht also indicated the treaty could be reintroduced at the next parliament in 2015 should it be rejected in the current one.[303]

Washington also indicated its contempt for Congress, which has the power under the Constitution to ratify treaty agreements. Reportedly the Office of the US Trade Representative (USTR) stated they will use the form of a "sole executive agreement" to implement ACTA, an unconstitutional process that bypasses Congressional approval entirely.[304]

When a citizens' organization requested that the US Trade representative office provide a list of the US corporations which were given secret advance copies of ACTA for comment, the Obama Administration refused, stating that the documents were "information that is properly classified in the interest of national security pursuant to Executive Order 12958."[305] To invoke US government secrecy under the pretext of "national security" reminds one of the Cold War. It also suggests ACTA and the US corporate interests behind it are devising it as a weapon of economic warfare.

> In March 2010, a leaked draft negotiation text showed that the European Commission had proposed language in ACTA to require criminal penalties for "inciting, aiding and abetting" certain offenses, including "at least in cases of willful trademark counterfeiting and copyright or related rights piracy on a commercial scale."[306]

The vagueness of the language would allow an aggressive government such as Washington to fabricate any excuse to launch criminal action against, for example, Chinese solar companies. ACTA would lead to increased governmental interference in intellectual property rights issues.

It is suspicious that negotiations for the ACTA treaty were not conducted under the aegis of any international body. ACTA was first developed by the United States and Japan in 2006. Canada, the EU and Switzerland joined the preliminary talks. Official negotiations began in June 2008, with Australia, Mexico, Morocco, New Zealand, the Republic of Korea and Singapore joining the talks. The Senate of Mexico later voted unanimously to withdraw Mexico from ACTA negotiations.

ACTA: Criminalizing generic medicine

> According to French European Parliament member Kader Arif, "The problem with ACTA is that, by focusing on the fight against violation of intellectual property rights in general, it treats a generic drug just as a counterfeited drug. This means the patent holder can stop the shipping of the drugs to a developing country, seize the cargo and even order the destruction of the drugs as a preventive

measure." He continued, "Generic medicines are not counterfeited medicines; they are not the fake version of a drug; they are a generic version of a drug, produced either because the patent on the original drug has expired, or because a country has to put in place public health policies," he said.

A number of countries such as China, India and African nations have histories of seeking generic medicines — cheaper versions of expensive drugs for infections — something that has often been historically resisted by pharmaceutical companies. "There are international agreements, such as the TRIPS Agreement, which foresees this last possibility," he said. "They're particularly important for developing countries which cannot afford to pay for patented HIV drugs, for example." Arif stated ACTA would limit the freedom of countries such as India [and China[307]] to determine their own medical choices.[308]

The non-governmental organization Médecins Sans Frontières has opposed ACTA, as part of their Access Campaign promoting the development and access to "life-saving and life-prolonging medicines." In their report, *A blank cheque for abuse: ACTA & its Impact on Access to Medicines,* Médecins Sans Frontières concluded that ACTA had "fatal consequences on access to medicines," that the agreement "does nothing to address the problem of poor quality and unsafe medicines," and finally that ACTA "undermines existing international declarations to protect public health," circumventing the Doha Declaration. Michael Gylling Nielsen, the executive of the Danish division of Médecins Sans Frontières, said in a statement to the media, "In the end, this is a question of life and death," elaborating his point by mentioning the "possible consequences" of the treaty that "the hundreds of thousands of people who for example have HIV/AIDS not will get the treatment they need."[309]

Similarly, the 2014 ebola outbreak will spread because Africa is denied access to new drugs.

TRIPS, the Trade Related Intellectual Property Rights agreement signed in 1994, requires a minimum level of observance of intellectual property rights by WTO members. Developing countries felt it was interpreted too strictly in favor of patent holders, and initiated negotiations leading to the Doha Declaration, which "reaffirmed flexibility of TRIPS member states in circumventing patent rights for better access to essential medicines."[310] ACTA was an attempt to roll back TRIPS and make poor nations pay license fees on drugs even when generic versions were available.

Nate Anderson with Ars Technica pointed out that ACTA encourages service providers to collect and provide information about suspected infringers by giving them "safe harbor from certain legal threats." Similarly, it provides for criminalization of copyright infringement on a commercial scale, granting law enforcement the powers to perform criminal investigation, arrests and pursue criminal citations or prosecution of suspects who are alleged to have infringed on copyright on a commercial scale. It also allows criminal investigations and invasive searches to be performed against individuals for whom there is no probable cause, and in that regard weakens the presumption of innocence and allows what would in the past have been considered unlawful searches.

Since ACTA is an international treaty, it is an example of policy laundering used to establish and implement legal changes. Policy laundering allows legal provisions to be pushed through via closed negotiations among private members of the executive bodies of the signatories. This method avoids use of public legislation and its judiciary oversight. Once ratified, companies belonging to non-members may be forced to follow the ACTA requirements, since they will otherwise fall out of the safe harbor protections. Also, the use of trade incentives and the like to persuade other nations to adopt treaties is a standard approach in international relationships. Additional signatories would have to accept ACTA's terms without much scope for negotiation.

In June 2010, a conference was held at the Washington College of Law, attended by over 90 academics, practitioners and public interest organizations from six continents. Their conclusions were published on the American University Washington College of Law website. They found "that the terms of the publicly released draft of ACTA threaten numerous public interests, including every concern specifically disclaimed by negotiators." Over 75 law professors signed a letter to President Obama demanding a host of changes to the agreement. The letter alleges that no meaningful transparency has been in evidence.[311]

While discussion of ACTA is less noticeable at present, the project is anything but dead. In fact, the Obama Administration has taken the key provisions of ACTA and secretly inserted them into the anti-China Trans-Pacific Partnership (TPP) for creating a US-dominated Asia-Pacific Free Trade region that explicitly refuses entry to China.

Washington's new TPP

The US Trade Representative has called TPP an

> "ambitious, next-generation, Asia-Pacific trade agreement that reflects US priorities and values." President Obama, who announced the goal of creating TPP in November 2009, said that TPP will "boost our economies, lowering barriers to trade and investment, increasing exports, and creating more jobs for our people, which is my No. 1 priority."[312]

Since that time all negotiations and content of the TPP have been kept secret, as with ACTA, by the Office of the US Trade Representative (USTR). TPP is an ominous project that bodes no good for China. It is an anti-China trade effort, a bid to co-opt earlier bilateral and multilateral regional Asian and Latin American trade agreements into a US-led anti-China economic coalition.

> In May 2012, some 30 US legal scholars critical of the USTR's "biased and closed" TPP negotiation process and proposed intellectual property-related provisions, publicly called upon USTR Ambassador Kirk to uphold democratic ideals by reversing the "dialing back" of stakeholder participation and to release negotiating texts for public scrutiny.

> The law professors claimed that leaked documents show that the USTR was "pushing numerous standards that could require changes in current US statutory law," and that the proposal was "manifestly unbalanced – it predominantly proposes increases in proprietor rights,

with no effort to expand the limitations and exceptions to such rights that are needed in the US and abroad to serve the public interest." The group claimed that the negotiations excluded stakeholders such as "consumers, libraries, students, health advocacy or patient groups, or others users of intellectual property," and that it only offered "minimal representation of other affected businesses, such as generic drug manufacturers or Internet service providers."[313]

The main point of TPP however is that the USTR in Washington is, according to leaked information, simply secretly inserting all the key provisions of the stalled ACTA and other trade schemes into the text of the TPP treaty. No members of the US Congress have even been informed. The second salient fact is that China was excluded by design from Obama's TPP club. It is an attempt by Washington to control Asian trade to the detriment of China.

According to reports, the terms of the TPP membership will include

"customs, cross-border services, telecommunications, government procurement, competition policy, and cooperation and capacity building," as well as investment and financial services. Technically, TPP would only take effect in the ten negotiating countries: Australia, Brunei, Chile, Malaysia, New Zealand, Peru, Singapore, United States, and Vietnam. Mexico joined recently, and Canada and Japan may soon follow. But in reality, it would affect citizens of China or any nations that interact with at least one of those ten.[314]

If the TPP is considered in the context of the currency wars, and the Pentagon's "String of Pearls" military strategy against China's oil trade routes, it becomes clear that Washington has moved step by step to create a web of control around China, attempting to cripple any independent Chinese sovereign development. The US-led Arab Spring destabilizations, and the attempt to bring Syria and then Iran into chaos, are integral parts of that strategy. China is Washington's new "enemy image," replacing Osama Bin Laden and the earlier enemy image of "Soviet Communism."

Chapter Nine:
Media Wars – Google, YouTube, Facebook and Embedded Global Media

Since President Woodrow Wilson openly enlisted the cooperation of Hollywood filmmakers to create propaganda to stir war fever among Americans, Hollywood and US media have been intimately linked with shaping consensus for US national strategy. By 2012 that combination was being turned to slowly make the Peoples' Republic of China into what in perhaps a few short years would be portrayed as the new "Hitler Germany," the new adversary. The US Pentagon and the military industrial complex, together with the New York Council on Foreign Relations and other select organizations of powerbrokers, developed a form of culture and media warfare which China was very susceptible to.

CIA and Control of US Media

With the creation of the Cold War came the NATO alliance, and the US Central Intelligence Agency (CIA). One of the first priorities of the first CIA Director in 1948, at the recommendation of US State Department Cold War strategist George Kennan, was to appoint Frank Wisner as first Director of the newly-created CIA Office of Special Projects (OSP), soon renamed the Office of Policy Coordination (OPC).

The OPC became the covert action branch of the Central Intelligence Agency. Wisner was told to create an organization that concentrated on "propaganda, economic warfare; preventive direct action, including sabotage, anti-sabotage, demolition and evacuation measures; subversion against hostile states, including assistance to underground resistance groups, and support of indigenous anti-Communist elements in threatened countries of the free world."³¹⁵

Later in 1948 Wisner established what was code-named Operation Mockingbird, a CIA covert program to influence foreign media. Wisner recruited Philip Graham from the *Washington Post* to run the project. By the early 1950's when Allen Dulles took over control of the CIA, Wisner "owned" key journalists of *The New York Times*, *Newsweek*, CBS and other communications majors."[316]

That early CIA link to influential American and international private media was merely the early stage of what became by 2012 a nearly complete control of major global "mainstream" media.

US Pentagon Perfects "Culture" warfare

During the aftermath of the US invasion of Iraq, US Army Colonel Ralph Peters made a remarkably accurate military assessment of the awesome effectiveness of the interconnected US media and culture offensive in the world. The culture offensive included a cartel of Hollywood movie studios, the mainstream TV and print media, such as CNN and *The New York Times*. It includes, more recently, the enormously influential Internet and social media, including Google, YouTube, Facebook and Twitter.

Since President Woodrow Wilson openly enlisted the cooperation of Hollywood filmmakers to create propaganda to stir war fever among Americans, Hollywood and the US media have been intimately linked with shaping consensus for US national strategy. By 2012 that combination was being applied to slowly transform the Peoples' Republic of China into what would be portrayed, within perhaps a few short years, as the new "Hitler Germany" adversary.

The US Pentagon and the military industrial complex, together with the New York Council on Foreign Relations and other organizations of powerbrokers, developed a form of culture and media warfare to which China was very susceptible. One of the clearest and most outspoken Pentagon analysts of this US cultural warfare, Colonel Ralph Peters, wrote in the *US Army War College Quarterly*:

> Information destroys traditional jobs and traditional cultures; it seduces, betrays, yet remains invulnerable. How can you counterattack the information others have turned upon you? There is no effective option other than competitive performance. For those individuals and cultures that cannot join or compete with our information empire, there is only inevitable failure (of note, the internet is to the techno-capable disaffected what the United Nations is to marginal states: it offers the illusion of empowerment and community)...

Hollywood goes where Harvard never penetrated, and the foreigner, unable to touch the reality of America, is touched by America's irresponsible fantasies of itself; he sees a devilishly enchanting, bluntly sexual, terrifying world from which he is excluded, a world of wealth he can judge only in terms of his own poverty.

...It is fashionable among world intellectual elites to decry "American culture..." But traditional intellectual elites are of shrinking relevance, replaced by cognitive-practical elites – figures such as Bill Gates, Steven Spielberg, Madonna, or our most successful politicians – human beings who can recognize or create popular appetites, recreating themselves as necessary. Contemporary American culture is the most powerful in history, and the most destructive of competitor cultures... The genius, the secret weapon, of American culture is the essence that the elites despise: ours is the first genuine people's culture. It stresses comfort and convenience – ease – and it generates pleasure for the masses. We are Karl Marx's dream, and his nightmare.

Secular and religious revolutionaries in our century have made the identical mistake, imagining that the workers of the world or the faithful just can't wait to go home at night to study Marx or the Koran. Well, Joe Sixpack, Ivan Tipichni, and Ali Quat would rather "Baywatch." America has figured it out, and we are brilliant at operationalizing our knowledge, and our cultural power will hinder even those cultures we do not undermine. There is no "peer competitor" in the cultural (or military) department. Our cultural empire has the addicted – men and women everywhere – clamoring for more. And they pay for the privilege of their disillusionment.

American culture is criticized for its impermanence, its "disposable" products. But therein lies its strength. All previous cultures sought ideal achievement which, once reached, might endure in static perfection. American culture is not about the end, but the means, the dynamic process that creates, destroys, and creates anew. If our works are transient, then so are life's greatest gifts – passion, beauty, the quality of light on a winter afternoon, even life itself. American culture is alive. This vividness, this vitality, is reflected in our military; we do not expect to achieve ultimate solutions, only constant improvement. All previous cultures, general and military, have sought to achieve an ideal form of life and then fix it in cement. Americans, in and out of uniform, have always embraced change...

The films most despised by the intellectual elite – those that feature extreme violence and to-the-victors-the-spoils sex – are our most popular cultural weapon, bought or bootlegged nearly everywhere. American action films, often in dreadful copies, are available from the Upper Amazon to Mandalay. They are even more popular than our music, because they are easier to understand. The action films of a Stallone or Schwarzenegger or Chuck Norris rely on visual narratives that do not require dialog for a basic understanding. They deal at the level of universal myth, of pre-text, celebrating the most fundamental impulses (although we have yet to produce a film as violent and cruel as the Iliad). They feature a hero, a villain, a woman to be defended or won – and violence and sex. Complain until doomsday; it sells. The enduring popularity abroad of the shopworn Rambo series tells us far more about humanity than does a library full of scholarly analysis.

...We use technology to expand our wealth, power, and opportunities. The rest get high on pop culture. If religion is the opium of the people, video is their crack cocaine.

There will be no peace. At any given moment for the rest of our lifetimes, there will be multiple conflicts in mutating forms around the globe. Violent conflict will dominate the headlines, but cultural and economic struggles will be steadier and ultimately more decisive. The de facto role of the US armed forces will be to keep the world safe for our economy and open to our cultural assault. To those ends, we will do a fair amount of killing.[317]

This disguised and extremely effective weapon of US cultural warfare was targeting China ever more. Google was a major part of that.

CIA and US Government behind Google

In March 2010, US-based Internet search engine colossus Google Inc. left mainland China for Hong Kong over a dispute with the Chinese government concerning restrictions on Google's search engine inside China.

Google had earlier alleged on its blog in January 2010 that it had been the victim of a cyber-attack which they claimed originated from China. As a result of the attack, Google said it was reviewing its business in China. On that same day, United States Secretary of State Hillary Clinton condemned the attacks and requested a response from China. Earlier the Chinese government had secured cooperation with Google on restricting access to certain Google sites. The Beijing Government had begun to place more restrictions on Google's search engine, with some sensitive searches blocked altogether.[318]

The attempt by the Chinese Government to restrict Google was more than a mere superficial conflict. It involved an effort to restrict one of the most important new weapons of Pentagon and CIA media control: control of information found on the Internet.[319]

What the US Secretary of State did not say to the public in the Google affair is the reality that Google and its subsidiaries such as YouTube are an integral part of the US Government cyber-warfare apparatus.

The California-based Internet giant Google was founded by two Stanford University students, Sergey Brin and Larry Page. They received covert financial support from the CIA who realized that the two entrepreneurs had come up with an ingenious search technology that could dominate the emerging Internet. Former CIA officer Robert David Steele told US media in 2006 that CIA seed money helped get Google established. He went so far as to name the CIA contact with Google: "Let me say very explicitly - their contact at the CIA is named Dr. Rick Steinheiser, he's in the Office of Research and Development," said Steele.[320]

In addition to the CIA funding, Google had deep ongoing ties to Washington's top secret spy agency, National Security Agency (NSA). According to investigations and public information, Google had a close working relationship with the National Security Agency. Google provided the software, hardware and technology support to NSA and other US intelligence agencies to create a vast closed source database for global spy networks to share information.[321]

Furthermore, Google and the CIA were partners in a cyber joint-venture. Google had jointly invested with the CIA in an Internet monitoring project that scours Twitter accounts, blogs and websites for all sorts of information, and can also predict the future. Google Ventures, the investment arm of Google, injected $10 million, along with the CIA's In-Q-Tel – which handled investments for the CIA and the wider intelligence network – into a company called Recorded Future.[322]

Moreover Google executives have even boasted of playing a major role in the Egyptian Facebook "revolution" of 2011. During the 2011 uprising in Egypt, Google took the opportunity to insert itself into key news stories about the mass protests. Eric Schmidt, then CEO of Google admitted that Google senior executive, Egyptian cyber-activist, Wael Ghonim, played a significant role in building up and organizing the Tahrir Square and other protests via Facebook and Twitter. That was critical in the early days of the anti-Mubarak protests.

Without Facebook, without Twitter, without Google, without You Tube, the regime change would never have happened, Ghonim told the media, suggesting that the search engine was responsible for an entire revolution. Google's Egyptian executive Ghonim was administrator of the Facebook page, "We are all Khaled Saeed," which helped spark the revolution.[323]

It was clear that China had good reason to be overly cautious about letting Google have free reign in Chinese cyberspace.

Control of Major US media

In addition to the intimate links between Google, Facebook, Twitter and YouTube with the US intelligence community, the major mainstream US media formed a giant information cartel in which freedom of speech had become a relic of the pre-September 11, 2001 era.

The wartime Prime Minister of Great Britain, Sir Winston Churchill, a former Lord of the Admiralty, once remarked, "In war-time, truth is so precious that she should always be attended by a bodyguard of lies." A bodyguard of lies was the best description of the version of reality doled out by the major globalized media controlled out of the United States in 2012.

As the Iraq war demonstrated openly, major US and international media were allowed access to warzones only if they were "embedded" journalists travelling with US military forces. Propaganda control was complete. US media had become an essential accomplice in creation of the permanent War State, the Washington doctrine of "pre-emptive wars" to "spread democracy."

So long as the perceptions of reality of ordinary Americans could be manipulated to support the global agenda of the establishment, the American population could be manipulated into being unwitting implementers of that New World Order, sending their sons and daughters to die in a senseless brutal slaughter in places such as Iraq and Afghanistan.

That powerful and controlled US media propaganda machine was now being turned against China, the new "adversary" as President Obama termed China in the Presidential debate of October 2012.

US Global Media Cartel

Since World War II and creation of the Psychological Strategy Board in the CIA and State Department, the CFR and the inner circles of the US elite have devoted enormous resources to the control of global media. By the year 2000, the American media were more tightly controlled behind the scenes by members of the elite Council on Foreign Relations than were the openly state-owned media of either Russia or the People's Republic of China. The control was subtle so that most Americans were blind to the fact that their every political thought was being spoon-fed and manipulated from above.

To reflect changing priorities in the era of globalization of their control since the early 1990's, the major media giants were reorganized, centralized and globalized in a tiny few hands with Government approval and anti-monopoly laws removed to allow it, as follows:

AOL-TimeWarner: The largest US media group today is AOL-TimeWarner, which in turn controls: CBS television; CNN; HBO, the largest US pay-TV network; *Time* magazine group, the largest magazine publisher, which includes *Sports Illustrated* and numerous others; Warner Bros. and other Hollywood film studios. AOL is the largest private Internet provider in the US. Gerald Levin is the Chairman of AOL-TimeWarner.

Walt Disney Co.: The second largest US media giant is the Walt Disney Co. headed by CEO Michael Eisner, an outsider with no ties to the Disney family. Disney today controls several TV production companies, including Touchstone TV and Buena Vista TV; Hollywood film companies, including Walt Disney Motion Pictures, Touchstone, Caravan and Hollywood Pictures. It also owns Capital Cities/ABC the second largest TV network with many subsidiaries in Europe.

Viacom Inc.: The third member of the US media cartel is Viacom Inc. It also owns the cable sports network ESPN, *Women's Wear Daily*, Viacom Inc., Paramount Pictures, and it recently bought CBS from TimeWarner. Viacom controls the worldwide youth market through its cable network MTV, which promotes violence and sex via song videos, and Nikelodeon, and Showtime. MTV shows its rock-rap videos to 210 million homes in 71 countries. It is one of the world's most influential communications companies.

News Corporation : Australian-born media mogul Rupert Murdoch is the owner of the fourth largest US media group, News Corporation. He owns Fox TV, whose programs are dominated by neo-conservative propaganda in favor of Israel. Murdoch also owns the *New York Post* and numerous other newspapers including the neo-conservative *Weekly Standard* of William Kristol. Murdoch's former business associate, Haim Saban, a Hollywood billionaire who was close to Ariel Sharon and Benjamin Netanyahu and a pro-Israel hawk, recently bought Germany's largest TV group, Pro-7 Media.

Newhouse Group: The fifth largest media conglomerate is the Newhouse Group, owned by billionaire Si Newhouse. Newhouse owns 12 TV stations, 87 cable TV systems, the largest circulation Sunday magazine *Parade*, the *New Yorker, Vogue, Mademoiselle, Vanity Fair* magazines; and the Cleveland *Plain-Dealer*, Newark *Star-Ledger*, and New Orleans *Times-Picayune* newspapers.

The striking fact about this concentration of media power today in America is that all the top companies, from Disney to AOL-TimeWarner to Fox News to Viacom, are controlled by individuals affiliated with the Council on Foreign Relations (CFR). The fact remains that US media today is more concentrated than ever in history, and that the control is held by a small clique. It is little wonder that most Americans have a lopsided view of world events or of the Iraq war. They have little chance to see a larger, more neutral view of news.

Because of the control of small local or regional newspapers by these giant media companies, no newspaper is able to afford independent journalists, let alone international news bureaus. They must buy their "news" from services such as AP, Reuters, the *New York Times*, Dow Jones-*Wall Street Journal*, or the *Washington Post* Company. All are controlled by this same cartel of interests.

The New York Times: The *New York Times* is owned by the Arthur Sulzberger family. The New York Times Corp. owns the *Boston Globe* and 33 other regional papers as well as *McCalls'* and *Family Circle* magazines, radio and TV stations. New York Times News Service sells news stories to 506 papers around the US.

The Washington Post Corporation: The *Washington Post*, the most influential paper in Washington, is run by the descendants of banker Eugene Meyer, a former partner of Bernard Baruch, through the late Catherine Meyer Graham's son, Donald. The *Washington Post* owns TV stations, 11 military publications, *Newsweek* magazine, Cable One TV, and until recently, it co-published the largest foreign English language newspaper, *International Herald Tribune* with the *New York Times*.

Under the rules passed by the Bush Administration's Federal Communications Commission chairman, Michael Powell, son of Secretary of State Colin Powell, this handful of media giants were being allowed to merge and control even more local TV and media across America, making their control of public opinion, outside the worldwide web, virtually total, as total as under Stalin in the wartime Soviet Union. The control was more subtle, however, so that evident differences of opinion were allowed, in order to give the illusion of genuine debate. The parameters of that debate were all within the parameters of support for the

American Century agenda of Bush, Cheney, and the permanent establishment driving for global empire – "Full Spectrum Dominance."

Since the communications industry pressed Congress to give it a deregulated open field in 1996, newspapers, radio, TV, cable and telecommunications had all been allowed to create giant global monopolies of information control, all in the name of "free" enterprise. Their control of the media is one of the hidden levers of control of the US-based establishment in their push for global empire. Yet they did it in such a way that most Americans believe they enjoy a "free press."

Through their creation of a mass-based, ideologically-driven movement driving towards war – the American people, underpinned by a deluded belief that they were fighting a new Holy Crusade – the leading circles of the American Century appeared to be nearing their goal of a global New World Order. China was about to feel the heat of that massive media machine as it increasingly tried to assert national Chinese interests, whether over its rights in the South China Sea, over freedom of speech or its restraints in China, over Chinese economic and currency policies and other spheres of vital activity.

When the totality of the assault by NATO and allied agencies on the Peoples' Republic of China is understood, only then is it possible to plan a sovereign strategy to defend against this total warfare form of outside aggression. It is a strategy drawing on the marvelous principles of Sun Tzu. This is what we will now discuss.

Chapter Ten:
A Chinese Strategy for Victory

The seeds of a counter to NATO and the Pentagon's strategic threat to force China into unwilling submission to their New World Order plans – sometimes politely called "globalization" – fortunately exist in an active form. It is implicit in the membership and associate nations in the Shanghai Cooperation Organization, most emphatically Russia and Iran.

"If you know the enemy and know yourself, you need not fear the result of a hundred battles. If you know yourself but not the enemy, for every victory gained you will also suffer a defeat. If you know neither the enemy nor yourself, you will succumb in every battle"...

"If your enemy is secure at all points, be prepared for him. If he is in superior strength, evade him... Attack him where he is unprepared, appear where you are not expected."

— Sun Tzu, The Art of War

Part I: The Strategic Reality

China faces a strategic reality in 2013 that is unlike any challenge faced in the history of the Peoples' Republic. The previous eight chapters of this work are by no means a complete review of the threats to the future existence of China as a sovereign nation-state. They are, however, intended to be a catalyst to a broader debate on the true dangers China faces. Such a debate is urgently necessary not only for the future well-being of China and the Chinese people. It is urgent for the future well-being of the entire world population, including most emphatically the population of the United States and of Western Europe, as China has become a vital actor in the effort to create a counter-pole to a one-world totalitarian control.

In effect China's leadership has already begun reacting to many of the threats or forms of disguised or overt warfare outlined. China's Central Bank has engaged in a renminbi strategy to make the currency less and less dependent on the US dollar, and potentially leading to its acceptance as an alternative reserve currency, at least for China's Asian and Eurasian trading partners. China has led the world's most active oil acquisition strategy since at least 2001 in Africa, the Middle East, Latin America and elsewhere. In the process, with mistakes along the way, China has enabled numerous African nations to begin to invest in their national economic development free from the shackles of IMF debt conditionalities.

Yet if we look at the totality of the threats confronting China in the second decade of the 21st Century, China is anything but secure. Maintaining a stable and secure China to the end of this Century will require extraordinary effort and resources on the part of the entire Chinese people.

The Arab Spring was launched by NATO countries, above all by the USA and France, in order to redraw the map of the Middle East to the detriment of China's main oil import sources.[324] As chronicled herein, the Pentagon's AFRICOR was created in 2008 specifically to rob China of its oil security from Africa. The issue of Chinese food security has been a disaster, as GMO soybeans contaminated with glyphosate comprise at least 61% of all soybeans consumed by animals and humans in China. Chinese crops are being massively sprayed with neo-nicotinoids that are doing untold damage to insect, bee colony and bird species and ultimately the human population that consumes crops sprayed with the toxic insecticides.

The industrialization of Chinese agriculture along the model of the American, is destroying the food quality of the Chinese diet, creating epidemics of allergies and illnesses such as Diabetes II. The decision to proliferate the drugs and vaccines patented by the American and Swiss pharmaceutical cartel is creating a generation with illnesses and chronic health problems worse than the illnesses they theoretically were designed to prevent. The Pentagon military deployments around the Obama 2012 China "Pivot" confront China with a severe challenge to defend her oil and sea supply lines as well as her own borders.

The rising provocations of Western trade wars and WTO challenges to Chinese exports or domestic manufacture is binding China into the rules of a game, the globalization game, where ultimately, rather than being the "winner" as in the last three decades, China increasingly will be forced to be the loser.

The decision by the Government of China to open earthquake-prone regions of China for US, UK and French oil companies that introduce toxic shale gas fracking methods to extract gas threatens not only China's scarce fresh water supply, but also threatens to detonate deadly and destructive earthquakes in the country. This is a consequence likely far more costly to the national economy than the gain in a few billion cubic meters of gas. The open circulation across China of Hollywood films and even the semi-controlled Internet pose challenges to China's cultural sovereignty and integrity that have not been fully appreciated.

What should a concerned and patriotic national consensus seek to do in order to roll-back all or most of these threats? What we propose here is intended as mere illustration from abroad, and not any blueprint. Chinese people are the only qualified people to make sovereign decisions for their future in the most beneficial way. The following are intended as suggestions from a friend of China for broader debate.

As the leading American geopolitical strategist Zbigniew Brzezinski openly admitted, the sole threat to unchallenged American Superpower hegemony since the collapse of the Soviet Union in 1990-1991 has been the emergence of an economically and politically integrated Eurasian land-space which draws China and Russia into a common alliance of shared strategic interests.[325]

Brzezinski, still today in his late 80's a senior American strategist, made several statements in his 1998 book, *The Grand Chessboard*, regarding the geopolitical threat that a vibrant growing Eurasia posed for America: "Ever since the continents started interacting politically, some five hundred years ago, Eurasia has been the center of world power."[326]

Brzezinski added, "It is imperative that no Eurasian challenger emerges capable of dominating Eurasia and thus of also challenging America…"[327] Then he summed up the true threat to American sole superpower hegemony seen in the aftermath of the collapse of the Soviet Union:

> How America 'manages' Eurasia is critical. A power that dominates Eurasia would control two of the world's three most advanced and economically productive regions. A mere glance at the map also suggests that control over

Eurasia would almost automatically entail Africa's subordination, rendering the Western Hemisphere and Oceania geopolitically peripheral to the world's central continent. About 75 per cent of the world's people live in Eurasia, and most of the world's physical wealth is there as well, both in its enterprises and underneath its soil. Eurasia accounts for about three-fourths of the world's known energy resources.[328]

Part II: Eurasian Military Defense

The seeds of a counter to NATO and the Pentagon's strategic threat to force China into unwilling submission to their New World Order design, sometimes politely called "globalization," fortunately exist in an active form. It is implicit in the membership and associate nations in the Shanghai Cooperation Organization.

The Shanghai Cooperation Organization, today in many respects still an embryo, contains within its membership the seed-crystal for just such a cohesive Eurasian challenge to a destructive one-world dictatorship. The Shanghai Cooperation Organization (SCO) was established in 2001 as a regional economic and trade organization which increasingly is assuming the role of a "counter-NATO" as Washington expands the war in Afghanistan and the Middle East.

SCO includes, in addition to Russia and China, Kazakhstan, Kyrgyzstan, Tajikistan and Uzbekistan. Iran, Pakistan and India have observer status, but are not yet admitted as members for a variety of reasons, not the least that SCO includes a mutual defense component requiring all to defend an attack against any member.

Eurasian mutual cooperation, especially between the two great powers, Russia and China, is rapidly assuming a strategic depth. The mutual decision by China and Russia to refuse to agree to a UN-sanctioned military intervention into Bashar al-Assad's Syrian regime has already begun to reveal the deep fault lines within the members of the NATO anti-Assad coalition. The longer China and Russia as a combined opposition hold firm, the more fault ruptures and divisions among the nations of the Western NATO globalist faction will emerge, presenting China with new, even unexpected opportunities to forge new alliance or cooperation partners against the forces of a nominally superior NATO military opposition.

It is instructive to recall the wisdom of Sun Tzu: "If your enemy is secure at all points, be prepared for him. If he is in superior strength, evade him... Attack him where he is unprepared, appear where you are not expected." If China understands these words not in the sense of direct military attack but rather in terms of countermeasures in an undeclared war of ideas and opposing visions of the world future, China can "win" the war against a militarily far superior adversary, one internally deeply divided and confused.

Part III: Countering the US Missile "Defense" Threat

The vital component of a viable military defense is already in the making. It involves separate and combined efforts by China, Russia and Iran to counter the US offensive Missile "Defense" Shield's global deployment. Since the last years of the past decade, the Washington administrations of both Bush and Obama had made a priority the deployment of an anti-missile array of radars and missile sites to cripple Chinese, Russian and Iranian military potentials to launch any missile strike.

What few outside a handful of military strategic experts realized was that in war and nuclear military strategy, if one side has even a primitive anti-missile deployment and the opponent none, the missile defense side has *de facto* won a potential nuclear war.

That presents the prospect of a potential nuclear first strike that would destroy the missile strike force of the opponent, in this case, China or Russia or Iran, and most likely all three simultaneously.

During the Cold War, the ability of both sides – the Warsaw Pact and NATO – to mutually annihilate one another, led to a nuclear stalemate dubbed by military strategists, MAD – Mutually Assured Destruction. It was scary but, in a bizarre sense, more stable than what would come later with a unilateral US pursuit of nuclear primacy. MAD was based on the prospect of mutual nuclear annihilation with no decisive advantage for either side; it led to a world in which nuclear war had been "unthinkable."

The first nation with a nuclear missile "defense" shield (NMD) would *de facto* have "first strike ability." Quite correctly, Lt. Colonel Bowman, who had been Director of the US Air Force Missile Defense Program during the Reagan era, called missile defense, "the missing link to a First Strike."[329]

The US nuclear missile defense shield, which had been under top secret development by the Pentagon since the 1970s, involved a ground-based system that could respond to a limited missile attack. There were five parts to the NMD system, including phased array radar installations that could detect a launch of enemy missiles and track them. Such a first strike has been the dream of Washington since the 1950's, when Russia's nuclear strike force was not yet fully operational.[330]

A Eurasian "Iron Triangle'?

In the Indian Ocean China is developing her military infrastructure under what the Pentagon calls, as noted above, the Chinese "string of pearls." Iran is going through a process of naval expansion, which is seeing it deploy its maritime forces further and further from its home waters in the Persian Gulf and Gulf of Oman. All three Eurasian powers, along with several of their allies, also have naval vessels stationed off the shorelines of Yemen, Djibouti, and Somalia in the geo-strategically important maritime corridor of the Gulf of Aden.

Despite repeated warnings that US deployment of its missile shield offensive system would trigger a new arms race, Washington has relentlessly pushed ahead. That provides China with more than ample justification to actively pursue its own anti-missile defense and active countermeasures to protect its homeland from any possible US or NATO nuclear attack.

China, logically, given the military reality, must be assumed to be already making large scale improvements to the survivability and penetration capabilities of its strategic weapons by increasing the amount of weapons, developing nuclear attack submarines and turning every type of Chinese missile into a strategic deterrent that no anti-missile shield can stop. The larger strategic defense involves China's quiet coordination with friendly states also threatened by US missile deployments, including Russia and North Korea and Iran.

In late October 2012 just before the US national elections, the Chinese Defense Ministry officially dismissed reports that its armed forces, the People's Liberation Army or PLA, were about to conduct anti-satellite missile tests. They issued a cryptic statement that neither confirmed nor denied: "Such reports did not conform to the fact," Ministry spokesman Yang Yujun stated. China is reportedly test-targeting satellites with a high orbit altitude, such as reconnaissance satellites and navigation satellites.[331]

In 2010 as Washington announced sale of US Patriot missiles to Taiwan over vehement Chinese protest, the Xinhua official news agency announced that China had successfully tested its first land-based missile defense system.[332]

Two weeks before the Chinese defense Ministry statement, on October 12, 2012, the Government of North Korea announced it planned to boost its missile capability to strike US forces. Pyongyang's announcement was a response to a presidential statement from South Korea that it would develop ballistic missiles with a range of 800 km – compared with a previous limit of 300 km – under a revised pact with the United States. The new range could cover the entire peninsula and enable Seoul to better respond to perceived missile threats from the Democratic Peoples' Republic of Korea.

The South Korea extension plan contradicts its commitment to a global arms control agreement, the Missile Technology Control Regime (MTCR), to curb the spread of missiles and unmanned aerial vehicles that could deliver weapons of mass destruction. The Obama White House defended South Korea's pursuit of longer-range missiles as "absolutely legitimate to respond to a threat posed by the DPRK's ballistic missile program."[333]

If Japan, South Korea and Australia continue to participate in the US anti-missile program, Asia will undergo a runaway arms race. In such a context China is far better suited to undertake such a race given its stronger economic resources. It also has indirect resources of potential economic sanctions to Japan, South Korea and Australia, all of whose economies have become dependent on China for their survival in recent years.

The fact that it is the USA which is imposing its Missile Defense Shield on Asian countries directed against China gives Beijing the moral "high ground" which it must use in shaping world public opinion against the provocative US deployment. A significant investment by Beijing CCTV or a special new TV broadcast source along the lines of the Russian state-owned RT TV broadcasts in English, using native English-speaking journalists to get an accurate version of events across to the peoples of Australia, or broadcasting in Korean and Japanese would be an important part. China must cleverly adapt the superior Western propaganda techniques to turn them against the dangerous Western plans.

The US global missile shield is a component of the Pentagon's strategy to encircle Eurasia and specifically China, Russia and Iran.

In the first instance, this military system is aimed at establishing the nuclear primacy of the US by neutralizing any Russian or Chinese nuclear response to a US or NATO attack. The global missile shield is aimed at preventing any reaction or nuclear "second strike" by the Russians and Chinese to a nuclear "first strike" by the Pentagon.

The US missile shield was designed to be a global system with components strategically positioned across the world from the onset. The Pentagon had planned this in the 1990s and maybe much earlier. Japan and the Pentagon's NATO allies have more or less been partners in the military project from the start.[334]

For several years both China and Russia were aware of the Pentagon's global ambitions for the missile shield and made joint statements condemning it as a destabilizing project that would disturb the global strategic balance of power. China and Russia even jointly issued multilateral statements in July 2000 with Kazakhstan, Kyrgyzstan, and Tajikistan warning that the creation of the Pentagon's global missile shield would work against international peace, and that it contravened the Anti-Ballistic Missile (ABM) Treaty. The US government was repeatedly warned that the steps it was taking would polarize the globe with hostilities that would be reminiscent of the Cold War. Washington has ignored these warnings. Now Russia, China and Iran are quietly taking asymmetrical steps to counter the US missile deployment.

Closer cooperation on countermeasures to the US missile shield is vital for China's future sovereignty. Russia has great resources to bring to the project as do China and Iran, each in different areas of strength. Combined, the three nations have a formidable strategic response that could make a nuclear war avoidable.

Russia is involved in expansion of its presence on the high seas and an upgrade of its naval capabilities. Moscow plans opening new naval bases beyond its home waters and outside both the shorelines of the Black Sea and Mediterranean Sea. The Russian Federation already has two naval bases outside of Russian territory; one is in the Ukrainian port of Sevastopol in the Black Sea and the other is in the Syrian port of Tartus in the Mediterranean Sea. The Kremlin is now looking at the Caribbean Sea, South China Sea, and eastern coast of Africa (in close proximity to the Gulf of Aden) as suitable locations for new Russian bases. Cuba, Vietnam, and the Seychelles are the prime candidates to host new Russian naval bases in these waters.

Russia had a presence in Vietnam's Cam Ranh Bay until 2002. The Vietnamese port was home to the Soviets since 1979 and then hosted Russian forces after the breakup of the Soviet Union in 1991. Russia also had a post-Soviet military presence in Cuba until 2001 through the Lourdes intelligence signal base that monitored the US.

The Kremlin is additionally developing its military infrastructure on its Arctic coast. New Arctic naval bases in the north are going to be opened. This is part of an overlap with a careful Russian strategy that includes the Arctic Circle. It is drawn with two dual functions in mind. One function is to protect Russian territorial and energy interests against NATO states in the Lomonosov Ridge. The other purpose is to serve Russian global maritime strategy.[335]

Moscow realizes that the US and NATO want to restrictively hem in its maritime forces in the Black Sea and Mediterranean Sea. US and EU moves to control and restrict Russian maritime access to Syria is an indicator of this strategic inclination and objective. The moves to strategically hem in Russian marine forces are one of the reasons that the Kremlin wants naval bases in the Caribbean, South China Sea, and eastern coast of Africa.

The development of Russia's Arctic naval infrastructure and the opening of Russian naval bases in places like Cuba, Vietnam, and the Seychelles would virtually guarantee the global presence of Russian naval forces. Russian vessels would have multiple points of entry into international waters and secure docking bases abroad. These bases will give the Russians permanent docking facilities in both the Atlantic Ocean and Indian Ocean too.

Russia's naval infrastructure in the Russian Far East, on the shores of the Pacific Ocean, has the greatest access to open international waters. The addition of naval infrastructure in places like Cuba would effectively guarantee that Russia's naval forces will have a free hand and not be hemmed in by the US and its allies.

Historically, the mandate of the naval forces of the Russian Armed Forces had been to protect the Russian coast. Thus, the Russian naval fleet has not been structured as an offensive attack force. This, however, is changing as part of Moscow's reaction to the Pentagon's strategy of encirclement. Russia, like China and Iran, is now focusing on sea power.

Russia is upgrading and expanding its nuclear naval fleet. The Russian media has referred to this as a new bid for their country's "naval dominance." Moscow's aims are to establish the nuclear superiority of its naval fleet with sea-based nuclear attack capabilities. This is a direct reaction to the Pentagon's global missile shield and the encirclement of Russia and its allies.

Over fifty new warships and more than twenty new submarines will be added to the Russian fleet by 2020. About 40% of the new Russian submarines will have lethal nuclear strike capabilities. This process started after the Bush Jr. White House began taking steps to establish the US missile shield in Europe.[336]

In the last few years, Russia's counter-measures to the US missile shield have begun to manifest themselves. Trials of Russia's Borey class submarine in the White Sea, where the port of Archangel (Arkhangelsk) is situated, began in 2011. In the same year the development of the submarine-launched Liner ballistic nuclear missile was announced, which was said to be able to pierce through the US missile shield. A Russian submarine would secretly test the Liner from the Barents Sea in 2011.[337]

Russia's new nuclear naval posture actually allows it to cleverly station multiple mobile nukes around the US. In other words, Russia has "multiple Cubas" in the form of its floating mobile nuclear naval vessels that can deploy anywhere in the world. This is also why Russia is developing its naval infrastructure abroad. Russia will have the option of surrounding or flanking the United States with its own sea-based nuclear strike forces.[338]

Russia's clever naval strategy is meant to counter the Pentagon's global missile shield. Included in this process is the adoption of a pre-emptive nuclear strike policy by the Kremlin as a reaction to the aggressive pre-emptive post-Cold War nuclear strike doctrine of the Pentagon and NATO. In the same year as the test of the Liner by the Russians, the commander of the Strategic Rocket Forces of the Russian Federation, Colonel-General Karakayev, said that Russia's inter-continental ballistic missiles would become "invisible" in the near future.[339]

Iranian missiles in test

Iran, Russia and China cooperation

Russia has quietly and quite legally been supplying Iran with vital military hardware for its defense as Western economic sanctions tightened on the Persian Gulf country. Iran has not only upgraded its own defenses but now possess, according to sources in the Israeli regime, three Russian advanced S-400 launchers, state-of-the-art air defense systems.

In October 2012, Russia's Chairman of the Russian Defense Ministry's Public Council, Igor Korotchenko, made it clear that defensive military hardware, including air defense systems, are not covered by UN sanctions. Russia had recently sold Iran an amount of advanced defensive military equipment totaling $13 billion, a fact kept out of all Western press outlets. The S-400 uses three different missiles with a range up to 250 miles. It is between 96% and 98% effective against stealth aircraft that Israel has yet to take delivery of and is equally effective against ICBMs and "cruise type" missiles.[340]

In October 2012 the US Navy Times journal admitted: "Iran's high-flying ballistic missiles could overwhelm US missile defenses in the Persian Gulf, where much of the world's oil passes. Its fast-attack boats could swarm a large warship and sink it. And its fleet of hard-to-find submarines carry torpedoes faster than any torpedo in the US fleet."[341] Clearly, despite the colossal US military size and budget, it is by no means invincible in such a war game scenario, a fact which at some point could lead to a decision in Washington to back away globally from its offensive missile defense strategy.

China-Iran relations in recent years have become strategic and close for both. China has become Iran's biggest oil customer and biggest economic partner. Iran is China's third most important oil import source despite recent US sanctions on Iran. Iranian officials explicitly emphasize the strategic nature of the partnership. According to Iranian Foreign Minister Ali Akbar Salehi, "Tehran-Beijing ties are strategic and their prospects are bright."[342] Tehran views China as an emerging economic, political, and military power that can offset US power globally and in the Middle East specifically.

China has played a crucial role in starting up Iran's indigenous military-industrial sector, greatly helping Iran's military modernization efforts. Chinese design and technology were seen in many Iranian missile series, from the short-range Oghab and Nazeat missiles to the long-range Shahab 3.13 In addition, Iran developed its own relatively sophisticated antiship cruise missiles with Chinese help. These included the Nasr, which is reported to be nearly identical to the Chinese C-704. According to some reports, China even helped Iran establish a plant for the manufacture of the Nasr in 2010. China is also reported to have provided Iran with advanced antiship mines and fastattack boats.

The total value of those transfers was estimated by some analysts to range possibly as high as $10 billion.[343]

This suggests very broadly how essential it is for Chinese military deployments and plans to mesh with Russian and Iranian. The basis for this exists. The necessity exists as well. This cooperation could be the one force that prevents a nuclear world war.

Chapter Eleven:
China's Land Bridge to Europe[344]

The prospect of an unparalleled Eurasian economic boom lasting into the next Century and beyond is at hand. The first steps binding the vast economic space are being constructed with a number of little-publicized rail links connecting China, Russia, Kazakhstan and parts of Western Europe. Rail infrastructure is a major key to building vast new economic markets across Eurasia.

Strategic Role of Economic Infrastructure

The cohesion of the landmass of Eurasia and a future market for Chinese export growth to counter the declining markets in North America and the EU depends on the creation of new markets. In turn, new markets in and across Eurasia and beyond into Africa and Western Europe depend on the construction of massive new links among high-speed rail, modern highways, telecommunications, electricity and energy infrastructures.

Financing construction of such infrastructures, with state backing from China, from Russia and the nations of Eurasia, including Kazakhstan and even Iran, is not a question of money. It never is. Money is a political creation of sovereign governments issuing credits.

China still retains an enormous advantage over the USA and EU nations in terms of the ability of the State to issue bonds for such long-term infrastructure. Were China and Russia and the other states of the SCO to genuinely cooperate and mutually plan such infrastructure and fund it internally, and not on dollar or Euro capital markets, it would generate an economic renaissance not only for the next three or more decades for Chinese industry, but also for Russia and Central Asia, as well as into the economically troubled economies of the EU in Western Europe.

China's Strategic Land Bridge

The prospect of an unparalleled Eurasian economic boom lasting into the next Century and beyond is at hand. The first steps binding the vast economic space are being constructed with a number of little-publicized rail links connecting China, Russia,

Kazakhstan and parts of Western Europe. Rail infrastructure is a major key to building vast new economic markets across Eurasia.

China and Turkey are in discussions to build a new high-speed railway link across Turkey. If completed it would be the country's largest railway project ever, even surpassing the pre-World War I Berlin-Baghdad Railway link. The project was an important agenda item in early April 2012 talks between the Turkish and Chinese governments. The proposed rail link would run from Kars on the easternmost border with Armenia, through the Turkish interior on to Istanbul where it would connect to the Marmaray rail tunnel now under construction that runs under the Bosphorus strait. Then it would continue to Edirne near the border to Greece and Bulgaria in the European Union. It will cost an estimated $35 billion. The realization of the Turkish link would complete a Chinese Trans-Eurasian Rail Bridge project that would bring freight from China to Spain and England.[345]

The Kars-Edirne line would reduce travel time across Turkey by two-thirds from 36 hours down to 12. Under an agreement signed between China and Turkey in October 2010, China has agreed to extend loans of $30 billion for the planned rail network.[2] In addition a Baku-Tbilisi-Kars (BTK) railway connecting Azerbaijan's capital of Baku to Kars is under construction, which greatly increases the strategic importance of the Edirne-Kars line. For China it would put a critical new link in its railway infrastructure across Eurasia to markets in Europe and beyond.

The visit of Turkey's President Erdogan to Beijing was significant for other reasons. It was the first such high level trip of a Turkish Prime Minister to China since 1985. The fact that Erdogan was also granted a high-level meeting with Chinese Vice President Xi Jinping, and was granted an extraordinary visit to China's oil-rich Xinjiang Province also shows the high priority China is placing on its relations with Turkey, a key emerging strategic force in the Middle East.

Xinjiang is a highly sensitive part of China as it hosts some 9 million ethnic Uyghurs who share a Turkic heritage with Turkey as well as nominal adherence to the Turkish Sunni branch of Islam. In July 2009 the US government, acting through the National Endowment for Democracy, the regime-change NGO it finances, backed a major Uyghur uprising in which many Han Chinese shop owners were killed or injured.

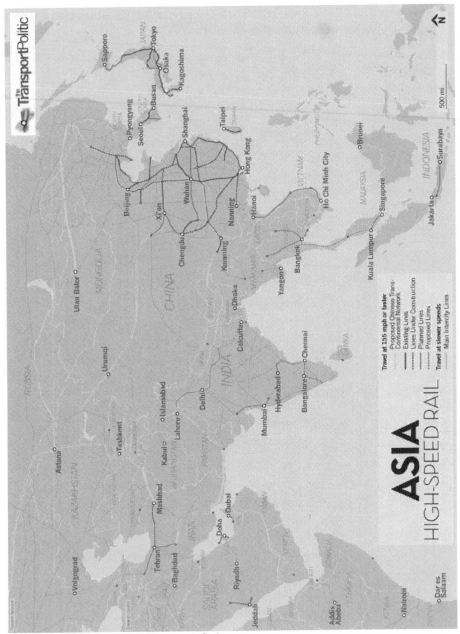

(Map: Yunus Emre Hatuno lu)

Washington in turn blamed the riots on Beijing as part of a strategy of escalating pressure on China.[346] During Uyghur riots in Xinjiang in 2009, Erdogan accused Beijing of "genocide" and attacked the Chinese on human rights, a dicey issue for Turkey given their ethnic Kurd problems. Clearly economic priorities from both sides have now changed the political calculus.

Building the world's greatest market: Eurasia

Contrary to the dogma of Milton Friedman and his followers, markets are never "free." They are always man-made. The essential element to create new markets is building infrastructure, and for the vast landmass of Eurasia railroad linkages are essential to those new markets.

With the end of the Cold War in 1990 the vast under-developed land space of Eurasia became open again. This space contains some forty percent of total land in the world, much of it prime unspoiled agriculture land; it contains three-fourths of the world's population, an asset of incalculable worth. It consists of some eighty eight of the world's countries and three-fourths of known world energy resources as well as every mineral known needed for industrialization. North America as an economic potential, rich as she is, pales by comparison.

The Turkish-China railway discussion is but one part of a vast Chinese strategy to weave a network of inland rail connections across the Eurasian Continent. The aim is to literally create the world's greatest new economic space and in turn a huge new market for not just China but all Eurasian countries, the Middle East and Western Europe. Direct rail service is faster and cheaper than either ships or trucks, and much cheaper than airplanes. For manufactured Chinese or other Eurasian products the rail land bridge links are creating vast new economic trading activity all along the rail line.

Two factors have made this prospect realizable for the first time since the Second World War. First the collapse of the Soviet Union has opened up the land space of Eurasia in entirely new ways, as has the opening of China to Russia and its Eurasian neighbors, overcoming decades of mistrust. This is being met by the eastward expansion of the European Union to the countries of the former Warsaw Pact.

The demand for faster rail transport over the vast Eurasian distances is clear. China's container port activities, and that of its European and North American destinations, are reaching a saturation point as volumes of container traffic explode at double-digit rates. Singapore recently displaced Rotterdam as the world's largest port in volume terms. The growth rate for container port throughput in China in 2006, before the world financial crisis, was some 25% annually. In 2007 Chinese ports accounted for some 28% of world container port throughput.[347]

However there is another aspect to the Chinese and, to an extent, the Russian land bridge strategies. By moving trade flows over land, it is more secure in the face of escalating military tensions between the nations of the Shanghai Cooperation Organization, especially China and Russia on one hand, and NATO on the other. Sea transport must flow through highly vulnerable narrow passageways or chokepoints such as the Malaysian Straits of Malacca.

The Turkish Kars-Edirne railway would form an integral part of an entire web of Chinese-initiated rail corridors across the Eurasian landmass. Following the example of how rail infrastructure transformed the economic space of Europe and later of America during the late 19th Century, the Chinese government, which today stands as the world's most efficient railroad constructor, has quietly been extending its rail links into Central Asia and beyond for several years. They have proceeded in segments, which is one reason the vast ambition of their grand rail infrastructure has drawn so little attention to date in the West outside the shipping industry.

China builds Second Eurasian Land Bridge

By 2011 China had completed a Second Eurasian Land Bridge running from China's port of Lianyungang on the East China Sea through to Kazakhstan's Druzhba, and on to Central Asia, West Asia and then to various European destinations and finally to Rotterdam Port of Holland on the Atlantic coast.

The Second Eurasian Land Bridge is a new railway connecting the Pacific and the Atlantic that was completed by China to Druzhba in Kazakhstan. This newest Eurasia land bridge extends west in China through about 360,000 square kilometers, some 37% of the total land space of China. About 400 million people live in these provinces, which accounts for 30% of the total population of the country. Outside of China, the land bridge covers over 40 countries and regions in both Asia and Europe, and is particularly important for the countries in Central and West Asia that don't have sea outlets.

In 2011 China's Vice Premier Wang Qishan announced plans to build a new high-speed railway link within Kazakhstan, linking the cities of Astana and Almaty, to be ready in 2015. The Astana-Almaty line, with a total length of 1050 kilometers, employing China's advanced rail-building technology, will allow high-speed trains to run at 350 kilometers per hour.

> DB Schenker Rail Automotive is now transporting auto parts from Leipzig to Shenyang in northeastern China for BMW... "With a transit time of 23 days, the direct trains are twice as fast as maritime transport, followed by over-the-road transport to the Chinese hinterland"... The route reaches China via Poland, Belarus, and Russia... Containers have to be transferred by crane to different gauges twice – first to Russian broad gauge at the Poland-Belarus border, then back to standard gauge at the Russia-China border in Manzhouli.[348]

In May 2011 a daily direct rail freight service was launched between the Port of Antwerp, Europe's second-largest, and Chongqing, the industrial hub in China's southwest. That greatly speeded rail freight transport across Eurasia to Europe. Compared to the 36 days for maritime transport from east China's ports to west Europe, the Antwerp-Chongqing Rail Freight service now takes 20 to 25 days, and the aim is to cut that to 15 to 20 days.

Westbound cargo includes automotive and technological goods; eastbound shipments are mostly chemicals. The project was a major priority for the Antwerp Port and the Belgian government in cooperation with China and other partners. The service is run by Swiss inter-modal logistics provider Hupac, their Russian partner Russkaya Troyka, and Eurasia Good Transport over a distance of more than 10,000km, starting from the Port of Antwerp through to Germany and Poland, and further to Ukraine, Russia and Mongolia before reaching Chongqing in China.[349]

The Second Eurasian Land Bridge runs 10,900 kilometers in length, with some 4100 kilometers of that in China. Within China the line runs parallel to one of the ancient routes of the Silk Road. The rail line continues across China into Druzhba where it links with the broader gauge rail lines of Kazakhstan – the largest inland country in the world. As Chinese rail and highways have expanded west, trade between Kazakhstan and China has been booming. From January to October 2008, goods passing through the Khorgos port between the two nations reached 880,000 tons – over 250% growth compared with the same period a year before. Trade between China and Kazakhstan is expected to grow 3 to 5 fold by 2013. As of 2008, only about 1% of the goods shipped from Asia to Europe were delivered by overland routes, meaning that the room for expansion is considerable.[350]

From Kazakhstan the lines continue via Russia and Belarus over Poland to the markets of the European Union.

Another line goes to Tashkent in Uzbekistan, Central Asia's largest city of some two millions. Another line goes west to Turkmenistan's capital Asgabat and to the border of Iran.[351] With some additional investment, these links, now tied to the vast expanse and markets of China, could open new economic possibilities in much-neglected regions of Central Asia.

The Shanghai Cooperation Organization (SCO) could serve as a well-suited vehicle for coordinating a broad Eurasian rail infrastructure coordination to maximize these initial rail links. The members of the SCO, formed in 2001, include China, Kazakhstan, Russia, Kyrgyzstan, Tajikistan, and Uzbekistan, while Iran, India, Mongolia and Pakistan have observer status.

Russia's Land Bridge

Russia is well-positioned to benefit greatly from such an SCO strategy. The First Eurasian Land Bridge runs through Russia along the Trans-Siberian Railway, first completed in 1916 to unify the Russian Empire. The Trans-Siberian remains the longest single rail line in the world at 9,297 kilometers, a tribute to the vision of Russian finance minister Sergei Witte in the 1890s. The Trans-Siberian Railway, also called the Northern East-West Corridor, runs from the Russian Far East port of Vladivostok, with connections in Europe linking to the Port of Rotterdam, some 13,000 kilometers away. At present it is the less attractive for Pacific-to-Atlantic freight because of maintenance problems and maximum speeds of 55 km.

There are attempts to better use the Trans-Siberian Land Bridge. In January 2008 a long distance Eurasian rail freight service, the "Beijing-Hamburg Container Express" was successfully tested by the German railway Deutsche Bahn. It completed the 10,000 km (6,200 miles) journey in 15 days to link the Chinese capital to the German port city of Hamburg, going through Mongolia, the

Russian Federation, Belarus and Poland. By ship to the same markets takes double the time or some 30 days.

Were the Trans-Siberian railway passage across Russian Eurasian space to be modernized and upgraded to accommodate high-speed freight traffic, it would add a significant new dimension to the economic development of Russia's interior regions. The Trans-Siberian is double-tracked and electrified. By minimally improving some segments to insure a better integration of all the elements, it would be a more attractive option for Eurasian freight to the west.

There are strong indications the new Putin presidency will turn more of its attention to Eurasia. Modernization of the First Eurasian Land Bridge would be a logical way to accomplish much of that development by literally creating new markets and new economic activity. With the bond markets of the United States and Europe flooded with toxic waste and state bankruptcy fears, issuance of Russian state bonds for modernizing existing rails – or even building a new parallel high-speed rail land bridge – based on the certainty of growing freight traffic across Eurasia would have little difficulty finding eager investors.

Russia is currently in discussion with China and Chinese rail constructors who are bidding on construction of a planned $20 billion of new high-speed Russian rail track to be completed before the 2018 Russian hosting of the FIFA World Cup soccer summit. China's experience in building some 12,000 km of high speed rail in record time is a major asset for China's bid. Significantly, Russia plans to raise $10 billion of the cost by issuing new railroad bonds.[352]

A Third Eurasian Land Bridge?

In 2009 at the Fifth Pan-Pearl River Delta Regional (PPRD) Cooperation and Development Forum, a government-sponsored event, the Yunnan provincial government announced its intention to accelerate construction of needed infrastructure to build a third Eurasian continental land bridge that will link south China to Rotterdam via Turkey over land. This is part of what Turkey's President Erdogan and Chinese Prime Minister Wen Jiabao discussed in Beijing in April 2014.

The network of inland roads for the land bridge within Yunnan province will be completed by 2015, said Yunnan governor Qin

Guangrong. The project starts from coastal ports in Guangdong, with the Port of Shenzhen being the most important. It will ultimately go all the way through Kunming to Myanmar, Bangladesh, India, Pakistan and Iran, entering Europe from Turkey.[353]

The route would cut some 6,000-km from the sea journey between the Pearl River Delta and Rotterdam, and allow production from China's eastern manufacturing centers to reach Asia, Africa and Europe. The proposal is for completing a series of rail and highway links totaling some 1,000 Km.

In neighboring Myanmar a mere 300 km of railways and highways are lacking in order to link the railways in Yunnan with the highway network of Myanmar and South Asia. It will help China pave the way for building a land channel to the Indian Ocean.

The third Eurasian Land Bridge will cross 20 countries in Asia and Europe and have a total length of about 15,000 kilometers, which is 3,000 to 6,000 kilometers shorter than the sea route entering at the Indian Ocean from the southeast coast via the Malacca Straits. The total annual trade volume of the regions the route passes through was nearly US$300 billion in 2009. Ultimately the plan is for a branch line that would also start in Turkey, cross Syria and Palestine, and end in Egypt, facilitating transportation from China to Africa.

Clearly the Pentagon's AFRICOM and the US-backed Arab Spring unrest directly impact that extension, though for how long at this point is unclear.[354]

The geopolitical dimension

Not every major international player is pleased about the growing linkages binding the economies of Eurasia with western Europe and Africa. In his book, *"The Grand Chessboard: American Primacy and its Geostrategic Imperatives,"* former Presidential adviser Zbigniew Brzezinski noted,

> In brief, for the United States, Eurasian geo-strategy involves the purposeful management of geo-strategically dynamic states... To put it in a terminology that harkens back to the more brutal age of ancient empires, the three grand imperatives of imperial geo-strategy are to prevent collusion and to maintain security dependence among the

vassals, to keep tributaries pliant and protected, and to keep the barbarians from coming together.355

The "barbarians" that Brzezinski refers to are China and Russia and all in between. The Brzezinski term "imperial geo-strategy" refers to US strategic foreign policy. The "vassals" he identifies in the book include countries like Germany, Japan and other NATO "allies" of the US. Brzezinski's geopolitical perspective remains US foreign policy today.

The prospect of an unparalleled Eurasian economic boom lasting into the next Century and beyond is at hand.

The first sinews of binding the vast economic space have been put in place or are being constructed with these rail links. It is becoming clear to more people in Europe, Africa, the Middle East and Eurasia – including China and Russia – that their natural tendency to build these markets faces only one major obstacle: NATO and the US Pentagon's Full Spectrum Dominance obsession.

In the period prior to World War I it was the decision in Berlin to build a rail land link to and through the Turkish Ottoman Empire, from Berlin to Baghdad, that was the catalyst for British strategists to incite events that plunged Europe into the most destructive war in history to that date. This time we have a chance to avoid a similar fate with the Eurasian development. More and more the economically stressed economies of the EU are beginning to look more to the east and less to their west across the Atlantic for Europe's economic future.

Chapter Twelve:
The West's Achilles Heel

For China to pursue a further road to peaceful national and international economic growth and development, she must be keenly aware of the West's Achilles Heel – The reality no one dares to say, namely that the United States and in a large part also the European Union economies of Western Europe are in terminal economic and demographic decline as hegemonic powers.

China's Internal Achilles Heel

Before any serious discussion of the West's Achilles Heel, it is important to introduce constructively how geopolitical strategists in the West view China's domestic Achilles Heel. First and foremost, the West through its vast propaganda apparatus and "humanitarian" NGOs seeks to exploit a growing sense of alienation between the senior members of the ruling Communist Party of China and the people it is mandated to serve.

The emergence of such vast wealth potential inside China in such a brief span of three decades has understandably tempted more than one party senior official or municipal and local official to accumulate vast fortunes. It has reached such proportions that the London *Economist* magazine recently noted that there were more millionaires inside the Chinese Politburo than in the US Senate or Congress. Much of that clearly is owed to the rapidity of China's ascent as a global economic force.

So long as the Party tolerates such vast wealth accumulation, it threatens its own ultimate demise as the legitimate governing political force. This reality was openly identified at the recent 18th Party Congress by President Hu. A collapse of CPC authority and legitimacy would spell catastrophe for China and for the world. Precisely to encourage such a collapse in perceived legitimacy is the goal of leading Western intelligence circles that use their politicized "pro-democracy" NGOs to encourage dissidence and discord.

There are several ways the Party leadership could respond to these growing pressures. One would be to deny there exists any legitimacy problem, or any officials who have misused their positions of public trust to unduly enrich themselves or their families. That would be a dangerous course today. A second way would be to single out one or several cases, label them exceptional, and punish them severely as in the recent excommunication of Bo Xilai.

The most uncomfortable but clearly more convincing approach would be to introduce financial transparency of party officials and family members, and to take convincing measures prohibiting unjust enrichment owing to misuse of party position. Genuine moral leadership in the new party leaders is the only convincing way. And it is possible. Leadership of the dominant political body in a land so vast and populous is one of the greatest responsibilities in this world today, and it requires men and women of the greatest integrity and concern for their people. China certainly has such men and women in influential positions, as I have had the good fortune to know.

How the Party and the Chinese people deal with the evident abuses of power is a matter for them and only them to decide. It is only important to note that the Western intelligence agencies and their NGOs are exploiting the scandals and abuses of power to the utmost to foster a growing climate of distrust towards the central government in Beijing. To ignore the real problems that exist will threaten the future not just of the CPC but also of China as a sovereign nation.

The experience of Putin in Russia, and the Iranian government after the US-incited "Green Revolution" of 2009, should also be taken seriously in Beijing to make it more difficult for NATO intelligence agencies to use real or imaginary corruption or dissidence. That would mean that China would ban all western-financed Non-Governmental-Organizations (NGOs), as well as ban all US and EU government aid, including USAID, Human Rights watch, National Endowment for Democracy or programs inside China which have any conceivable subversive role such as Western-financed Tibetan or Uyghur "culture preservation" programs.

So-called "pro-freedom" NGOs have become one of the most strategic NATO weapons for destabilizing opponent regimes over the past two decades or more. In Egypt the military leaders reacted too late, and today have lost power to dangerous Muslim Brotherhood elements around president Mohamed Morsi.

In the period of opening to the West initiated in 1979, in many cases China unwittingly allowed Western intelligence services to take advantage of China's openness. That can no longer be risked. China is in an undeclared war with a Western globalist adversary and must take measures appropriate to that reality. However, along with clamping down on such Western intervention, the Government has a great responsibility to educate the population, especially the youth as to what the concerns are, and what dangers to China's stability are posed by the US and EU NGOs.

The West's Financial Achilles Heel

The primary weakness of the West as represented most concretely by the sole superpower, the United States, is that the people, and their political and spiritual and business leaders, have lost their moral compass. At first glance this might sound silly as immoral empires from Caligula's Rome to Hitler's Germany have been fierce engines of destruction of other nations.

That moral erosion over the past thirty years and more has resulted from the early 1980's "Reagan Revolution" – the introduction of "free market" unregulated capitalism, and the removal of prudent government controls on banking. It has laid the seeds of the greatest financial and banking crisis in world history. US and EU banks, despite reassuring public comments to the contrary, are deeper in their crisis than in 2007 when the US real estate bubble first collapsed. Little has changed since except the fact that the US Federal Reserve has engaged in unprecedented Quantitative Easing and buying up from the banks their toxic bad debts, in effect debasing the dollar as world reserve currency by the printing press as in 1923 Weimar Germany.

Decline and Fall[356]

A brief glance into the economic reasons for the fall of the Roman Empire some sixteen centuries ago was instructive. The roots of the decline and ultimate collapse of the Roman Empire – in its day also the world's sole superpower – lay in the political decision by a ruling aristocracy, more accurately an oligarchy of wealth, to extend the bounds of empire through wars of conquest and plunder of foreign lands. They embarked on this to feed their private wealth and personal power, not for the greater good of the state. The economic model of the Empire of Rome was based on the plunder of conquered territories. As the empire expanded, it installed remote military garrisons to maintain control and increasingly relied on foreign mercenaries to man those garrisons.

In the process of military expansionism the Roman empire's peasantry, the heart of the empire, became impoverished. They were forced to leave their farms, often for years to fight foreign wars of conquest. The south of Italy was devastated as one result. Those with money were able to buy land as the only stable investment, becoming huge *latifundistas* or landowners.

Internal decadence destroyed Rome

That led to the huge concentration of land in a few hands, and the land in turn was run by slaves captured in wars of conquest. Small farmers were bankrupted and forced to flee to Rome to attempt a living as proletarians, wage laborers. They had no voting rights or other civil rights. In the eyes of the rich, they were simply the "mob" that could be bought, manipulated, and directed to attack an opponent; they were the "demos," the masses, the public. Roman "democracy" was all about mass manipulation in the service of empire.[357]

The government of Imperial Rome didn't have a proper budget system, and squandered resources maintaining the empire while producing little of value. When the spoils from conquered territories were no longer enough to cover expenses, it turned to higher taxes, shifting the burden of the immense military structure onto the citizenry. Higher taxes forced many more small farmers to let their land go barren. To distract its citizens from the worsening conditions, the Rome's ruling oligarchy handed out free wheat to the poor and entertained them with circuses, chariot races, throwing Christians to the lions and other entertainments – the notorious "bread and circuses" strategy of keeping unrest at bay.

Political offices increasingly were sold to those with wealth. The masses, in turn, "sold" their votes to various politicians for favors, the charade of democracy.

The next fundamental change that vitally wounded the Roman Empire was the shift from a draft army made up of farmer soldiers to one of paid professional career soldiers as the ever-more distant wars became more unpopular. That was not unlike what took place in America in the years after the Vietnam War when President Nixon abolished the draft in favor of an "all volunteer" Army.

As conditions for Roman soldiers in faraway wars became more onerous, more incentives were needed to staff the legions. Limiting of military service to citizens was dropped and Roman citizenship could be won in exchange for military service, not unlike what is taking place now as immigrant teenagers are being promised US citizenship if they risk their lives for America's wars in Afghanistan, Iraq or elsewhere. At a certain point, Roman soldiers were forced to take an oath of service to their commander, not to the state.

Small farms were gradually replaced by huge *latifundia*, bought for booty, and the gap between the Roman rich and the poor increased. When the two brothers Gracchus tried in the second century AD to ease the growing gap between rich and the rest by introducing agriculture reforms that limited the powers of the wealthy Senators, they were assassinated by the men of wealth.

The Roman oligarchy grew increasingly degenerate. Towards the end of the reign of Roman emperors, gluttony was so commonplace among the rich that vomitoriums were constructed, so that people who had eaten or drunk too much could throw up and go and eat and drink some more.

Emperor Nero at one point declared, "Let us tax and tax again. Let us see to it that no one owns anything!" The purchasing of exotic spices, silks, and other luxuries from the Orient bled Rome of its gold, gold that didn't return. Soon Rome didn't have enough gold to produce coins. And so it debased its coins with lesser metals until there was no gold left. Another emperor, in order to reduce production and raise the price of wine, ordered the destruction of half of the vineyards in Rome's provinces.

Over time the costs of maintaining this huge global Roman military structure became overwhelming. By the Third Century people were seeking every means to avoid the onerous taxes imposed to maintain the military. The army itself had doubled in size from the time of Augustus to the time of Diocletian, in the course of an inflationary spiral, inflation brought on by a systematic debasing of the gold and silver content of the Roman currency and a resulting chronic inflation. In addition, costs of the state administration had grown enormously. By the time of Diocletian there was not one emperor, but four emperors – which meant four imperial courts, four Praetorian Guards, four palaces, four complete imperial staffs. The cost of policing the Roman state became increasingly enormous.[358]

Ultimately, as its territorial expansion stalled and began to contract, less and less loot was available to support the empire's global ambitions as well as its domestic economy. The outsourcing of the military led to lethargy, complacency, and decadence. Comparisons with the United States since the fruitless wars of Vietnam, Iraq and Afghanistan are only too clear.

The Roman Empire gradually lost power. Barbarians in the north frequently went on raids against the disintegrating empire. The Roman Empire became steeped in debt as emperors tried desperately to buy the loyalty of the army, and the moral condition of its subjects continued to spiral downward. Christians were persecuted, and large, bloodthirsty crowds would gather in arenas to cheer as various people died violent deaths. "Bread and circus" was the method of control.

The systematic debasement of the value of the Roman currency in the Third Century was the final destruction of the Empire. As confidence in the currency's value declined, trade declined, crops failed and the military suffered what must have seemed like constant defeat.

The US dollar since the 1970's has also undergone a massive debasement which has been partly hidden by the abandonment of the dollar gold standard in 1973 and the decision to float the dollar against other currencies. Only the fact that the US was the global military Superpower and the dollar still the reserve currency allowed Washington to force other nations such as Japan and in the past 20 years increasingly China to "finance" the US Government's wars in Iraq and elsewhere, involuntarily, by allowing China to buy US Treasury debt, today well over $1.1 trillion. The hidden US dollar inflation of the past thirty or so years has reached a point where it is creating the greatest wealth divide in the American population in history as the wealthiest 1% get more and the 99% lose more, resulting in deep social splits, and protests such as Occupy Wall Street.

Since the senseless Vietnam War of the late 1960's the American people have become more and more numb to the purpose of what had been a nation founded on the idea of liberty and freedom for all. The wars in Iraq and in Afghanistan and later against Libya find a nation deeply in debt with an economic base that gradually has been outsourced to Mexico, Eastern Europe and especially to China.

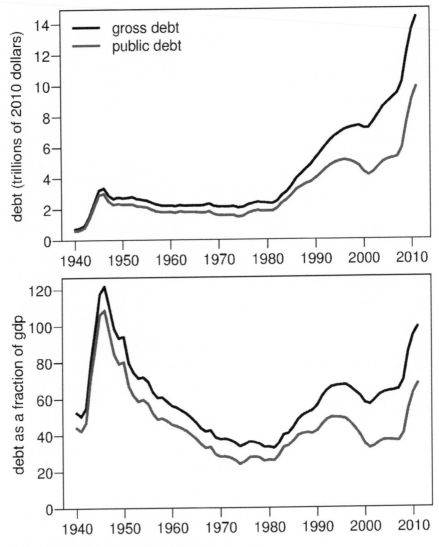

The American Debt Trap

America and Americans are caught increasingly in a devastating debt trap. Her politicians in Washington allowed major Wall Street banks free reign to loot and create fictitious wealth without regulation beginning in the 1970's. Towards the close of 2012 in

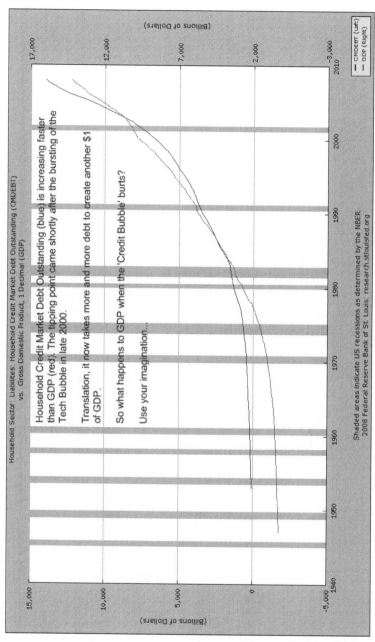

Household Sector: Liabilities: Household Credit Market Debt Outstanding (CMDEBT) vs. Gross Domestic Product, 1 Decimal (GDP)

Household Credit Market Debt Outstanding (blue) is increasing faster than GDP (red). The tipping point came shortly after the bursting of the Tech Bubble in late 2000.

Translation, it now takes more and more debt to create another $1 of GDP.

So what happens to GDP when the 'Credit Bubble' bursts?

Use your imagination...

Shaded areas indicate US recessions as determined by the NBER.
2008 Federal Reserve Bank of St. Louis. research.stlouisfed.org

— CMDEBT (Left)
— GDP (Right)

the wake of a re-election of a weary President Obama, Americans faced the greatest debt burden as a share of its GDP in its history. Including private and public government debt, total US debt burden stood at 336% of annual GDP. From 2005 through 2007 when the financial crisis began, US total debt, including real estate, increased by a staggering $11 trillion or almost 30% in only three years.[359]

As the two graphs show, US government debt as a nominal sum remained relatively constant from the end of World War II in 1945 until the end of the 1970's. At that point the debt began an astronomical explosion from some $3 trillion to $14 trillion by 2011, an increase of some 500% in just 30 years. Government debt as a share of GDP by 2011 was as high as it was during the heavy debt years of the Second World War.

Much of the US Government debt is held by foreign governments, above all China, Japan, Saudi Arabia and Russia. Already in 2007 the US Comptroller General warned:

> Foreign interests have more control over the US economy than Americans, leaving the country in a state that is financially imprudent. More and more of our debt is held by foreign countries – some of which are our allies and some are not. The huge holdings of American government debt by countries such as China and Saudi Arabia could leave a powerful financial weapon in the hands of countries that may be hostile to US corporate and diplomatic interests.[360]

That suggests China has potential leverage on the US financial system were she to decide to dump even a small portion of its holdings of US Treasury debt.

Private US debt is much higher now than during the Great Depression, and has been allowed to grow as if there were no consequences to borrowing, and no limit to what can be paid back in the future. After the Great Depression the US debt was about 20% of the GDP, by the end of World War II it was 40% (although during the war the gross debt was 100% of GDP). By the 1970s it was back down to 20%. Then during the Presidency of George W. Bush and two wars, US federal debt doubled from some $6 trillion in 2001 to $11 trillion in 2008.

The Achilles Heel of record debt levels exposes the US to risk on many levels. Savings go towards purchases of government debt, rather than investments in productive capital goods such as factories and computers, leading to lower output and incomes. Rising interest costs to sell the debt to the world will force reductions in government programs.

The greatest risk for the US economy is that the world will boycott future US debt sales, forcing dramatic rises in US interest rates to place its debt. That in turn will force major debt defaults and a crisis in the fragile US banking system. America is frequently called the "richest nation on earth," but the reality is that the American people are living on borrowed money. Across the US economy, Government, corporate, and consumer debt are all at record levels. Private debt, which is debt from a private entity, such as a bank, has skyrocketed in the last three decades alone. The purchase of homes, automobiles, stocks, and other consumer goods on credit increased consumer spending, but compounded debt. Unlike in the 1930s Great Depression when the level of Federal Government debt was tiny, today that debt is well over 103% of GDP and rising rapidly.

US Fiscal "Cliff"

At the end of 2012 and the beginning of 2013, many major fiscal events were set to occur all at once in a foolish "shock therapy" attempt by the US Congress to bring the exponential rise of the Federal deficit and debt under control. They include the expiration of the 2001 and subsequent tax cuts, the ending of Government jobs programs and activation of a $1.2 trillion across-the-board "sequester," an immediate and steep reduction in Medicare physician payments, the end of current Alternative Minimum Tax (AMT) patches, and the need to once again raise the country's debt ceiling. This combination of pre-planned actions is what Federal Reserve Chairman Ben Bernanke called a "fiscal cliff."

The planned combination of automatic Federal Budget cuts and tax increases will amount to $700 billion in 2013. Unless avoided, this could contract US gross domestic product by around 4.5 percent and plunge the economy back into depression.[361]

That pre-programmed new economic shock to the US economy would come on top of the continuing negative effect of the US real estate speculation bubble that burst in 2007 and is far from over in terms of its negative effects of mortgage payment defaults or home repossession by banks. More than five years into the first mortgage crisis, more than five million private homes across America are still in default or non-payment to banks of mortgages.[362]

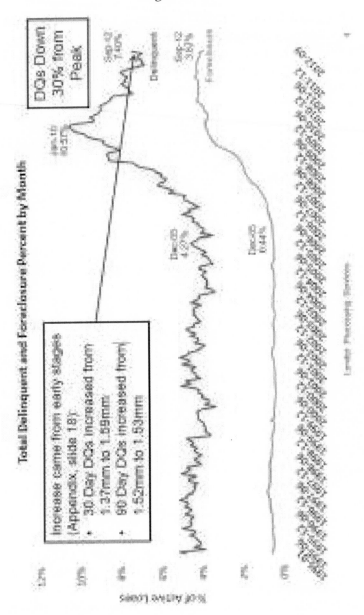

Mortgage defaults have yet to return to normal after more than five years of crisis. Add to the real estate collapse across America the collapse of state revenues from the 50 states making up the United States. The worst case is the nation's largest state economically, California, whose own GDP would make it the eighth largest GDP in the world were California a nation. Almost six years into the crisis, the California state budget deficit has doubled to $16 billion for 2012. By law California cannot run a deficit meaning either $16 billion of state budget cuts or $16 billion of new taxes or both. The 2012 California budget crisis followed three straight budgets that made deep cuts in aid to public education, the state university system and social welfare programs, as well as repeated worker layoffs as California tried, in vain, to find its balance.[363]

The US dollar at the beginning of 2013 was dangerously near to conditions for a dollar panic selloff. The US has a massive current account deficit, meaning the US needs investment from abroad simply to stop the dollar from falling. As a result, the US is required to generate economic growth to attract capital from abroad. The euro doesn't have this same pressure as most of its trade is within the EU. Only the constant attention to the Euro crisis in the past three years has prevented a dollar free-fall.

And a worsening Eurozone crisis

Simultaneously, pressed on by a Troika consisting of the EU, European Central Bank and IMF, Greece and other weak Eurozone economies are being forced into a ruthless self-defeating austerity that has resulted in official unemployment above 25% in both Greece and Spain. EU major banks are on the brink of insolvency, held afloat only via emergency measures from the ECB.

The EU countries are themselves in a different but every bit as grave debt trap, fed by the surplus of cheap dollar credit from the US Federal Reserve during the Greenspan era. The deeper Eurozone structural crisis by the end of 2012 was still getting worse. Loan demand had crashed 50% in Italy and France. Spain's unemployment was 26% and headed to 30% in 2013. The strategy of Berlin, of the European Central Bank and IMF was to save the Euro and the major banks tied to the Euro at all costs, even to that of the population and economies of the EU.[364] Recent IMF reports indicated that EU major banks could face a credit contraction of more than €4 trillion if the overall economic situation continues to decline. That would plunge all EU countries into deep recession, including Germany which depends on the export market of the EU for some 60% of all its exports.

The essential point to understand from the vantage point of China was that the once-great economic powerhouses of the United States and Western Europe by 2013 were choking in unpayable debt, corruption and economic and moral decline. That reality was essential for China to formulate an effective economic strategy going forward that could effectively defuse EU complicity in any future NATO provocations against China.

Afterword:
Washington Foments a Color Revolution against China in Hong Kong

On September 27, 2014, Washington's State Department and the bevy of "democracy" NGOs it controls issued the order to begin a full-scale Color Revolution protest in China's Hong Kong.

The Washington neo-cons and their allies in the US State Department and Obama Administration are clearly furious with China, as they are with Russia's Vladimir Putin. As both Russia and China in recent years have become more assertive about defining their national interests, and as both Eurasian powers draw into a closer cooperation on all strategic levels, Washington has decided to unleash havoc against Beijing, as it has unleashed the Ukraine disorder against Russia and Russian links to the EU. The flurry of recent deals binding Beijing and Moscow more closely – the $400 billion gas pipeline, the BRICS infrastructure bank, trade in rubles and renminbi by-passing the US dollar – has triggered Washington's response. It's called the Hong Kong 'Umbrella Revolution' in the popular media.

The Hong Kong Special Administrative Region of the People's Republic of China was targeted for a color revolution, one that was dubbed in the media as the Umbrella Revolution, after the umbrellas that protesters use to block police tear gas.

The "umbrellas" for Hong Kong's ongoing Umbrella Revolution were planned in Washington. Proof of that lies not only in the rapid White House open support of Occupy Central just hours after it began, following the same model they used in Ukraine.[365] The US State Department and NGOs it finances had been quietly preparing these protests for years.

Same dirty old cast of characters...

Washington unleashed another of its infamous Color Revolutions, as it had done since 2000 in Yugoslavia, in Ukraine, Georgia, Iran, Egypt and beyond. The aim in Hong Kong was to challenge Beijing's right to politically control future elections, and to unleash similar protests inside China itself, as the CIA had done in the 1989 Tiananmen Square student protests.

US Government-steered NGOs and US-trained operatives were running the entire Hong Kong "Occupy Central" protests, ostensibly in protest against the rules Beijing has announced for Hong Kong's 2017 elections. The Occupy Central Hong Kong "spontaneous" protest movement was being nominally led by a 17-year-old student, Joshua Wong, who resembles a Hong Kong version of Harry Potter, a kid who was only just born the year Britain reluctantly ended its 99-year colonial occupation, ceding the city-state back to the Peoples' Republic. Wong is accompanied in Occupy Central leadership by a University of Minnesota-educated hedge fund money man for the protests, Edward Chin; by a Yale University-educated sociologist, Chan Kin-man; by a Baptist minister who is a veteran of the CIAs 1989 Tiananmen Square destabilization, Chu Yiu-ming; and by a Hong Kong University law professor, Benny Tai Yiu-ting, or Benny Tai.

Behind these Hong Kong faces, the US State Department ran the Occupy Central destabilization, through its favorite NGO, the US Congress-financed National Endowment for Democracy (NED), and its daughter, the National Democratic Institute (NDI).

The US State Department role began at the top with Chu Yiu-ming, the Baptist minister chosen to head Occupy Central. The most reverend Chu Yiu-ming was also a founder and member of the executive committee of a key NGO, the Hong Kong Human Rights Monitor (HKHRM). HKHRM, as they openly admit on their website, was mainly financed by the US State Department via its neo-conservative Color Revolution NGO (NED).

As they state their purpose: "HKHRM briefs the press, the United Nations, local and overseas governments and legislative bodies on Hong Kong human rights issues both orally and through written reports."[366] In their 2013 Annual Report, the NED reported giving Rev. Chu Yiu-ming's HK Human Rights Monitor a grant of US $145,000. You can buy a boatload of umbrellas for that.[367] Chu's HKHRM also worked with another NED-financed creation, the Alliance for Reform and Democracy in Asia (ARDA).[368]

When Occupy Central top figures decided to (undemocratically) name Chu as their leader in January, 2014, Chu himself said it was because "I have more connections with different activist groups, and experience in large-scale social campaigns."[369] He should have named NED as activist group and the CIA's 1989

Tiananmen Square as a "large-scale social campaign, to be more specific. The Baptist preacher admitted that he was named de facto leader of Occupy Central by two other leading organizers of the civil disobedience movement, Benny Tai Yiu-ting and Dr Chan Kin-man, who wanted him "to take up" the role.[370] It was an insider move, "with no broad voting.

Benny Tai was also familiar with the US State Department. Tai, law professor at the University of Hong Kong and co-founder of Hong Kong Occupy Central, worked with the Hong Kong University Centre for Comparative and Public Law, which receives grants from the NED subsidiary, National Democratic Institute, for projects like Design Democracy Hong Kong. The Centre Annual Report states, "With funding assistance from the National Democratic Institute, the Design Democracy Hong Kong website was built to promote a lawful and constructive bottom-up approach to constitutional and political reform in Hong Kong."[371] On its own website, NDI describes its years-long Hong Kong law project, the legal backdrop to the Occupy demands which essentially would open the door for a US-picked government in Hong Kong, just as Victoria Nuland hand-picked a US-loyal coup regime in Ukraine in February 2014. The NDI boasts,

> The Centre for Comparative and Public Law (CCPL) at the University of Hong Kong, with support from NDI, is working to amplify citizens' voices in that consultation process by creating Design Democracy Hong Kong (www.designdemocracy.hk), a unique and neutral website that gives citizens a place to discuss the future of Hong Kong's electoral system.[372]

The Hong Kong *wunderkind* of the Color Revolution Washington destabilization, 17-year-old student, Joshua Wong, founded a Facebook site called *Scholarism* when he was 15, with support from Washington's neo-conservative National Endowment for Democracy via its left branch, National Democratic Institute and NDI's *NDItech* project.[373] And another Occupy Central leading figure, Audrey Eu Yuet-mee, recently met with Vice President Joe Biden.[374]

Cardinal Zen and cardinal sin…

Less visible in the mainstream media but identified as one of the key organizers of Occupy Central was Catholic Cardinal Emeritus

Joseph Zen Ze-kiun, the sixth bishop of Hong Kong, a perennial thorn in the side of the Chinese authorities. Cardinal Zen, a veteran protestor though in his 80's, was playing a key role in the US-financed protests against Beijing's authority.[375] Cardinal Zen also happened to be the primary Vatican adviser on China policy. It looked as though the first Jesuit Pope in history, Pope Francis, was making a US-financed retry at the mission of Society of Jesus founder (and, incidentally, the Pope's real namesake) Francis Xavier, to subvert and take over the Peoples' Republic of China, using Hong Kong as the Achilles Heel.

Vice President Joe Biden, whose own hands were soaked with the blood of thousands of eastern Ukraine victims of the neo-nazi civil war; Cardinal Zen; Reverend Chu; Joshua Wong; Benny Tai and the neo-conservative NED and its NDI and a bevy of other State Department assets and NGO's too numerous to name here, ignited a full-blown Color Revolution aimed to target China – the Umbrella Revolution. The timing of the action, a full two years before the Hong Kong 2017 elections, suggested that some people in Washington and elsewhere in the West were getting nervous.

The growing Eurasian economic space of China in conjunction with Putin's Russia and their guiding role in creating a peaceful and very effective counter-pole to Washington's New World (dis-) Order, acting through organizations such as the Shanghai Cooperation Organization and BRICS, was the real target of their Occupy disorders. That was really quite stupid of them, but then, they are fundamentally stupid people who despise intelligence, and who fail to see the connections of their actions to the global totality.

– F. William Engdahl, October 6, 2014

Endnotes

[1] http://www.worldsecuritynetwork.com/China/Erich-Marquardt-and-Yevgeny-Bendersky-/The-Significance-of-Sino-Russian-Military-Exercises

[2] Paul Bowles and Wang Baotai, "China-US Economic Tensions Expected to Endure," *China Daily*, February 27, 2007, http://www.china.org.cn/english/international/200895.htm

[3] Andrew Leung, "Currency War and the RMB: Monetary Policy, Imbalances, and the Global Reserve Currency System," http://www.andrewleunginternationalconsultants.com/files/currency-war-and-the-rmb.pdf

[4] Ibid.

[5] Paul Bowles et al, *op. cit.*

[6] For details on the 1973 US dollar manipulation and oil shock see F. William Engdahl, *A Century of War: Anglo-American Oil Politics and the New World Order*, edition.engdahl, Wiesbaden, 2010.

[7] Ibid.

[8] Ibid.

[9] "China's Leader Says He Is 'Worried' Over U.S. Treasuries," *New York Times*, 13 March 2009, http://www.nytimes.com/2009/03/14/business/worldbusiness/14china.html

[10] Andrew Leung, *op. cit.*

[11] Ibid.

[12] "US Presses China on Value of Its Currency," *Bloomberg News*, May 3, 2012.

[13] Keith Bradsher, "China Lets Currency Weaken Risking New Trade Tensions," *New York Times*, May 31, 2012, http://www.nytimes.com/2012/06/01/business/global/china-lets-its-currency-slip-raising-trade-tension.html.

[14] Peter Pham, "ASEAN and Looming Currency Wars," April 30, 2012, http://beta.fool.com/peterpham8/2012/04/30/asean-and-looming-currency-wars/4083/

[15] *United Press International*, "Sudan says oil discovered in impoverished Darfur," http://sudanwatch.blogspot.de/2005/04/sudan-says-oil-discovered-in.html.

[16] F. William Engdahl, "China and USA in New Cold War over Africa's Oil Riches: Darfur? It's the Oil, Stupid...", *GlobalResearch*, May 20, 2007, http://www.globalresearch.ca/index.php?context=va&aid=5714

[17] Ibid.

[18] Ibid.

[19] Ibid.

[20] Ibid.

[21] Ibid.

22 John Cherian, "Scramble for Africa," *Frontline: India's National Magazine*, Volume 28 , Issue 23, Nov. 05-18, 2011.

23 Aly-Khan Satchu , "South Sudan's oil cutoff: brilliant negotiating or suicide?" *Christian Science Monitor*, January 30, 2012, http://www.csmonitor.com/World/Africa/Africa-Monitor/2012/0130/South-Sudan-s-oil-cutoff-brilliant-negotiating-or-suicide.

24 *Sudan Tribune*, "UN officials hold heated discussion about UNAMID movement," June 14, 2012, http://www.sudantribune.com/spip.php?iframe&page=imprimable&id_article=42920.

25 AFRICOM, "US Africa Command Fact Sheet", September 2, 2010, http://www.africom.mil/fetchBinary.asp?pdfID=20101109171627

26 Ibid.

27 F. William Engdahl, "NATO's War on Libya is Directed against China: AFRICOM and the Threat to China's National Energy Security," September 26, 2011, http://libyaagainstsuperpowermedia.com/2011/09/26/natos-war-on-libya-is-directed-against-china-africom-and-the-threat-to-chinas-national-energy-security/

28 F. William Engdahl, Nov. 25, 2008, "AFRICOM, China and Congo Resource Wars," http://www.oilgeopolitics.net

29 "China's copper deal back in the melt," June 12, 2009, http://www.atimes.com/atimes/China_Business/KF12Cb02.html

30 "China - DRC Sicomines deal back on track," Aug. 4, 2014, http://www.theafricareport.com/

31 *Xinhua*, "China-Chad joint oil refinery starts operating," July 1, 2011, http://english.peopledaily.com.cn/90001/90776/90883/7426213.html. *BBC News*, "Chad pipeline threatens villages," October 9, 2009, http://news.bbc.co.uk/2/hi/8298525.stm.

32 F. William Engdahl, *op. cit.*

33 F. William Engdahl, "The Yemen Hidden Agenda: Behind the Al-Qaeda Scenarios, A Strategic Oil Transit Chokepoint," *Global Research*, January 5, 2010.

34 Ibid. This section is reproduced from the above cited article by the author.

35 Ibid. Cited in *Terrorism Monitor*, "Yemen President Accuses Iraq's Sadrists of Backing the Houthi Insurgency," Jamestown Foundation, Volume: 7 Issue: 28, September 17, 2009.

36 Ibid. Cited in *Yemen Observer*, September 10, 2009.

37 US Department of Energy, Energy Information Administration, "Bab el-Mandab," http://www.eia.doe.gov/cabs/World_Oil_Transit_Chokepoints/Full.html.

38 F. Wm. Engdahl, "Myanmar's "Saffron Revolution": The Geopolitics behind the Protest Movement," Oct. 15, 2007 http://www.globalresearch.ca/

39 Ibid.

40 Ibid.

41 Ibid.

42 Ibid.

43 Ibid.

44 Ibid.

45 Ibid.

46 Ibid.

47 Ibid. This section reproduced from the article by the author.

48 Ibid. This section on India reproduced from "Myanmar's "Saffron Revolution" by the author.

49 Ibid.

50 This section on Tibet is reproduced from the author's article "Risky Geopolitical Game: Washington Plays 'Tibet Roulette' with China"

51 "Ex-Nazi, Dalai's tutor Harrer dies at 93," *The Times of India*, 9 Jan 2006, in http://timesofindia.indiatimes.com/articleshow/msid-1363946,prtpage-1.cms.

52 Nicholas Goodrick-Clarke, *Black Sun: Aryan Cults, Esoteric Nazism and the Politics of Identity*, New York University Press, 2001, p. 177.

53 Colin Goldner, "Mönchischer Terror auf dem Dach der Welt Teil 1: Die Begeisterung für den Dalai Lama und den tibetischen Buddhismus," March 26, 2008, excerpted from the book *Dalai Lama: Fall eines Gottkönigs*, Alibri Verlag, April 2008, reproduced in http://www.jungewelt.de/2008/03-27/006.php.

54 Michael Parenti, "Friendly Feudalism: The Tibet Myth," June 2007, in www.michaelparenti.org/Tibet.html.

55 Ibid.

56 Jim Mann, "CIA funded covert Tibet exile campaign in 1960s," *The Age* (Australia), Sept. 16, 1998.

57 David Ignatius, "Innocence Abroad: The New World of Spyless Coups," The Washington Post, 22 September 1991.

58 William Blum, "The NED and 'Project Democracy,'" January 2000, in www.friendsoftibet.org/databank/usdefence/usd5.html

59 Michael Barker, "'Democratic Imperialism': Tibet, China and the National Endowment for Democracy," *Global Research*, August 13, 2007, www.globalresearch.ca.

60 Ralph McGehee, Ralph McGehee' s Archive on JFK Place, "CIA Operations in China Part III," May 2, 1996, in www.acorn.net/jfkplace/03/RM/RM.china-for.

61 US Tibet Committee, "Fifteen things you should know about Tibet and China," in http://ustibetcommittee.org/facts/facts.html.

62 Colin Goldner, "Mönchischer Terror auf dem Dach der Welt Teil 2: Krawalle im Vorfeld der Olympischen Spiele," *op cit.*

63 Jonathan Mowat, "The new Gladio in action?", *Online Journal*, March 19, 2005

64 Ibid.

65 Ibid.

66 Zbigniew Brzezinski, "A Geostrategy for Eurasia," *Foreign Affairs*, 76:5, September/October 1997.

[67] F. William Engdahl, "Washington is Playing a Deeper Game with China," July 12, 2009, http://www.globalresearch.ca/index.php?context=va&aid=14327.

[68] Ibid.

[69] Ibid.

[70] Ibid.

[71] Catherine T. Yang, "China Drills Into Shale Gas, Targeting Huge Reserves Amid Challenges," *National Geographic News*, August 8, 2012, http://news.nationalgeographic.com/news/energy/2012/08/120808-china-shale-gas/.

[72] Ibid.

[73] Ibid.

[74] Ibid.

[75] Ibid.

[76] *Trefis*, "Can ConocoPhillips Help China Tap Its Shale Gas Reserves?", September 18, 2012, http://www.trefis.com/stock/cop/articles/144078/can-conocophillips-help-china-tap-its-shale-gas-reserves/2012-09-18.

[77] Vello Kuuskraa, et al, "World Shale Gas Resources: An Initial Assessment of 14 Regions Outside the United States," Advanced Resources International, Inc., prepared for US Energy Information Administration, Office of Energy Analysis, US Department of Energy, Washington, DC, April, 2011.

[78] *Earthworks*, "The Halliburton Loophole," http://www.earthworksaction.org/issues/detail/inadequate_regulation_of_hydraulic_fracturing

[79] Ibid.

[80] Lisa Sumi, "Our Drinking Water at Risk: What EPA and the Oil and Gas Industry Don't Want Us to Know About Hydraulic Fracturing," April 7, 2005, http://www.earthworksaction.org/files/publications/DrinkingWaterAtRisk.pdf

[81] Ibid.

[82] John Deutch, quoted in "Shale Gas Has Challenges But Study Group Holds Out Hope," November 18, 2012, http://globalresourcesnews.com/getp.php?needle=deutchshale

[83] Ibid.

[84] Bill Mckibben, "Why Not Frack?", *The New York Review of Books*, March 8, 2012, http://www.nybooks.com/articles/archives/2012/mar/08/why-not-frack/?pagination=false&printpage=true.

[85] Cited in "Water Contamination from Shale Gas Drilling," http://www.water-contamination-from-shale.com/

[86] Ibid.

[87] Abrahm Lustgarten, "New Study Predicts Frack Fluids Can Migrate to Aquifers Within Years," May 2, 2012, http://www.commondreams.org/headline/2012/05/02-3.

88 Ibid.

89 *BBC News*, "Fracking water pollution in Lancashire 'extremely unlikely,'" http://www.bbc.co.uk/news/uk-england-lancashire-16494766.

90 John Daly, "UK Government Seismic Fracking Report Certain to Sharpen Debate," 20 April 2012, http://oilprice.com/Energy/Energy-General/UK-Govt.-Seismic-Fracking-Report-Certain-to-Sharpen-Debate.html

91 Marianne Lavelle, "Tracing Links Between Fracking and Earthquakes," *National Geographic*, January 4, 2012, http://www.greatenergychallengeblog.com/2012/01/04/tracing-links-between-fracking-and-earthquakes/

92 Ibid.

93 Amber Moore, "Chinese Children Facing Diabetes Epidemic," July 06, 2012

94 Carla Sharetto, "Study Exposes Fast Food Health Dangers," *The Lancet*, 31 December, 2004, http://www.eurekalert.org/pub_releases/2004-12/uom-1ss123004.php

95 Ibid.

96 Ibid.

97 Andrea Bennett, "Can Fast Food Change Your Brain?", January 20, 2012, http://responsibility-project.libertymutual.com/blog/can-fast-food-change-your-brain

98 Ibid.

99 Joshua P. Thaler, Chun-Xia Yi, et al, "Obesity is associated with hypothalamic injury in rodents and humans," *Journal of Clinical Investigation*, Volume 122, Issue 1 (January 3, 2012)

100 Wendy Brundige and Eric Noll, "The Science of Food Cravings," *ABC News*, November 14, 2009, http://abcnews.go.com/GMA/Weekend/junk-food-addictive-illegal-drugs/story

101 Graeme J. Sills, PhD, "Glutamic acid (glutamate): An amino acid that is a particularly potent nerve cell killer," *Epilepsy Currents*, Vol. 6, No. 1 (January/February) 2006 pp. 6-7.

102 "Ajinomoto Group History," http://www.ajinomoto.com/about/history/1990_1999.html

103 Aspartame and Nutrasweet Toxicity Info Center, "Toxicity Effects of Aspartame Use," http://www.holisticmed.com/aspartame/

104 "Michael R. Taylor," *Wikipedia*, http://en.wikipedia.org/wiki/Michael_R._Taylor

105 F. William Engdahl, *Seeds of Destruction: The Hidden Agenda of Genetic Manipulation*, Global Research, 2007, p. 153.

106 Ibid. p.153 ff.

107 Ibid., pp. 160-166.

108 Ibid.

109 Ibid.

[110] Maria Domnitskaya, "Russia says genetically modified foods are harmful," April 16, 2010, http://english.ruvr.ru/2010/04/16/6524765.html

[111] Ibid.

[112] Tony C. Dreibus, "China Soybean Imports to Jump by 14% on Demand", February 21, 2012, http://www.bloomberg.com/news/2012-02-21/china-soybean-imports-to-jump-by-14-on-demand-oil-world-says.html

[113] Zhou Siyu, "Soybean imports from US to decline", *China Daily*, July 6, 2012, http://www.chinadaily.com.cn/bizchina/2012-06/07/content_15481765.htm .

[114] F. William Engdahl, *op. cit.*, pp. 216-227.

[115] Boris Cambreleng, "GM rice spreads, prompts debate in China," *AFP*, June 15, 2011

[116] Zhang-Liang Chen and Li-Jia Qu, "The Status of Agriculture Biotechnology in China: Two strains of GM rice were approved for open-field trials", Peking University, Beijing 100871, P. R. China

[117] Boris Cambreleng, *op. cit.*

[118] Ibid.

[119] F. William Engdahl, "The GMO Dangers in Rice Varieties: The Strategic Context of GMO Agriculture – The fraud of 'substantial equivalence'," unpublished research report, May 1, 2007.

[120] Ibid.

[121] Ibid.

[122] Ibid.

[123] GRAIN, "USAID in Africa: 'For the American Corporations'," *Seedling*, 24 April 2005, http://www.grain.org/article/entries/493-usaid-in-africa-for-the-american-corporations

[124] F. William Engdahl, "The GMO Dangers...", *op. cit.*

[125] *Reuters*, "End of the line: GMO production in China halted," August 21, 2014, http://rt.com/news/181860-gm-china-rice-stopped/

[126] Ibid.

[127] Jacob Bunge, "US Corn Exports to China Dry Up Over GMO Concerns," April 11, 2014, *Wall Street Journal*, http://online.wsj.com/news/articles/SB10001424052702303873604579493790405023808

[128] Ibid.

[129] Ibid.

[130] Ibid.

[131] Ibid.

[132] Ibid.

[133] Ibid.

[134] F. William Engdahl, "Monsanto Buys 'Terminator' Seeds Company," *Global Research*, August 27, 2006, http://www.globalresearch.ca/index.php?context=va&aid=3082

[135] Ibid.

[136] Ibid.

137 Ibid.

138 Gilles-Eric Seralini, et al., "Long term toxicity of a Roundup herbicide and a Roundup tolerant genetically modified maize," *Journal of Food and Chemical Toxicology*, 19 September, 2012, http://www.sciencedirect.com/science/article/pii/S0278691512005637#F CANote

139 *Food Product Design*, "Russia Bans Monsanto GM Corn Over Food-Safety Concerns," September 26, 2012, http://www.foodproductdesign.com/news/2012/09/russia-bans-monsanto-gm-corn-over-food-safety-con.aspx

140 Ibid.

141 Ibid.

142 Dirk Brändli and Sandra Reinacher, "Herbicides found in Human Urine," *Ithaka Journal*, 1 | 2012: 270-272 | ISSN 1663-0521, http://www.ithaka-journal.net/druckversionen/e052012-herbicides-urine.pdf.

143 Ibid.

144 Rady Ananda, "Genetic Engineering Scientists warn of link between dangerous new pathogen and Monsanto's Roundup," *Global Research*, February 21, 2011, http://www.globalresearch.ca/index.php?context=va&aid=23303.

145 Rady Ananda, "Genetic Engineering Scientists warn of link between dangerous new pathogen and Monsanto's Roundup," *Global Research*, February 21, 2011, http://www.globalresearch.ca/index.php?context=va&aid=23303

146 Ibid.

147 Ibid.

148 Ibid.

149 Carey Gillam, "Roundup ingredient glyphosate found in water, air," *Reuters*, August 31, 2011.

150 J.S. de Vendômois JS, et al, "A Comparison of the Effects of Three GM Corn Varieties on Mammalian Health," *International Journal of Biological Sciences*, 2009; 5(7):706-726. http://www.biolsci.org/v05p0706.htm.

151 Andrés Carrasco, "Michael Antoniou, et al, GM Soy: Sustainable? Responsible?", *GM Watch*, 13 September, 2010, http://www.gmwatch.org/reports/12479-gm_soy_sustainable_responsible_report.

152 Ibid.

153 Rady Ananda, *op. cit.*

154 F. William Engdahl, "Monsanto Herbicide Deadly to Human Cells," 26 June 2009.

155 Ibid.

156 Amy Dean, D.O. and Jennifer Armstrong, M.D. , "Genetically Modified Foods," American Academy of Environmental Medicine, May 8, 2009, http://www.aaemonline.org/gmopost.html

157 Ibid.

158 The sections "Death of Birds and the Bees" through "Banned in Many EU Countries" are reproduced from the author's article "Death of the Birds and the Bees Across America," July 1, 2012,

http://www.globalresearch.ca/death-of-the-birds-and-the-bees-across-america/31699

159 AgroPages.com, Neonicotinoid Insecticides Insight, http://www.agropages.com/BuyersGuide/category/Neonicotinoid-Insecticide-Insight.html

160 Ibid.

161 Anon. Neo-nicotinoids, http://beesalive.com/honey-bee-deaths/neo-nicotinoids/

162 Foreign Trade Department, "China Crop Protection Industry Association Delegates Visited Japan for the Second Time," January 30, 2012, http://en.sdupi.com/

163 Coalition against BAYER Dangers (Germany), "Countermotion to shareholder meeting: BAYER Pesticides causing bee decline," Press Release, April 11, 2012.

164 F. William Engdahl, "Scary Facts about Birds and the Bees and Bayer AG," July 1, 2012, http://www.veteranstoday.com/2012/07/01/214009/

165 Louise Gray, "Beekeepers lose one fifth of hives," 24 August, 2009, *The Telegraph*, http://www.telegraph.co.uk/earth/earthnews/6069218/Beekeepers-lose-one-fifth-of-hives.html

166 Anon., "Clothianidin a Neonicotinoid Pesticide Highly Toxic to Honeybees and other pollinators," March 20, 2007, http://www.theenvironmentalblog.org/2007/03/clothianidin-a-neonicotinoid-pesticide-highly-toxic-to-honeybees-and-other-pollinators/

167 Ibid.

168 Ibid.

169 Ibid.

170 Michael McCarthy, "Government to reconsider nerve agent pesticides," *The Independent*, 31 March 2012, http://www.independent.co.uk/environment/nature/government-to-reconsider-nerve-agent-pesticides-7604121.html

171 Henk Tennekes, "They've turned the Environment into the Experiment and WE are all the Experimental Subjects," January 19, 2011, http://www.boerenlandvogels.nl.

172 Ibid.

173 Ibid.

174 Jeffrey S. Pettis, et al, "Pesticide exposure in honey bees results in increased levels of the gut pathogen Nosema," *Naturwissenschaften-The Science of Nature*, 13 January, 2012, http://www.springerlink.com/content/p1027164r403288u/fulltext.html

175 Henk Tennekes, "Honey Bees Living Near Maize Fields Are Exposed To Neonicotinoids Throughout The Growing Season," January 5, 2012, http://www.farmlandbirds.net/en/taxonomy/term/3.

176 Henk Tennekes, "Prenatal exposures to pesticides may increase the risk of neurological disease later in life," March 20, 2012, http://www.farmlandbirds.net/en/content/prenatal-exposures-pesticides-may-increase-risk-neurological-disease-later-life

177 Henk Tennekes, "The neonicotinoids may adversely affect human health, especially the developing brain," March 20, 2012, http://www.farmlandbirds.net/en/taxonomy/term/

178 Brian Moench, "Autism and Disappearing Bees: A Common Denominator?", April 2, 2012, *Common Dreams*, http://www.commondreams.org/view/2012/04/02.

179 Coalition against BAYER Dangers (Germany), *op. cit.*

180 Richard Askwith, "How aspirin turned hero: A hundred years ago Heinrich Dreser made a fortune from the discovery of heroin and aspirin," Sunday Times, 13 September 1998, http://opioids.com/heroin/heroinhistory.html.

181 Coalition against BAYER Dangers (Germany), op cit.

182 *ENS*, "German Coalition Sues Bayer Over Pesticide Honey Bee Deaths," August 25, 2008, http://www.ens-newswire.com/ens/aug2008/2008-08-25-01.asp

183 Roberta Cruger, "Nicotine Bees Population Restored With Neonicotinoids Ban," May 15, 2010, http://www.treehugger.com/clean-technology/nicotine-bees-population-restored-with-neonicotinoids-ban.html .

184 Henk Tennekes, "EU response to bee death pesticide link questioned," April 24, 2012, http://www.farmlandbirds.net/en/taxonomy/term/3 .

185 Olivier Hoedeman, *Corporate Europe Observatory*, "Open letter regarding conflicts of interest EFSA's Management board," Brussels, March 4, 2011, http://www.corporateeurope.org

186 Andrew Olsen, "Chemical Cartel," June 28, 2010; see also, F. William Engdahl, *Seeds of Destruction: The Hidden Agenda of Genetic Manipulation.*

187 Henk Tennekes, "Imidacloprid and Colony Collapse Disorder – Scientists Call for Global Ban on Bee-Killing Pesticides," April 5, 2012, http://www.farmlandbirds.net/en/taxonomy/term/3.

188 Aldous Huxley, speech before Tavistock Group, California Medical School, 1961, http://modernhistoryproject.org/mhp?Article=Quotes

189 Burton Hersh, *The Old Boys- The American Elite & The Origins of the CIA*, page 41.

190 Tavistock Agenda, "In The Shadow of the Counterculture Revolution: Radical Change & Counterculture: Huxley, Esalen & Human Potential Movement," http://tavistockagenda.iwarp.com/whats_new_43.html

191 A.D.A.M. Medical Encyclopedia, "Attention deficit hyperactivity disorder (ADHD); ADD; ADHD; Childhood hyperkinesis," March 25, 2012, http://www.ncbi.nlm.nih.gov/pubmedhealth/PMH0002518/.

192 Mitch Moxley, "China: Wave Of Anger Rises Over Vaccine Scandal," *IPS*, April 6, 2010.

193 Ginger Taylor, "Gardasil Injury Victims Hold Press Conference at the GOP Debate," October 17, 2011, http://www.naturalnews.com/033899_gardasil_injury_victims.html.

194 Eustace Mullins, *Murder by Injection: The Story of the Medical Conspiracy Against America*, National Council for Medical Research,

Staunton, Virginia, http://www.bibliotecapleyades.net/archivos_pdf/murderinjection.pdf.

195 Ibid.

196 Ethan A. Huff, "Study: Polio vaccine campaign in India has caused 12-fold increase in deadly paralysis condition," *NaturalNews*, April 17, 2012, www.naturalnews.com/035588_polio_vaccine_India_paralysis.html

197 Ibid.

198 Ibid.

199 Ibid.

200 F. William Engdahl, "Secret Good Club holds first meeting in New York," 2 June 2009, www.engdahl.oilgeopolitics.net

201 F. William Engdahl, Bill Gates in video talks about vaccines to reduce population, 25 February 2010, www.engdahl.oilgeopolitics.net

202 P.H. Duesberg, *Inventing the AIDS Virus*, Washington, DC, Regnery Publishing, 1996.

203 Robert Herron, "Why are the NSC and CIA Managing America's Global Campaign Against Aids?", October, 2001, http://www.virusmyth.com/aids/hiv/rhaids.htm

204 John C. Gannon, et al, "The Global Infectious Disease Threat and Its Implications for the United States," NIE 99-17D, January 2000, http://www.fas.org/irp/threat/nie99-17d.htm

205 Robert Herron, *op. cit.*

206 Ibid.

207 Ibid.

208 Ibid.

209 Cited in "Rethinking AIDS," http://www.virusmyth.com/aids/controversy.htm.

210 http://www.rethinkingaids.com, "Rethinking AIDS (RA) History"

211 S. Krimsky, "Biotechnology Regulation," *Science*, 17 February 1995: 945.DOI:10.1126/science.7863335.

212 http://www.rethinkingaids.com, "Rethinking AIDS (RA) History"

213 D.T. Chiu, P.H. Duesberg, "The toxicity of azidothymidine (AZT) on human and animal cells in culture at concentrations used for antiviral therapy," *Genetica* 1995; 95: 103-109.

214 P.H. Duesberg & D. Rasnick, "The AIDS dilemma: drug diseases blamed on a passenger virus," *Genetica* 1998; 104: 85-132.

215 Anthony Gucciardi, "Follow the Trend: Batman Shooter James Holmes Was On Hardcore Pharmaceutical Drugs," July 23, 2012, http://naturalsociety.com/batman-shooter-james-holmes-on-pharmaceutical-drugs.

216 Ibid.

217 Anthony Gucciardi, "Asthma Drugs Kill More than Asthma, FDA Ignores Risk," November 17, 2011, http://naturalsociety.com/asthma-drugs-kill-more-than-asthma-fda-ignores-risk/

218 Ibid.

[219] The Vaccine Initiative, "Margaret Chan Continues to Deny WHO Incompetence Behind the Pandemic-That-Never-Was," October 4, 2010, http://www.vaccineinitiative.org/?p=206.

[220] F. William Engdahl, "The WHO Plays with Pandemic Fire: The Continuing Saga of the Flying Pigs Pandemic Flu," *Global Research*, June 5, 2009, http://www.globalresearch.ca/index.php?context=va&aid=13856.

[221] Chelsea Schilling, "How U.N. redefined 'pandemic' to heighten alarm over H1N1: World Health Organization quietly changed qualification of term in case of 'swine flu'," November 12, 2009, *WorldNetDaily*, http://www.wnd.com/2009/11/115719/

[222] Ibid.

[223] F. William Engdahl, "Now legal immunity for swine flu vaccine makers," *Global Research*, July 19, 2009, http://www.globalresearch.ca/index.php?context=va&aid=14487.

[224] Ibid.

[225] Ibid.

[226] *The Daily Mail*, "Drug firms drove swine flu pandemic warning to recoup £billions spent on research," 27 January 2010, http://www.dailymail.co.uk/news/article-1246370/Drug-firms-drove-swine-flu-pandemic-warning-recoup-billions-spent-research.html

[227] Jon Rappoport, "CDC whistleblower Thompson in grave danger now," August 21, 2014, http://jonrappoport.wordpress.com/2014/08/22/breaking-cdc-whistleblower-thompson-in-grave-danger-now/.

[228] GMI Reporter, "Whistleblower Names CDC Scientists In Covering Up Vaccine Autism Link," August 20, 2014, http://www.activistpost.com/2014/08/whistleblower-names-cdc-scientists-in.html.

[229] Jon Rappoport, *op. cit.*

[230] Ibid.

[231] Harris Coulter PhD, Medical Historian, cited in http://www.vaccinesuncensored.org/autism.php

[232] Sharyl Attkisson, "How Independent Are Vaccine Defenders?", *CBS News*, July 25, 2008, http://www.cbsnews.com/news/how-independent-are-vaccine-defenders/.

[233] Sharyl Attkisson, "Vaccines and autism: a new scientific review," *CBS/I*, *CBS News*, April 1, 2011, http://www.cbsnews.com/news/vaccines-and-autism-a-new-scientific-review/

[234] Jon Rappoport, *op. cit.*

[235] He Na, "Families struggle to cope with autistic children," *China Daily*, 21 November, 2011, http://usa.chinadaily.com.cn/china/2011-11/21/content_14128634.htm

[236] Francis Collins, Witness appearing before the House Subcommittee on Labor-HHS-Education Appropriations, April 6, 2006, http://www.genome.gov/18016846

[237] He Na, *op. cit.*

238 Sanjay Gupta, "Unraveling the Mystery of Autism; Talking With the CDC Director," *CNN*, March 29, 2008, http://transcripts.cnn.com/TRANSCRIPTS/0803/29/hcsg.01.html

239 *Wikipedia*, "MMR Vaccine," http://en.wikipedia.org/wiki/MMR_vaccine

240 Walter A. Orenstein, M.D. US Assistant Surgeon General, Director National Immunization Program, in a letter to the UK's Chief Medical Officer 15 February 2002, cited in http://sanevax.org/vaccination-causes-autism-say-us-government-mercks-director-of-vaccines/

241 Mark Rockwell, "Ten million H1NI flu vaccines produced in one month, says DARPA," July 27, 2012, *GSN: Government Security News*, http://www.gsnmagazine.com/aboutgsn/history.

242 "Ivan Fraser and Mark Beeston, The Pharmaceutical Racket," http://educate-yourself.org/nwo/brotherhoodpart9.shtml

243 Ibid.

244 Eustace Mullins, *op. cit.*, p. 136.

245 *Wikipedia*, "List of pharmaceutical companies," http://en.wikipedia.org/wiki/List_of_pharmaceutical_companies

246 Winslow Wheeler, "The Military Imbalance: How The US Outspends the World," March 16, 2012, http://www.iiss.org/publications/military-balance/the-military-balance-2012/press-statement/figure-comparative-defence-statistics/.

247 Ibid.

248 F. William Engdahl, *Full Spectrum Dominance: Totalitarian Democracy in the New World Order*, 2010, edition.engdahl, Wiesbaden.

249 President Barack Obama, "Remarks By President Obama to the Australian Parliament," November 17, 2011, http://www.whitehouse.gov/the-press-office/2011/11/17/remarks-president-obama-australian-parliament.

250 Ibid.

251 Otto Kreisher, "UK Defense Chief to NATO: Pull Your Weight in Europe While US Handles China," July 22, 2012, http://defense.aol.com/2012/07/19/uk-defense-chief-to-nato-pull-your-weight-in-europe-while-us-ha/.

252 *BBC*, "China military 'closing key gaps', says Pentagon," 25 August 2011, http://www.bbc.co.uk/news/world-asia-pacific-14661027.

253 Ibid.

254 Greg Jaffe , "US Model for a Future War Fans Tensions with China and inside Pentagon," *Washington Post*, August 2, 2012, http://www.turkishweekly.net/news/139681/us-model-for-a-future-war-fans-tensions-with-china-and-inside-pentagon.html.

255 Erik Slavin, "Analysts: Air-Sea Battle concept carries risks in possible conflict with China," *Stars & Stripes*, September 28, 2014, http://www.stripes.com/news/analysts-air-sea-battle-concept-carries-risks-in-possible-conflict-with-china-1.305505

256 Matt Siegel, "As Part of Pact, U.S. Marines Arrive in Australia, in China's Strategic Backyard," *The New York Times*, April 4, 2012, http://www.nytimes.com/2012/04/05/world/asia/us-marines-arrive-darwin-australia.html.

257 Greg Jaffe, *op. cit.*

258 F. William Engdahl, *Full Spectrum Dominance: Totalitarian Democracy in the New World Orde*r, Wiesbaden, 2009, edition.engdahl, p. 190.

259 Ibid., p. 190.

260 US-China Economic Security and Review Commission, *2005 Report to Congress of the US-China Economic and Security Review Commission*, US Government Printing Office, Washington, DC, November 2005, http://www.uscc.gov/annual_report/2005/annual_report_full_05.pdf, pp. 115, 118.

261 Ibid., p. 120.

262 *The Washington Times*, "China Builds up Strategic Sea Lanes," January 17, 2005, http://www.washingtontimes.com/news/2005/jan/17/20050117-115550-1929r.

263 Ibid.

264 Ibid.

265 *Wall Street Journal*, "An Opening in Burma: The regime's tentative liberalization is worth testing for sincerity," November 22, 2011, http://online.wsj.com

266 *Radio Free Asia*, "US to Invest in Burma's Oil," 7 November, 2011, http://www.rfa.org/english/news/burma/sanctions-07112012185817.html

267 Shaun Tandon, "US eases Myanmar restrictions for NGOs," *AFP*, April 17, 2012

268 http://www.eastasiaforum.org/2014/06/18/china-is-a-big-winner-from-thailands-coup/

269 http://www.bangkokpost.com/most-recent/429285/u-tapao-prepares-for-take-off

270 Craig Whitlock, U.S. eyes return to some Southeast Asia military bases, Washington Post, June 23, 2012, http://www.washingtonpost.com/world/national-security/us-seeks-return-to-se-asian-bases/2012/06/22/gJQAKP83vV_story.html

271 http://csis.org/publication/secretary-defense-leon-panetta-visits-australia-thailand-and-cambodia.

272 http://www.stripes.com/news/pacific/us-deploys-first-advanced-drones-to-japan-1.286185

273 *Zeenews*, "US-India ties are global in scope: Pentagon," August 02, 2012, http://zeenews.india.com/news/world/us-india-ties-are-global-in-scope-pentagon_791212.html

274 Ibid.

275 Gregoire Lalieu, Michael Collon, "Is the Fate of the World Being Decided Today in the Indian Ocean?", November 3, 2010,

http://dissidentvoice.org/2010/11/is-the-fate-of-the-world-being-decided-today-in-the-indian-ocean/

276 Zbigniew Brzezinski, *The Grand Chessboard: American Primacy and Its Geostrategic Imperatives*, 1997, Basic Books, p. xiv.

277 Ibid., p. 30.

278 Ibid., p. 31.

279 Cas Group, "Background on the South China Sea Crisis," http://casgroup.fiu.edu/pages/docs/3907/1326143354_South_China_Sea_Guide.pdf

280 Ibid.

281 *GlobalSecurity.org*, "South China Sea Oil and Natural Gas," http://www.globalsecurity.org/military/world/war/spratly-oil.htm

282 *Agence France Presse*, "US, Vietnam Start Military Relationship," August 1, 2011, http://www.defensenews.com/article/20110801/DEFSECT03/108010307/U-S-Vietnam-Start-Military-Relationship

283 Zacks Equity Research, "Oil Majors Eye South China Sea," June 24, 2010, www.zacks.com/stock/news/36056/Oil+Majors+Eye+South.

284 PRC General Administration of Customs, *China's Customs Statistics*, Beijing, 2009.

285 Sam Hornblower, "Walmart and China: A Joint Venture," http://www.pbs.org/wgbh/pages/frontline/shows/walmart/secrets/wmchina.html

286 F. William Engdahl, "Monsanto Buys 'Terminator' Seeds Company," *Global Research*, Montreal, August 27, 2006, http://www.globalresearch.ca/index.php?context=va&aid=3082.

287 Ibid.

288 Ibid.

289 Ibid.

290 Ibid.

291 Richard A. McCormack, "China's Entry Into The WTO 10 Years Later Is Not What President Clinton Promised," *Manufacturing & Technology News*, June 15, 2010, Volume 17, No. 10, http://www.manufacturingnews.com/news/10/0615/WTO.html.

292 Thierry Baudet, *The Significance of Borders*, Brill, Leiden, 2012, pp. 127-138.

293 F. William Engdahl, *Seeds of Destruction: The Hidden Agenda of Genetic Manipulation*, Global Research.ca, 2007, pp. 221-227.

294 Ibid.

295 Bradley S. Clapper, "WTO Chief: U.S.-China Trade Friction Rising," January 21, 2010, http://www.huffingtonpost.com/2010/01/22/wto-chief-us-china-trade_n_432620.html

296 Hillary R. Clinton, "Statement on Google Operations in China," US State Department, Washington DC, January 12, 2010, http://www.state.gov/secretary/rm/2010/01/135105.htm.

297 Paul Joseph Watson, "Ex-Agent: CIA Seed Money Helped Launch Google. Steele goes further than before in detailing ties, names Google's

CIA liaison," *Prison Planet*, December 6, 2006, http://www.prisonplanet.com/articles/december2006/061206seedmoney.htm

[298]William McQuillen, "Chinese Distorting Policies Causing Trade Friction, U.S. Says," *Bloomberg*, December 13, 2011, http://www.bloomberg.com/news/2011-12-13/chinese-distorting-policies-causing-trade-friction-u-s-says.html.

[299] *Global Times*, "Show some bite in US solar trade frictions," May 19, 2012, http://www.globaltimes.cn/NEWS/tabid/99/ID/710249/Show-some-bite-in-US-solar-trade-frictions.aspx

[300] http://en.wikipedia.org/wiki/Anti-Counterfeiting_Trade_Agreement

[301] Ibid.

[302]Zack Whittaker, "'Last rites' for ACTA? Europe rejects antipiracy treaty," *CNet*, July 4, 2012, http://news.cnet.com/8301-13578_3-57466330-38/last-rites-for-acta-europe-rejects-antipiracy-treaty/.

[303] Ibid.

[304] Eddan Katz and Gwen Hinze, "The Impact of the Anti-Counterfeiting Trade Agreement on the Knowledge Economy: The Accountability of the Office of the U.S. Trade Representative for the Creation of IP Enforcement Norms through Executive Trade Agreements," *Yale Journal of International Law*, November 2009.

[305] *KEI*, "White House says ACTA text a State Secret. EU parliament says time for more transparency," March 12, 2009, http://keionline.org/blogs/2009/03/12/acta-state-secret

[306] *Wikipedia*, "Anti-Counterfeiting Trade Agreement (ACTA)," http://en.wikipedia.org/wiki/Anti-Counterfeiting_Trade_Agreement

[307] *TechDirt*, "Why The Chances of China Joining ACTA Or TPP Are Practically Zero," http://www.techdirt.com/articles/20120308/09284118036/why-chances-china-joining-acta-tpp-are-practically-zero.shtml

[308] *Out-Law.com*, "ACTA restricts developing economies, India tells WTO: Secret IP treaty not a sweetie," June 15, 2010, http://www.theregister.co.uk/2010/06/15/acta_wto/

[309] Wikipedia, *op. cit.*

[310] http://en.wikipedia.org/wiki/Doha_Declaration

[311] *Wikipedia*, "Anti-Counterfeiting Trade Agreement (ACTA)," http://en.wikipedia.org/wiki/Anti-Counterfeiting_Trade_Agreement

[312] *Slate.com*: "The TPP is The Most Important Trade Agreement That We Know Nothing About," https://openmedia.ca/blog/slatecom-tpp-most-important-trade-agreement-we-know-nothing-about

[313] http://en.wikipedia.org/wiki/Ron_Kirk

[314] David S. Levine, "The Most Important Trade Agreement That We Know Nothing About: The Trans-Pacific Partnership could completely change intellectual property law. But the details are being kept secret," July 30, 2012, http://www.slate.com/articles/technology/future_tense/2012/07/trans_pacific_partnership_agreement_tpp_could_radically_alter_intellectual_property_law.single.html.

315 *Wikipedia*, "Operation Mockingbird,"
http://en.wikipedia.org/wiki/Operation_Mockingbird#cite_note-2

316 Deborah Davis, *Katharine the Great: Katharine Graham and the Washington Post*, Harcourt Brace Jovanovich, 1979, pp. 137-138.

317 Ralph Peters, "Constant Conflict, Parameters," *US Army War College Quarterly*, Summer 1997, pp. 4-14, http://www.carlisle.army.mil/usawc/parameters/Articles/97summer/peters.htm.

318 Hillary Clinton, "Statement on Google Operations in China,: Secretary of State, Washington, DC, January 12, 2010,
http://www.state.gov/secretary/rm/2010/01/135105.htm.

319 Jessica Guynn and David Pierson, "China puts new limits on Google search results," Los Angeles Times, March 24, 2010, http://articles.latimes.com/2010/mar/24/business/la-fi-china-google24-2010mar24.

320 Paul Joseph Watson, "Ex-Agent: CIA Seed Money Helped Launch Google," Prison Planet, December 6, 2006, http://www.prisonplanet.com/articles/december2006/061206seedmoney.htm.

321 Steve Watson & Paul Watson, "Don't Be Evil: 10 Ways In Which Google Runs The World," Infowars.com, February 18, 2011, http://www.infowars.com/dont-be-evil-10-ways-in-which-google-runs-the-world/.

322 Ibid.

323 Ibid.

324 "Arab Spring is about controlling Eurasia," interview with the author on *Russia Today*, http://rt.com/news/arab-engdahl-us-africa-273/

325 Zbigniew Brzezinski, *The Grand Chessboard: American Primacy And Its Geostrategic Imperatives*, Basic Books, 1998.

326 Ibid., p. xiii.

327 Ibid., p. xiv.

328 Ibid., p. 31.

329 F. William Engdahl, *Full Spectrum Dominance: Totalitarian Democracy in the New World Order*, Wiesbaden, 2009, edition.engdahl, p. 162 ff.

330 Ibid.

331 "China dismisses reports about anti-satellite missile test," *Xinhua*, October 25, 2012

332 Andrew Jacobs and Jonathan Ansfield, "With Defense Test, China Shows Displeasure of U.S.", *The New York Times*, January 13, 2010

333 "DPRK bolsters missile capability to strike US force," *Xinhua*, October 11, 2012

334 Mahdi Darius Nazemroaya, "Military Encirclement and Global Domination: Russia Counters US Missile Shield from the Seas," *Global Research*, November 04, 2012, http://www.globalresearch.ca/russia-counters-the-us-missile-shield-from-the-seas/5310516

335 Ibid.

336 Ibid.

337 Ibid.

338 Ibid.

[339] Ibid.

[340] Gordon Duff, "Israel Loser of Any Anti-Iran Scenario," November 5, 2012, *Press TV*.

[341] Ibid.

[342] *Fars News Agency*, "Senior Analyst Underlines Iran's Geostrategic Importance to China," June 20, 2011.

[343] John W. Garver, *China and Iran: Ancient Partners in a Post-Imperial World*, Seattle: University of Washington Press, 2007, pp. 13-17;

[344] This chapter is reproduced from the author's original article, "Eurasian Economic Boom and Geopolitics: China's Land Bridge to Europe: The China-Turkey High Speed Railway," published April 27, 2012, on globalresearch.ca

[345] *Sunday's Zaman*, "Turkey, China mull $35 billion joint high-speed railway project," Istanbul, April 14, 2012, http://www.todayszaman.com/_turkey-china-mull-35-bln-joint-high-speed-railway-project_277360.html.

[346] F. William Engdahl, "Washington is Playing a Deeper Game with China," *Global Research*, July 11, 2009, http://www.globalresearch.ca/index.php?context=va&aid=14327.

[347] UNCTAD, "Port and multimodal transport developments," 2008, http://www.thefreelibrary.com/Chapter+5%3a+Port+and+multimodal+transport+developments.-a0218028142.

[348] "BMW Rides Orient Express to China," http://www.inboundlogistics.com/cms/article/global-logistics-october-2011/, cited in F. William Engdahl, "Eurasian Economic Boom and Geopolitics: China's Land Bridge to Europe: The China-Turkey High Speed Railway," *Global Research*, April 27, 2012, http://www.globalresearch.ca/eurasian-economic-boom-and-geopolitics-china-s-land-bridge-to-europe-the-china-turkey-high-speed-railway/30575

[349] Aubrey Chang, "Antwerp-Chongqing Direct Rail Freight Link Launched," May 12, 2011, http://www.industryleadersmagazine.com/antwerp-chongqing-direct-rail-freight-link-launched/

[350] Ibid.

[351] Shigeru Otsuka, "Central Asia's Rail Network and the Eurasian Land Bridge," *Japan Railway & Transport Review* 28, September 2001, pp. 42-49.

[352] *CNTV*, "Russian rail official: Chinese bidder competitive," November 21,2011, http://english.cntv.cn/program/bizasia/20111121/110092.shtml

[353] *Xinhua*, "Yunnan accelerates construction of third Eurasia land bridge," 2009, http://www.shippingonline.cn/news/newsContent.asp?id=10095

[354] Li Yingqing and Guo Anfei, "Third land link to Europe envisioned," *China Daily*, July 2, 2009, http://www.chinadaily.com.cn/china/2009-07/02/content_8345835.htm.

[355] Zbigniew Brzezinski, *The Grand Chessboard*, 1997, Basic Books, p. 40. See F. William Engdahl, *A Century of War: Anglo-American Oil Politics*

and the New World Order, Wiesbaden, 2011, edition.engdahl, for details of the role of the German Baghdad rail link in World War I.

356 This account of the fall of the Roman Empire is reproduced from the author's book *Gods of Money*, pp. 377-379

357 Mateusz Romanowski, "Ancient Rome: Downfall of the Empire," http://www.ancient-rome.biz/downfall.html.

358 Josef Peden, *Inflation and the Fall of the Roman Empire*, Mises Institute, October 27, 1984, http://www.marketoracle.co.uk/Article12831.html.

359 Rex Nutting, "U.S. debt load falling at fastest pace since 1950s," June 08, 2012, MarketWatch

360 David Walker, the US Comptroller General, 23 July 2007, http://business.timesonline.co.uk/tol/business/markets/united_states/art icle2120735.ece

361 *The Committee for a Responsible Federal Budget*, "Between a Mountain of Debt and a Fiscal Cliff," http://crfb.org/sites/default/files/ Between_a_Mountain_of_Debt_and_a_Fiscal_Cliff.pdf

362 Tom Lawler, "REO inventory of 'the F's' and PLS," November 8, 2012, http://www.calculatedriskblog.com/2012/11/lawler-reo-inventory-of-fs-and-pls.html

363 *New York Times*, "California Budget Crisis," November 6, 2012, http://topics.nytimes.com/topics/news/national/usstatesterritoriesandpo ssessions/california/budget_crisis_2008_09/index.html

364 Ambrose Evans Pritchard, "Who will stop the Sado-Monetarists as jobless youth hits 58pc in Greece?", *The Telegraph*, November 8, 2012, http://blogs.telegraph.co.uk/finance/ambroseevans-pritchard/ 100021180/who-will-stop-the-sado-monetarists-as-jobless-youth-hits-58pc-in-greece/

365 "White House Shows Support For Aspirations Of Hong Kong People," *Reuters*, September 29, 2014, http://www.huffingtonpost.com/2014/ 09/29/white-house-hong-kong_n_5901782.html.

366 *Wikipedia*, "Hong Kong Human Rights Monitor," http://en.wikipedia.org/wiki/Hong_Kong_Human_Rights_Monitor#Offic ers.2C_founders_and_staff.

367 NED, *2013 Annual Report*, "Grants, China (Hong Kong)," http://www.ned.org/where-we-work/asia/china-hong-kong

368 *Wikipedia*, "Hong Kong Human Rights Monitor," http://en.wikipedia.org/wiki/Hong_Kong_Human_Rights_Monitor#Offic ers.2C_founders_and_staff

369 *Asia News*, "Occupy Central chooses Rev Chu Yiu-ming as its new leader," January 3, 2014, http://www.asianews.it/news-en/%27Occupy-Central%27-chooses-Rev-Chu-Yiu-ming-as-its-new-leader-29951.html

370 Ibid.

371 Hong Kong University Centre for Comparative and Public Law, *Annual Report*, 2014, http://www.law.hku.hk/ccpl/Docs/Annual%20Report%202014.pdf.

372 Tony Cartalucci, "US Openly Approves Hong Kong Chaos it Created," September 30, 2014, *Land Destroyer Blog*, http://landdestroyer. blogspot.de/2014/09/us-openly-approves-hong-kong-chaos-it.html

373 NDI, "In Hong Kong Does Change Begin with a Single Step?", September27, 2012, National Democratic Institute for International Affairs, https://www.demworks.org/blog/2012/09/hong-kong-does-change-begin-single-step

374 Tony Cartalucci, op. cit.

375 Timmy Sung, Ernest Kao and Tony Cheung, "Occupy Central is on: Benny Tai rides wave of student protest to launch movement," September 27, 2014, *Hong Kong Morning Post*, http://www.scmp.com/news/hong-kong/article/1601625/hong-kong-students-beat-us-it-benny-tai-declares-start-occupy-central

Index

Three by Michel Chossudovsky

Towards a World War III Scenario: The Dangers of Nuclear War. The Pentagon is preparing a first-strike nuclear attack on Iran. 103 pp, $15.95.

The Global Economic Crisis: The Great Depression of the XXI Century, by Prof. Chossudovsky with a dozen other experts. 416 pp, $25.95.

The Globalization of Poverty and the New World Order. Brilliant analysis how corporatism feeds on poverty, destroying the environment, apartheid, racism, sexism, and ethnic strife. 401 pp, $27.95.

Two by Henry Makow

Illuminati: Cult that Hijacked the World tackles taboos like Zionism, British Empire, Holocaust. How international bankers stole a monopoly on government credit, and took over the world. They run it all: wars, schools, media. 249 pp, $19.95. *Illuminati 2: Deception & Seduction*, more hidden history. 285 pp, $19.95

History

Two by George Seldes, the great muckraking journalist, whistleblower on the plutocrats who keep the media in lockstep, and finance fascism. *1,000 Americans Who Rule the USA* (1947, 324 pp, $18.95) Media concentration is nothing new! *Facts and Fascism* (1943, 292 pp, $15.95) How our native corporatist élite aimed for a fascist victory in WW2.

Two by Prof. Donald Gibson. *Battling Wall Street: The Kennedy Presidency.* JFK: a martyr who strove mightily for social and economic justice. 208 pp, $14.95. *The Kennedy Assassination Cover-Up.* JFK was murdered by the moneyed elite, not the CIA or Mafia. 375 pp, $19.95.

Two by Stewart H. Ross. Global Predator: US Wars for Empire. A damning account of the atrocities committed by US armed forces over two centuries.

Propaganda for War: How the US was Conditioned to Fight the Great War Propaganda by Britain and her agents like Teddy Roosevelt sucked the USA into the war to smash the old world order. 350 pp and $18.95 each.

Afghanistan: A Window on the Tragedy. An eloquent photo essay on life amidst the ruins of war. 110 pp, $9.95.

Enemies by Design: Inventing the War on Terrorism. A century of imperialism in the Middle East. Biography of Osama bin Ladeen; Zionization of America; PNAC, Afghanistan, Palestine, Iraq. 416 pp, $17.95.

The Iraq Lie: How the White House Sold the War, by former congressman Joseph M. Hoeffel. Bush Lied about WMD — and went ahead with war. $14.95

The Nazi Hydra in America: Suppressed History of a Century by Glen Yeadon. US plutocrats launched Hitler, then recouped Nazi assets to erect today's police state. Fascists won WWII because they ran both sides. "The story is shocking and sobering and deserves to be widely read." – Howard Zinn. 700 pp, $19.95.

Inside the Gestapo: Hitler's Shadow over the World. Intimate, fascinating Nazi defector's tale of ruthlessness, intrigue, and geopolitics. 287 pp, $17.95.

Sunk: The Story of the Japanese Submarine Fleet, 1941-1945. The bravery of doomed men in a lost cause, against impossible odds. 300 pp, $15.95.

Terrorism and the Illuminati, A 3000-Year History. "Islamic" terrorists are tentacles of western imperialism—the Illuminati. 332 pp, $16.95.

Troublesome Country. US history is one of failure to live up to our guiding democratic creed. 146 pp, $12.95.

Psychology: Brainwashing

The Rape of the Mind: The Psychology of Thought Control, Menticide and Brainwashing. Conditioning in open and closed societies; tools for self-defense against torture or social pressure. 320 pp, $16.95. Classic study by Dr Joost Meerloo, who experienced both Nazism and McCarthyism first-hand.

The Telescreen: An Empirical Study of the Destruction of Consciousness, by Prof. Jeffrey Grupp. How mass media brainwash us with consumerism and war propaganda. Fake history, news, issues, and reality steal our souls. 199 pp, $14.95. Also by Grupp: ***Telemention: Cosmic Feeling and the Law of Attraction***. Deep feeling rather than thought or faith is our secret nature and key to self-realization. 124 pp, $12.95.

Conspiracy, NWO

The Money Power: Empire of the City and Pawns in the Game. Two classic geopolitics books in one. The illuminist Three World Wars conspiracy, to divide humanity on ethnic and political lines to conquer us. 320 pp, $16.95

Corporatism: the Secret Government of the New World Order by Prof. Jeffrey Grupp. Corporations control all world resources. Their New World Order is the "prison planet" that Hitler aimed for. 408 pp, $16.95.

Descent into Slavery. How the banksters took over America and the world. The Founding Fathers, Rothschilds, the Crown and the City, world wars, and globalization. 310 pp, $16. Also by Des Griffin: ***Fourth Reich of the Rich***, 316 pp, $16.

Dope Inc.: Britain's Opium War against the United States. "The Book that Drove Kissinger Crazy." Underground Classic, new edition. 320 pp, $12.95.

Ecology: Ideology and Power, by Donald Gibson. The reactionary elite interests pushing population and resource control. 162 pp., $13.95

Final Warning: A History of the New World Order by D. A. Rivera. Classic, in-depth research into the Great Conspiracy: the Fed, the Trilateral Commission, the CFR, and the Illuminati. 360 pp, $14.95.

How the World Really Works by A.B. Jones. Crash course in conspiracy. Digests of 11 classics like *Tragedy and Hope, Creature from Jekyll Island*. 336 pp, $15.

Killing us Softly: *the Global Depopulation Policy* by Kevin Galalae, 146 pp., color. Both the Why and How. $15.95.

The Triumph of Consciousness by Chris Clark. The real Global Warming and Greening agenda: more hegemony by the NWO. 347 pp, $14.95.

Conspiracy: False Flag Operations

9/11 on Trial: The W T C Collapse. 20 closely argued proofs that the World Trade Center was destroyed by controlled demolition. 192 pp, $12.95.

Gladio, NATO's Dagger at the Heart of Europe: The Pentagon-Mafia-Nazi Terror Axis. The blood-red thread of terror by NATO death squads in Europe, from WW2 up to 2012. 484 pp, $16.95.

Conspiracies, Conspiracy Theories and the Secrets of 9/11, German best-seller explores conspiracy in history, before tackling 9/11. 274 pp, $14.95.

Grand Deceptions: Zionist Intrigues. The Neocon World Order. 177 pp., $13.95.

In Search of the Truth: An Exposure of the Conspiracy, by Azar Mirza-Beg. A portrait of our times, society and religion, and the threat we face. 208 pp, $17

JFK-911: 50 Years of Deep State., by Laurent Guyénot. An Israeli strategy behind the JFK and 9/11 murders. 238 pp, $15.95.

Subverting Syria: How CIA Contra Gangs and NGO's Manufacture, Mislabel and Market Mass Murder. Syrian "uprising" is a cynical US plot using faked news, provocateurs, opportunists, mercenaries, and Wahhabi fanatics. 116 pp, $10.00

Terror on the Tube: Behind the Veil of 7/7, an Investigation, by Nick Kollerstrom. The glaring evidence that all four Muslim scapegoats were completely innocent. 7/7 clinched the assault on our rights. 3rd ed, 322 pp, $17.77.

The War on Freedom. The seminal exposé of 9/11. "Far and away the best and most balanced analysis of September 11th." – Gore Vidal. 400 pp, $16.95.

Truth Jihad: My Epic Struggle Against the 9/11 Big Lie. Kevin Barrett's outrageously humorous autobiographical testament. 224 pp, $9.95.

Coming Soon

A Prisoner's Diary, by Hussain Mohammed Al-Amily

Myth of the Arab Spring, by Chris Macavel

Subjugating the Middle East and *Ukraine: The Attack on Russia and the Eurasian Union* by Takis Fotopoulos.

E-Books

9/11 Synthetic Terror; Barack Obama Unauthorized Biography;
Gladio, NATO's Dagger at the Heart of Europe,
Grand Deceptions; In Search of the Truth; Iraq Lie; JFK-911; Just Too Weird;
Nazi Hydra; Subverting Syria; Surviving the Cataclysm; Target: China

Made in the USA
Monee, IL
15 December 2019

18749405R00150